Climate Change, Justice and
Future Generations

For
Ted and Jill

Climate Change, Justice and Future Generations

Edward A. Page

Department of Political Science and International Studies, University of Birmingham, UK

Edward Elgar
Cheltenham, UK • Northampton, MA, USA

Published by
Edward Elgar Publishing Limited
Glensanda House
Montpellier Parade
Cheltenham
Glos GL50 1UA
UK

Edward Elgar Publishing, Inc.
136 West Street
Suite 202
Northampton
Massachusetts 01060
USA

A catalogue record for this book
is available from the British Library

Library of Congress Cataloguing in Publication Data

Page, Edward, 1968–
    Climate change, justice and future generations / by Edward A. Page.
        p. cm.
        1. Climatic changes. 2. Climatic changes—Government policy—Economic
    aspects. 3. Global environment change. 4. Environmental management. I. Title.

    QC981.8.C5P34 2006   2005052714

ISBN-13: 978 1 84376 184 6
ISBN-10: 1 84376 184 X

Typeset by Cambrian Typesetters, Camberley, Surrey
Printed and bound in Great Britain by MPG Books Ltd, Bodmin, Cornwall

Contents

Acknowledgements

During the period of writing this book, I have been fortunate enough to bene-fit from the comments and suggestions of a wide range of people. Earlier versions of the chapters contained in the book were presented at academic seminars and conferences at the universities of Lund, Gothenburg, Stockholm, Birmingham, Keele, Luleå, Umeå, Manchester, Leeds and Ulster. I am grate-ful to the audiences on all of these occasions for their comments. I am also grateful to John Barry, Stephen M. Gardiner and Oluf Langhelle for detailed comments on an earlier version of the book. I would especially like to thank colleagues at Lund, Gothenburg and Birmingham who have contributed in numerous ways to the project over the course of the last three years. In partic-ular, I would like to thank Sverker Jagers, Johannes Stripple, Lars Göran Stenelo, Åsa Mattsson, Raimund Muscheler and Göran Duus-Otterström in Sweden; and Simon Caney, Derek Bell, Clare Heywood and Pia Halme in the UK. An equally great, and much longer-term, debt is owed to the supervisors of my doctoral research at Warwick University, Susan Hurley and Andrew Williams, whose ideas and comments improved my understanding of political philosophy on countless occasions. Finally, I would like to acknowledge the financial support of the European Commission, from whom I received a Marie Curie Research Fellowship to work at Lund University between 2002 and 2004, and the UK Arts and Humanities Research Council, which funds my present post at Birmingham University as part of the 'Global Justice and the Environment' research project.

1. Intergenerational justice in a warming world

Climate is what we expect, weather is what we get.

Mark Twain

By spraying deodorant at your armpit in your New York apartment, you could, if you use an aerosol spray propelled by CFCs, be contributing to the skin cancer deaths, many years later, of people living in Punta Arenas, Chile. By driving your car, you could be releasing carbon dioxide that is part of a causal chain leading to lethal floods in Bangladesh. How can we adjust our ethics to take account of this new situation?[1]

Peter Singer

1.1 WEATHER, CLIMATE AND THE ETHICS OF CLIMATE CHANGE

On 29 August 2005, Hurricane Katrina made landfall on the Gulf coast of the United States, with winds of up to 135 miles per hour and catastrophic storm surges of up to seven metres. Katrina went on to have a huge socio-economic, human health and environmental impact in Louisiana, Mississippi and Alabama. At the time of writing, Katrina had been widely recognised as the greatest weather disaster in the history of the United States, with over 1300 confirmed dead, many in flood-ravaged New Orleans, and an estimated cost to insurers of over $30 billion according to the reinsurance giant Munich Re.[2]

Between 2 and 24 September 2004, Hurricane Ivan, the most powerful of an unusual series of wind storms, hit the coast of Florida after devastating several countries throughout the Caribbean. The hurricane caused over $10 billion in damage in total, and led to 2 million evacuations in four US states. Ivan, with winds of up to 280 kilometres per hour, was particularly catastrophic for Haiti and the Cayman Islands where high winds and waves of 6 metres wrecked up to 90 per cent of homes, killing hundreds and making hundreds of thousands homeless.[3]

One year earlier, on 10 August 2003, whilst Europe was in the middle of a heatwave, the record for the highest surface temperature in England was broken. The Brogdale station in Kent reported a temperature of 38.5°C, a weather landmark. It was, in fact, the hottest day in the country that holds the longest unbroken temperature series, as scientists have collected data as part of the Central England Temperature record since 1659.[4] The year 2003 went on to be the third warmest recorded, surpassed only by 1998 and 2002. Not all were thrilled with the heat, however, and later studies confirmed that the heatwave caused at least 20 000 excess deaths in Europe through dehydration and heat stroke.[5]

One year earlier still, between 31 July and 26 August 2002, two high-altitude, low-pressure systems combined to cause torrential rain and flooding across Northern Europe, hitting Germany, Austria and the Czech Republic severely. Several hundred thousand people were evacuated temporarily from their homes, and there were over 100 deaths. The exceptional scale of the event led to total economic damage of 15 billion euros, according to Swiss insurance company Swiss Re.[6]

In different ways, each of these weather events was unusual and all were talked about as early indications of global climate change (or 'global warming' – the most widely discussed, but far from the only, dimension of climate change).[7] Were these events, and other extremes of weather being reported around the world, reflective of a new trend in global climate towards extreme events? Were they early warnings of even greater events to come?

Because of the complexity of (and inherent variability in) weather and climate, such questions will probably never be answered. It will, for example, never be established beyond doubt that the events described above led to the *first* deaths and economic losses attributable to global climate change. But as we shall see, the vast majority of physicists and climatologists active today predict large increases in the frequency and/or intensity of all three types of event. That is, they hold that intense rainfall events will become more frequent in Europe and elsewhere; the frequency of very hot days will increase throughout the world; and the intensity of wind storms, such as Ivan, will increase.

This, of course, raises great practical questions – not least, what *can* be done by individuals, and the countries to which they belong, to prevent the adverse changes in climate that can still reasonably be avoided or to adapt to the dangerous climate changes that cannot reasonably be avoided. But it also raises ethical questions, such as what *should* be done to mitigate, or adapt to, climate change? Who should be held responsible for climate change? How should the costs of climate change be distributed? Which parties should take the lead in international attempts to manage the causes and effects of climate change? Should the needs (or rights) of present persons be viewed as prior to those of the not yet born in our decisions about climate change?

This book will address many of these, as well as a number of related, questions. In doing so, it will be guided by two fundamental ideas, as well as a host of supplementary assumptions that will be explained later. The first idea is that a nuanced understanding of ethics is essential for the development of effective and legitimate policies to manage climate change. The second idea is that the part of ethics that is particularly useful in this regard is *distributive justice*, or the study of how benefits and burdens should be distributed across space and time. A theory of distributive justice is a central feature of any fully worked out ethical system, but, as will become clear, it is especially important in the debate about the impacts of climate change. Other aspects of ethics, which we might define broadly as the study of what we owe to each as a matter of duty, will also be relevant to our discussion, but will be secondary to the question of what division of benefits we should aim to bring about, as individuals and policymakers. We begin with a detailed look at some key concepts that will help us understand the causes and effects of climate change.

1.2 WEATHER AND CLIMATE: AN AWKWARD PARTNERSHIP

The *weather* – defined as the 'state or condition of the atmosphere at a particular place and time'[8] and comprised of 'weather elements' such as temperature, air pressure, wind, humidity, cloud and rain – has been a source of debate and discussion for millennia, possibly since the beginnings of human civilisation. Although by nature a transitory phenomenon, weather conditions play a key role in the lives of both individuals and states. Unusual weather conditions can profoundly affect a person's health, as well as their mental functioning. Extremes of heat are particularly dangerous, as has been shown by the numbers of heat related fatalities in unusually hot periods such as the heatwave of 2003; extremes of humidity are associated with a decrease in mental performance and general activity; and lack of sunshine has been associated with the deterioration of a range of functions, such as sleep and appetite. Weather is also a key contributor to a person's nutritional, clothing, shelter and recreational requirements on any given day. In fact, almost no feature of human life seems unaffected by weather.

Weather can also have unforeseen political consequences. Unexpected weather patterns have played an important role in a number of political events, in particular those concerning the timing, and outcome, of military conflicts.[9] It is well known, for example, that the D-Day landings were delayed repeatedly on the grounds of unfavourable weather conditions. In the event, the combined air and sea invasion of 6 June 1944 benefited not only by a forecasted opening of a window of relatively calm weather, but also by the relaxed readiness of the German defences as a result of the recent period of bad weather.[10] The brutal winter weather of 1941 that helped degrade the German army's mobility, morale and logistics was a critical factor in the failure of Hitler's invasion of the Soviet Union.[11] A third example concerns the timing, and causes, of the French Revolution of 1789. The bad harvest of 1788, and harsh winter of 1788/89, served to exacerbate existing social and political cleavages (bread prices soared over this period and existing inequalities widened) partly contributing to the subsequent revolution.

Given the above, it might seem surprising that there have been few scholarly works on the political and ethical implications of weather. However, the reason for this gap in the literature is in many respects clear. This is that, as phenomena apparently beyond the influence of human action, the importance of weather events for human civilisation and well-being was viewed until recently as a matter of luck and contingency. As in the case of other natural events such as the Indian Ocean Tsunami disaster of December 2004 (300 000 plus casualties) or the 1976 Earthquake in north-east China (240 000 casualties), the popular view has been that the bad effects of weather are regrettable but not unethical, inequitable or unjust (I use these terms interchangeably) since they are no one's fault. This is not to say that features of societies that exacerbate the impact of weather disasters are beyond ethical criticism. Nor that the societies that people belong to have no obligations to mitigate the worst effects of weather disasters when they occur. Rather, it is to observe that people do not seem to have ethical claims, in particular claims of justice, against others that they be protected from natural variations in weather. We might say that the notion of 'weather ethics' on this view is incoherent.

Ironically perhaps, the study of weather, *meteorology*, which we can define as the systematic study of the earth's atmosphere and its weather phenomena,[12] was pioneered by one of the founders of modern political and ethical theory. In his *Meteorologica* (which was written around 340 BC), Aristotle (384–322 BC) synthesised existing knowledge of weather and proposed explanations of weather phenomena in terms of his doctrine of four elements (earth, air, fire and water) as well as general principles of their interaction.[13] Although almost all of Aristotle's meteorological views have now been refuted, Aristotle's theories went on to form the basis of the discipline, and in particular weather forecasting, for nearly 2000 years. In the late 16th and 17th centuries, scientists such as Tycho Brahe (1546–1601) and Johannes Kepler (1571–1630) developed Aristotle's theories by arguing that the relative positions of planets were associated with different atmospheric conditions, albeit within the context of a striking metaphysics that attributed to the Earth a soul that was susceptible to planetary and solar influence.[14]

Despite the influence and apparent success of Kepler's methods, the notion of a direct coupling between astrology, astronomy and weather fell out of favour in the 17th and 18th centuries (the connection between astronomical variables, such as changes in the pattern of the Earth's orbit around the sun, were later shown to be a key factor in the timing of glacial and inter-glacial ages throughout earth's history by Milutin Milankovitch[15]). The new focus of meteorologists became the development of mathematical models that could explain observations of data made possible by a series of weather instrument inventions as well as conceptual improvements. Of particular importance were the introduction of the water thermometer (1593), mercury thermometer (1714), hygrometer (for measuring humidity, 1780), aneroid barometer (1843), and the development of cloud- (1803) and windspeed- (1806) classifications. The discipline also benefited indirectly from a number of other inventions, such as the telegraph (1830) which enabled the transmission and collection of weather data from large numbers of remote stations; supercomputers, such as the CRAY series of machines (1979–present), which could process increasingly complex forecast models within a reasonable time-period; and satellites, such as the US polar orbiting TIROS satellite (1960–66), that could make reliable observations of the Earth's cloud cover and other weather patterns from space.

Although these inventions have enabled great progress in weather forecasting, there has been a clear shift in outlook away from the ambitions of pioneer forecasters such as Aristotle and Kepler. Detailed forecasts that claim to model weather beyond ten days, for example, are highly controversial because of the many simplifying assumptions and uncertainties associated with weather models.[16] Nevertheless, an important assumption remained in place throughout this long period of meteorological innovation, namely, that although weather has a huge influence on human life and is to a certain extent predictable, it is not generally susceptible to direct human influence.

In contrast to weather, *climate* can be defined as 'a regional or global synthesis of weather extended through time'.[17] It is thus concerned with a range of data, such as the frequency and intensity of extremes of weather such as storms, floods and droughts mentioned earlier, as well as average measurements of weather elements such as temperature, over some extended period. Whereas meteorological forecasts typically refer to conditions in a region over a number of hours or days, climatologists analyse changes in atmospheric conditions over a much longer time-span, typically over several decades to millennia.

There have been numerous transformations of the Earth's atmosphere over its history, notably the successive glacial and inter-glacial periods that have characterised terrestrial climate for the last 2 billion years. The extremes of this period are staggering. Warmer periods (such as the period between 120 and 90 million years ago) were generally 5°C–15°C warmer than the colder periods that interspersed them (such as the numerous ice ages that have occurred in the last 15 million years) and sea levels were around 150 to 200 metres higher. In fact, mean temperatures have been much higher than they are today throughout most of the Earth's history.[18]

It appears from the evidence available that human life has been profoundly affected by each of the key climatic shifts that post-date modern man's evolution, notably the nine or more glacial ages of the last 750 000 years. Human societies have had to adapt continually to climatic events. Two prominent examples concern the human impacts of an unexpected cooling in the Northern Hemisphere. The first, the Younger Dryas Event, saw North America, Europe and Western Asia suffer a 1000 year temporary return to ice age conditions that started around 11 700 BC. Researchers believe that the event, which may have been caused by a disruption in the process that transports warm water to the northern latitudes, had a huge impact on animal and plant life in the Northern Hemisphere.[19]

A second example concerns the 'little ice age' that marked a pronounced cooling of Northern Europe between 1300 and 1850. The period witnessed a drop in temperature of between 1°C and 2°C relative to the average for the current, Holocene, climate period that began approximately 11 600 years ago, and appears to have been caused by a combination of reduced solar activity and raised volcanic activity. There were large advancements of glaciers in Scandinavia and Alpine Europe; crop failures throughout Europe; and massive cold and famine related mortality.[20] Moreover, like the Younger Dryas Event, some scholars claim that natural changes in climate during this period (and attempts to adapt to these changes) had large and unpredictable effects on human civilisation. There is increasing evidence, for example, that the cooling acted as a catalyst for the exploration and settlement of North America, as well as increased agricultural efficiency and the industrial revolution.[21] This raises the intriguing possibility that natural changes in climate themselves contributed to the development of institutions and practices that produced the anthropogenic greenhouse effect.

While a preoccupation with weather is arguably as central to the human condition as that of love, death and taxes – the Earth's climate has emerged as a much more recent feature of popular consciousness. If a non-specialist was asked 20 years ago what they thought about global warming or global climate change it is likely that they would have been baffled. As Mark Twain once quipped, everybody was talking about the weather but nobody could do anything about it for there was nothing one could do to affect it. The Earth's future climate was an even greater mystery. Tremendous advances in meteorology and climatology in the last 50 years, and in particular the greenhouse theory of climate change,[22] has changed this picture however. The vast majority of experts[23] now hold that we can affect, and are affecting, the global climate, and climate change is consistently reported as one of the greatest problems facing humanity in surveys of public opinion.[24]

1.3   THE INTERGOVERNMENTAL PANEL ON CLIMATE CHANGE

The international body charged with coordinating research into climate change is the Intergovernmental Panel on Climate Change (IPCC). The IPCC was founded by the World Meteorological Organization (WMO) and the United Nations Environment Programme (UNEP) in 1988. Its aim is to assess – on the basis of peer-reviewed literature – the scientific, technical and socio-economic information relevant to understanding the scientific basis of human-induced climate change; and its potential impacts and options for mitigation (the prevention of avoidable climate change) and adaptation (the modifying of human practices to fit in better with climate changes when and where they occur).[25]

In its influential Second Assessment Report (SAR), the IPCC found that 'the balance of evidence suggests discernible human influence on climate'.[26] The SAR went on to claim that, because of the way in which it will disturb biological and physical systems, climate change will have a range of, generally adverse, impacts on the health[27] and socio-economic resources[28] of future human populations.

The SAR's findings were developed, and in many ways strengthened, by the IPCC's Third Assessment Report (TAR) published in 2001. This found that 'there is new and stronger evidence that most of the warming observed over the last 50 years is attributable to human activities' and that 'human influences will continue to change atmospheric composition throughout the 21st century'.[29] The TAR argued that the distributive implications of climate change raise 'an important issue of equity, namely the extent to which the impacts of climate change or mitigation policies create or exacerbate inequities both within and across nations and regions'.[30]

It is within this context that public and governmental concern has grown regarding the way in which climate change will influence the pattern of distribution of social and economic benefits across generations and nations. This concern is reflected in both the policy documents of individual countries and of the United Nations. Article 3.1 of the United Nations Framework Convention on Climate Change (UNFCCC[31]), for example, states that those countries party to it:

> should protect the climate system for the benefit of present and future generations of humankind, on the basis of equity and in accordance with their common but differentiated responsibilities and respective capabilities.[32]

Considerations of ethics and justice are integral to the IPCC's assessments of climate change. According to the SAR, climate change raises 'particular questions of equity among generations'[33] and the TAR observes that any effective response to climate change must be consistent with ethical ideas of equity and fairness.[34] This claim, while not unchallenged, commands wide agreement amongst policymakers, ethicists, and scientists. In fact, the findings of the SAR and TAR commanded cross-party support in most industrialised countries.

The response of successive UK governments since 1992 is quite typical of the consensus. At the New York 'Rio Plus Five' Earth Summit held in June 1997, Tony Blair drew upon the SAR to urge all industrialised nations to set ambitious targets for the stabilisation, and eventual reduction, of greenhouse emissions. In his speech to the summit, Blair observed that:

> This Earth is the only planet in the solar system with an environment that can sustain life. Our solemn duty as leaders of the world is to treasure that precious heritage, and to hand on to our children and grandchildren an environment that will enable them to enjoy the same full life that we took for granted.[35]

Blair's speeches are mirrored by those of the then Secretary of State for the Environment, Margaret Beckett, who has claimed that:

> Climate change is the greatest and most urgent environmental challenge facing mankind today. For the sake of current and future generations and the future of the planet, let us rise to the challenge and take serious action to tackle it.[36]

Perhaps more surprisingly, achieving intergenerational equity was also a key aspect of the previous, Conservative, administration's approach to climate change. John Gummer (UK Environment Secretary 1993–7) was a firm supporter of the IPCC and played a key role in the UNFCCC negotiation process, and Margaret Thatcher (Prime Minister 1979–90) is credited as being one of the driving forces behind the establishment of the IPCC.[37]

It could, of course, be argued that the ideas contained in such speeches are motivated by political posturing, rather than by genuine concerns of environmental or intergenerational ethics. Blair's commitment to emissions reductions was criticised after it was confirmed in December 2004 that the UK would fail to meet the pledge contained in the Labour Party's 2001 manifesto to cut carbon dioxide emissions to 20 per cent below 1990 levels by 2010. Blair was also criticised when the UK Government increased the amount of greenhouse gases that businesses would be able to emit under the new European Emissions Trading Scheme (EU ETS) from 736 million tonnes to 756 million tonnes, mainly as a result of successful industry lobbying.[38] Nevertheless, such criticisms should not deflect attention from the growing emphasis on the ethical dimension of climate change, and in particular its impacts on the well-being of future generations.

There are a number of ethical arguments that might underwrite the expressions of concern about climate change surveyed above. The argument I wish to focus on concerns the consequences of failing to address climate change for the quantity and quality of human well-being in the future, and is presented in humanist terms.[39] The argument has three steps:

P1.   The changes in the climate system that are being brought about by human action threaten the well-being of members of future generations.
P2.   Human action that threatens the well-being of members of future generations is unjust and unethical (I use these terms interchangeably).
C.   The changes in the climate system that are being brought about by human action are unjust and unethical.[40]

We might call this the *Intergenerational Responsibility Argument*. This argument appears to be *valid*, as C clearly follows from P1 and P2. However, it is less clear if the argument is *true* as its premises are more controversial than they appear.

Much of the book will be devoted to a detailed investigation of this argument, which seems to underpin much common-sense thinking about the ethics of global climate change, as well as the ethical stance of the IPCC.[41] In particular, I will be investigating the debates that have emerged from both the popular and academic literature concerning P1 and P2 by applying the tools, techniques and methods of analytical philosophy. Consider premise P1. Some have claimed that this premise is false because the link between anthropogenic greenhouse gas emissions and climate change is unproven. The IPCC's assessments, it is argued, are little more than a 'scare story' and as such, there is insufficient evidence to claim that climate change exists, so the claim that climate change poses a clear and present threat to present or future well-being is false.[42]

The IPCC has also been criticised for being biased in the direction of mitigation as opposed to adaptation. This is because the IPCC, it is claimed, underplays the way in which climate change will be limited in the longer term by the logic of economic forces that will bring about the replacement of carbon intense activities (such as fossil fuel energy sources) with alternative, so-called 'clean', energy sources that involve little or no emissions of carbon (such as solar power) as and when they become more cost effective. In particular, the implicit support that the IPCC gives to the Kyoto Protocol, which is viewed as dangerous since it would damage economic development growth if implemented, is criticised.[43]

Still others have argued that climate change, while it certainly exists, will not have the range and depth of adverse effects on future generations that the IPCC suggest. They have also claimed that the *net* long-term impacts of climate change on humankind will either be negligible or mildly beneficial, as a result of localised reductions in cold-related deaths; improvements in agricultural yields; and benefits to tourism.[44]

While these 'sceptical' positions have been quite influential in some quarters, notably amongst administrations opposed to the Kyoto Protocol, it will be argued in Chapter 2 that they should not undermine our confidence in the IPCC's central findings or in the usefulness of the Kyoto Protocol.

Consider, next, the objections that might be directed towards premise P2, which will be the primary focus of the book. Whereas few deny that global environmental problems such as climate change pose a threat to the well-being of future generations, it might be claimed that such threats are simply not of genuine ethical concern. The requirements of ethics and justice, one might think, bind only contemporaries belonging to the same society, or only contemporaries whatever society they belong to. On the other hand, it might be conceded that the impacts of climate change are of ethical import, but only insofar as they threaten the well-being of those who will belong to the nearest of future generations. Such claims may appear to be unsound. However, it is an unsettling fact that there have been few systematic attempts to test the robustness of premise P2 (1) across different theories of distributive justice; (2) across the different accounts of human well-being that distributive theories adopt; or (3) in the light of some perplexing problems associated with extending the scope of distributive theories to cover persons belonging to different generations.

Regarding (1) and (2), I attempt to address this gap in the literature in Chapters 3 and 4, where I argue that climate change does indeed raise peculiarly important questions for a range of theories of the distribution of human well-being. The theories analysed are *impersonal* in the sense that they may view acts and social policies as wrong even if they harm no particular people. While such theories represent only a small range of the possible positions within ethics, they are important in that they provide the background to most discussions of what an ethical climate change policy would look like.[45]

Regarding issue (3), some preliminary comment is required. It appears to be the conviction of many that human activities that compound the climate change problem are inequitable, or unethical, because they *harm* the as yet unborn. Onora O'Neill, for example, writes that 'by burning fossil fuels prodigally we accelerate the green-house effect and may dramatically harm successors, who can do nothing to us'.[46] A similar view is held by Henry Shue.[47] Such views, because they urge us to benefit (or not to harm) particular persons, are often known as *person-affecting* views. The problem, as shown in Chapter 6, is that there are a number of difficulties in explaining exactly how our successors can be harmed either directly or indirectly by acts or policies which are also necessary conditions of their coming into existence.

Yet, even supposing that future persons can be harmed by actions or policies necessary for their coming into existence, some suggest that the lack of mutual benefit (or reciprocity) that characterises dealings between members of different generations undermines the claims of future persons to resources currently at the disposal of existing persons. This is because, it is claimed, the scope of ethics and justice is determined by a principle of *reciprocity*. Nevertheless, the discussion in Chapter 5 shows that even theories of distribution that appeal to reciprocity give rise to norms of intergenerational justice.

It is worth noting that, because I spend most of my time clarifying, and responding to, various *objections* that might be raised to premises P1 and P2, the bulk of the defence provided for the existence of intergenerational duties, and their application to climate change, is indirect. I set out to show that none of the objections to the Intergenerational Responsibility Argument are sound, rather than to provide a completely new theory of intergenerational distribution as such. Nevertheless, the book does seek to examine more closely one neglected normative approach to these issues, grounded in the principle of *sufficiency*, which holds that resources should be distributed so as that many persons as possible lead a decent life. The principle of sufficiency, I will claim, is a central element in a theory of distribution that is pluralist in the sense that it recognises that there are multiple sources of obligation.

1.4   SCIENCE, ETHICS AND THE ENVIRONMENT

It might be argued at this point that, whereas the theoretical issues raised so far may be of interest to the student of philosophy, the systematic study of ethical arguments and beliefs has little bearing on the pressing issue of how to manage our dealings with the environment. The sceptic claims that only 'sound science' can explain how complex physical processes work, what their likely consequences will be for future human life, and come to the aid of policy-makers faced with a bewildering range of alternative environmental policies. Ethical analyses of environmental problems, on the other hand, are viewed as too abstract to serve as a guide for environmental policymaking, or unnecessary since the appropriate aims of these policies are obvious and not in need of further discussion.

There are flaws in both of these sceptical lines of reasoning, however. The flaw in the latter is that the ethics of individual and state behaviour are more contested than they have ever been, both inside and outside the academic world. The flaw in the former line of argument is that, no matter how sophisticated one's natural scientific account of human–environmental interactions, empirical research can at best explain how things actually are and not how things ought to be. Since policymaking inevitably must aim for some desirable state of affairs – in democratic countries, this is usually developed in terms of the common good, subject to the constraints of personal freedom and democratic rights – policymakers will always rely on normative information in their decision-making.

This is not to say that there is an absolute demarcation between natural science and ethics, between facts and values. As we shall see in the next chapter, scientists, such as those working under the auspices of the IPCC, regularly invoke normative ideas such as the precautionary principle, that do not fit well with a traditional, positivist conception of scientific method. But even taking a stronger view of the science–ethics boundary, ethical theorising has a clear role to play in environmental research, critically to help us understand why (and which) environmental changes are bad, and how we might choose between mitigating and/or adapting to outcomes when at least some of these are unavoidable.

It is important also not to underestimate the importance of empirical research and the role it plays in our ethical theorising, or to overstate the importance of the fact–value distinction. This comes out clearly when we reflect on different types of ethical principles, and the way their application is shaped by empirical facts. Science itself plays a vital background role in our normative theorising because it is often necessary to acquire a detailed understanding of the likely consequences of our actions, with the exact relevance of empirical knowledge depending on the nature of the duty in question. So whereas science cannot prescribe what is, and is not, ethical or just it can help us investigate whether certain ethical norms have been violated by an act or social policy.[48]

To take an example, ethical duties have traditionally been separated into two camps: those that prohibit the infliction of suffering on others (negative duties), and those that involve furthering the well-being of others (positive duties). The distinction has clear relevance to the climate change issue. Climate change, the IPCC informs us, will result in numerous adverse impacts on future persons, and thus prima facie negative duty violations, directly through heatwaves, floods or infectious diseases and indirectly through making the conditions of life far harder than they would have been. However, climate change will also alter the pattern of benefits across both nations and generations in a way that is not obviously tied to particular people being made worse off. For those that believe in positive duties, then, it also will almost certainly violate a range of these duties as well.

The exact relationship between negative and positive duties is complex, and although the distinction seems obvious in some cases, it is much less clear in others. What is clear is that to give a full account of our negative duties, and the harms done to others, it will at some stage be necessary to understand the impacts of our actions on the quality of life enjoyed by other persons, nations and generations even if uncertainty and complexity mean that this understanding will never be perfect. The IPCC's assessments provide valuable assistance here, although a full picture of the harms that environmental problems inflict will take in a range of other sources as well.

To give a full account of our positive duties, on the other hand, we must not only explain their philosophical basis, which is more controversial that is the case with negative duties, but also explain how various phenomena will alter the distribution of benefits and burdens over time and space. This is because we need to know how we can best help people, or, in other words, how best to bring about the distribution of well-being that our theory of positive duties requires. Again, the IPCC provides useful information here since, although it attempts to stay neutral between different theories of distribution (or in its terms, theories of 'distributive equity'), it estimates the impacts of different possible climate scenarios on regional and global wealth, as well as its temporal distribution.

1.5 ETHICS, MORALITY, AND DISTRIBUTIVE JUSTICE

Before moving on to the methodological approach used in the book, it is worth saying something about the nature of ethics more broadly. What is ethics, and how is it distinguishable (if at all) from morality and other related concepts such as equity and justice? It was noted above that, for simplicity, ethics, equity and justice will be treated as interchangeable concepts. In general, however, I will be talking about theories of 'distributive justice' to reflect both the nomenclature and the focus of the expanding literature on ethics and climate change. Distributive justice, equity or ethics concern the way in which benefits and burdens should be distributed in a population comprising persons with competing claims. As such, it involves both the specification of the entitlements that people have (for example, to income and wealth) as well as the duties or obligations (I use these terms interchangeably) that persons or other agents are bound by to respect these entitlements.

Distributive justice, I will assume, is primarily, although not exclusively, a virtue of the basic social institutions of society – the political constitution, tax, education and health systems – which John Rawls has described as the 'basic structure of society'.[49] That is, it is a matter of what is owed to persons as a result of their engaging in cooperative behaviour with others but where social institutions, rather than individuals themselves, have the fundamental responsibility for enforcing entitlements. Unlike some contributors to the debate, however, I attempt to remain open to the possibility that norms of distributive justice also apply to individual behaviour as well as to the basic structure.[50]

What of the relation between morality and ethics? According to a useful distinction, morality concerns judgements about right and wrong that people hold and act upon in their daily lives. Ethics, on the other hand, concerns the systematic evaluation of such beliefs. The distinction has relevance across a wide range of debates in ethics, and this is also the case with environmental issues. We can, thus, distinguish between 'environmental ethics' as the academic study of the environment and our relation to it on the one hand, and 'environmental morality' as people's actual beliefs and values regarding the environment. Environmental morality has a much longer history in most countries life than environmental ethics. The development of a separate branch of ethics devoted to environmental issues in the developed world, for example, can largely be traced back to the period immediately after the Second World War and above all has developed rapidly since the late 1960s.

Consider next the ongoing debate concerning our obligations to future generations, which many see as a critical component of any legitimate, and politically feasible, solution to global climate change. It is in many respects clear that the vast majority of people possess moral convictions about the well-being of the not-yet-born and the extent to which the present generation should protect the environment that our successors will inherit, even if the scope and content of these convictions varies greatly from person to person and situation to situation. Nevertheless, it is less common for people to undertake a systematic evaluation of these convictions, and the modes of thought that lie behind them. When conflicts arise between the interests of present and future persons, as they appear to in the case of climate change, it appears that most reconcile competing convictions through an intuitive balancing process, and not by appealing to any underlying systematic theory of what is owed to others.

The problem with this otherwise practical and sensible approach to action, and which provides the motivation for the study of ethics, is that this 'intuitionism' cannot offer us a stable way to evaluate either ethical problems or the policies that are designed to manage them. Put simply, according to intuitionism, there simply is nothing more to ethics than people's actual moral convictions after they have been screened for clear breaches of some principle of basic human dignity.[51] An intuitionist approach, then, could not explain what was wrong with the claim that we have *no* responsibilities to future generations, if this conviction is not grounded in simple misanthropy.

I return to the possibility of a non-intuitionistic ethics in the next section, but it is enough at this point to say that a more systematic, critical, approach to people's actual beliefs about the environment will involve the analysis of a number of interesting and, until recently, neglected questions. Such questions can be ordered in terms of two levels of ethical theorising: *normative ethics* and *meta-ethics*.

Normative environmental ethics concerns the evaluation, and development, of fully worked out theories of how we ought to treat the environment and the natural world. Two types of normative theories are of interest here. First, those that single out a single fundamental ethical value and work out its implications for human conduct. A good example is utilitarianism, which holds that acts and social policies should maximise human welfare (defined as either conscious enjoyment or preference satisfaction). The 'principle of utility' that operates at the heart of this theory (described famously by Jeremy Bentham as requiring 'the greatest happiness of the greatest number'[52]) is held to be both absolute and non-revisable in the sense that its value is wholly independent of what people think about ethics.

The second sort of theory also generates principles that, like the utility principle, can be used to evaluate acts and social policies. But this sort of theory judges these principles to some extent by their fittingness with what people think is right or wrong in particular situations, or with other considerations such as facts of human psychology. The idea is that ethical theories should remain subject to continual scrutiny, and open to the possibility that the principles they embrace should be revised or even rejected in the light of reflection (more on this below).

Normative theories of both the above types endorse ethical principles that guide our environmental behaviour – such as that it is (1) wrong to despoil nature or (2) right to maximise social welfare – as well as rules for the application of these principles when they conflict (such as that (1) has strict priority over (2) or vice versa). There are, of course, several other aspects to normative ethics as described. Any fully worked out theory of ethics will, for example, appeal to principles concerning punishment, the ends of life, property and so forth.

Most theories of normative environmental ethics are coupled to a restriction on the scope of ethics such that only human beings possess ultimate moral value. They can, thus, be seen as natural extensions of normative theories that aim to regulate interactions between humans, such as liberalism, utilitarianism, or libertarianism.[53] However, other theories of environmental ethics have also been proposed that, for example, take certain non-human animals,[54] all living creatures[55] or nature as a whole[56] as their starting points. The point is that these normative theories are developed to the point that they provide us with both individual principles, and criteria for balancing these principles.

Whereas normative ethics involves the defence of a particular set of ethical claims within a systematic framework, *meta-ethics* concerns 'the status and nature of the ethical claims we make'.[57] A meta-ethical approach, therefore, involves the questioning of the assumptions that lie behind our selection of a normative theory.

Suppose a normative theory assumes that persons belonging to *all* generations possess distributive entitlements because they are all owners of interests of a comparable nature. A meta-ethical analysis of these issues would involve a closer look at what it means to claim that a person possesses interests that others should respect. According to one view, for example, a person can only possess interests if they also possess desires; and, as a result, any normative theory that claims that the not-yet-born possess interests (and thus claims and entitlements against others) must explain how these entities can 'possess' desires despite not yet existing. The problem is that this is much more difficult than it might seem. Some claim, for example, that meta-ethical considerations alone limit the scope of distributive entitlements to existing persons even before any substantive claims about right and wrong have been appealed to.[58] While such meta-ethical arguments can be challenged (more on this in Chapter 6 below), they remain a crucial component of theorising about the nature and extent of our obligations to the environment.

1.6   METHODOLOGY

In order to construct a manageable context for our investigation of ethics and justice in the context of climate change, I will be appealing to three method-ological assumptions. The first concerns the merits of egalitarian approaches to justice; the second concerns the method of reflective equilibrium; and the third concerns the merits of appealing to hypothetical, rather than imaginary, examples.

1.6.1   The Ideal of Equality

According to my first assumption, the range of theories of justice considered in later chapters is somewhat restricted. The theories I will be focusing on are what I will call 'broadly egalitarian'. Broadly egalitarian theories hold that benefits and burdens should be distributed according to the ideal of equality or some closely related ideal. The crucial point is that these theories reject the assumption behind libertarian theories of distributive justice that appeal only to 'historical principles'. Historical principles explain how resources should be distributed in terms of how those resources came to be owned, and how they were later transferred amongst persons.[59] It is the view of the author that egalitarianism, so long as it is defined broadly so that it includes 'non-histori-cal' views such as giving priority to the worst off or distributing so that all have enough, provides the basis of the most useful approach to distributive and environmental justice.

1.6.2   Wide Reflective Equilibrium

According to the reflective equilibrium approach, a cogent theory of distrib-utive justice must cohere with at least some of the most deeply held convic-tions about justice that people actually hold. This is not to say that the methodological strategy of the book will be to engage in what has been referred to disparagingly as 'piece-meal appeal to intuition'[60] – that the theories considered will be tested solely according to the extent to which they reflect people's everyday moral convictions and intuitions (I use these terms interchangeably). What it means is that we seek to take such intuitions seriously. There are a number of ways in which this might be achieved, the most useful approach being known as 'reflective equilibrium'.[61]

In *A Theory of Justice*, Rawls addresses the issue of how we might best characterise the relation between our common-sense beliefs and our ethical or political theories. Do the former stand in need of the latter for their justification? Or is the acceptability of these beliefs unconstrained by considerations of theory? Or is the justifiability of ethics constrained in some way by our considered common-sense beliefs? Rawls suggests that, rather than privileging either side of the equation, we should endeavour to find a balance, or equilibrium, between pre-theoretical and theoretical beliefs. The basic procedure for doing this is as follows.

- First, we start with our most considered pre-theoretical beliefs about an ethical issue (for example, intergenerational ethical responsibility) purged of basic inconsistencies.
- Second, we attempt to construct a more general ethical theory that will explain and give unity to these beliefs.
- Third, we establish the extent to which our beliefs and principles cohere with a range of additional normative and non-normative considerations that act as the background for our ethical reasoning (it is this stage in the process that makes reflective equilibrium much more than a systematisation of the particular beliefs that are held in our society, or in our ideological group).
- Fourth, we establish to what extent there exists coherence between these three levels of reasoning.
- Fifth, and depending on our answer to this question, we have basically two options to reduce incoherence: (1) to return to theory and modify it until it delivers greater coherence with our intuitions, or (2) to give up some elements of the pre-theoretical position. Adjustments to background beliefs are also possible.

Whether we choose (1) or (2), Rawls thinks, depends on the circumstances of the case. If the theory is particularly attractive and any modifications to it appear arbitrary, then we may decide to reject the common sense view (an approach which we might refer to as 'biting the bullet'). This is an attractive move if we can give a good explanation, independently of our theory, of why the common-sense view is obviously unsound. If, however, the common-sense view is very firmly held, then we might wish to modify the theory. Put simply, the aim of the procedure is to reach a balance, or 'equilibrium', between common-sense beliefs in particular cases and our theory of ethics or justice.

The achievement of a particular reflective equilibrium might seem rather arbitrary, until we remember that natural scientific research works in a surprisingly similar way. There is, even here, no simple rule that explains whether we should continue to endorse a scientific theory in the face of a falsifying observation. It is, at bottom, a matter of debate and conflict in the period where a consensus around one scientific theory takes over from a consensus around another.[62]

The method of wide reflective equilibrium seems well suited to issues of intergenerational justice and climate change, for these issues are now well rooted in both the media and in public life, and generate strong intuitions on the part of experts and non-experts. Most people have deeply felt convictions about the wrongness of despoiling the environment or of failing to bequeath some cultural and artistic heritage for the sake of future generations, even if these are not always given priority.

1.6.3   The Power of Examples

While a coherent approach to issues of intergenerational ethics requires extensive appeal to *hypothetical* examples (which, for example, attempt to tease out our convictions about the merits of climate change policies which will have differential impacts on the quality of life of future populations), it is my view that appeals to *imaginary* examples should be avoided wherever possible. Imaginary examples are those which 'involve logical possibilities that could occur only in a world very different from ours'.[63] The difference between these two types of examples is often difficult to draw, but it is important as the intuitions generated by imaginary examples are problematic.

Consider the series of imaginary science fiction examples that involve people being 'tele-transported' from one planet to another discussed by the influential philosopher Derek Parfit in his book *Reasons and Persons*.[64] Parfit, engaged in a particularly intricate instance of the reflective equilibrium approach, holds that, by appealing to people's intuitions about such examples, we can make progress in our characterisation of personal identity and its importance. The idea is that if one's intuition is that one dies as a result of being reconstituted somewhere many million miles away with the information provided by an imaginary scanner, then it means that one believes that personal identity is a matter of spatio-temporal continuity. If one believes that one *survives*, cutting months off an otherwise dull journey, this means one is drawn to a view of personal identity as psychological continuity. Either way, a cogent theory of personal identity, Parfit thinks, must generate a fit between a fully developed theory of what it is to be a person and people's intuitions when faced with both imaginary and hypothetical examples.

The problem with Parfit's methodological strategy is that even if people entertain clear and deeply held convictions about whether being teleported would involve the termination of their identity, it might be doubted that such convictions can be used to explain, and give unity to, the beliefs they hold about personal identity in more everyday contexts. The idea is that the imaginary case must not only generate intuitions on the part of the reader, but also be relevantly similar to everyday life for any important insight to be drawn. When we turn to hypothetical examples, that is to say, examples that are both conceptually and factually possible, these problems seem less serious. This is because they are much less prone to the objection that the set of circumstances that they describe are so dissimilar to those of the real world that our convictions cannot be transposed between these cases. In the book, we will be using these sorts of examples.

NOTES

1. Singer, 2002, p. 120.
2. See Munich Re, 2005, 'Press release on the costs of Hurricane Katrina', http://www.munichre.com/press_release, 28 September. See also BBC Online 2005, 'Hurricane damage to total $60 billion', http://news.bbc.co.uk?1?hi?business/4400288, 2 November.
3. Hecht, 2005.
4. The Meteorological Office provide an analysis of the record breaking summer 2003 temperature series online at <http://www.met-office.gov.uk/climate/uk/interesting/aug03maxtemps.html>.
5. Houghton, 2004, p. 177.
6. The company, which specialises in re-insurance, keeps a useful database of extreme weather events and natural disasters online at <http://www.swissre.com>.
7. See Nicola Jones, 2003 (http://www.newscientist.com/article.ns?id=dn4022).
8. Oliver and Fairbridge, 1987, p. 922.
9. See Winters et al., 2002.
10. Stagg, 1971, pp. 115ff.
11. Overy, 1997, pp. 112ff.
12. Ahrens, 2000, p. 16.
13. Aristotle, (1962 translation).
14. See, for example, Kepler, 1966; Ferguson, 2002, pp. 51–2.
15. See Milankovitch, 1920.
16. Longer-term experimental forecasts are, however, becoming increasingly common. The European Centre for Medium-Term Weather Forecasts (ECMWF), an international meteorological organisation supported by 25 European States, has recently added a monthly experimental forecast that operates on a timescale of 10–30 days (http://www.getweather.co.uk/).
17. Oliver and Fairbridge, 1987.
18. Aguado and Burt, 1999, pp. 408ff.
19. Fagan, 2004, pp. 90ff.
20. See Aguado and Burt, 1999, pp. 413–14; and Grove, 1988, especially pp. 379ff.
21. Fagan, 2004, pp. 247ff; and Fagan, 2002.

22. I refer to the definition of climate change given in the text of the United Nations Framework Convention on Climate Change (UNFCCC). According to this, climate change refers to changes in the atmosphere that are 'attributed directly or indirectly to human activity that alters the composition of the global atmosphere and which is in addition to natural climate variability observed over comparable time periods' (United Nations (Cm 2833), 1995, p. 4).

23. A widely cited article in December 2004's edition of *Science* reported that, of the 928 peer reviewed contributions to the debate on anthropogenic climate change, none disagreed with the 'consensus position' of the IPCC that the earth's climate has been changed, and will continue to change, as a result of human activity (see Oreskes, 2004, p. 1686).

24. An ICM survey for BBC TV in July 2004, for example, revealed that 64 per cent of people questioned viewed climate change as 'one of the most important issues facing the world today'. For a summary of the survey results and methodology used, see Alex Kirkby, 'Britons unsure of climate costs', *BBC Online* (http://news.bbc.co.uk/1/hi/sci/tech/3934363.stm).

25. Note that the focus of the IPCC, and of this book, is the changes in climate brought about by effects of greenhouse gas build-up since the start of the industrial revolution. It is much less concerned with other natural, or anthropogenic, causes of climate change such as volcanic activity, nuclear power, the possibility of nuclear winter, or recent attempts by the USA and other states to modify clouds to change rainfall patterns except, and in so far as, they modify the greenhouse effect. For a review of human activities that modify weather and climate, see Cotton and Pielke, 1995.

26. Houghton et al., 1996 (hereafter IPCC, 1996a), p. 5.

27. See McMichael et al., 'Human population health', in R.T. Watson et al., 1996 (hereafter IPCC, 1996b), pp. 561–84.

28. Bruce et al., 1996 (hereafter IPCC, 1996c), pp. 9ff.

29. Houghton et al., 'Summary for policymakers', Houghton et al., 2001, pp. 10, 12 (hereafter, IPCC, 2001a).

30. See 'Summary for policymakers', in Metz et al. 2001 (hereafter IPCC, 2001c), p. 3; see also 'Technical summary', in McCarthy et al. 2001 (hereafter IPCC, 2001b), pp. 21ff.

31. The UNFCCC was adopted at the United Nations Conference on Environment and Development, held in Rio de Janeiro in June 1992, and was designed to serve as the framework for further co-ordination and negotiation towards legally binding protocols on greenhouse emissions. The Kyoto Protocol to the FCCC, which was agreed in December 1997, requires the developed countries party to it to reduce their collective emissions of the six most important greenhouse gases to 5.2 per cent below their 1990 levels by 2012. The ratification of the protocol by Russia in November 2004 meant that the Protocol had received the support of countries that emit more than 55 per cent of the world's greenhouse gases, and the protocol entered into force on 16 February 2005 (three months after Russia handed ratification papers to the UN). The text of the Kyoto Protocol can be found online at <http://www.cop3.org/home.html>.

32. United Nations, 1995, p. 5. Article 2 of the same convention sets out an objective of stabilising atmospheric greenhouse concentrations at levels that 'would prevent dangerous anthropogenic interference with the climate system' and within a time-frame 'sufficient to allow ecosystems to adapt naturally to climate change, to ensure that food production is not threatened and to enable economic development to proceed in a sustainable manner.'

33. Arrow et al., 'Intertemporal equity, discounting and economic efficiency', in IPCC, 1996c, p. 130. See also, IPCC, 2001c, 'Summary for policymakers', p. 3. The IPCC use the notions of 'fairness', 'equity' and 'justice' interchangeably (Banuri et al., 'Equity and social considerations', IPCC, 1996c, p. 85).

34. See IPPC, 2001c, 'Setting the stage: climate change and sustainable development', pp. 73–114. In fact, according to the TAR's word search facility (http://www.grida.no/climate/ipcc_tar/) 'equity' issues are mentioned 211 times in the TAR's three volumes. The concepts of 'ethics' and 'justice' are much less frequently mentioned, which points to an idiosyncrasy of the debate on climate change that tends to avoid overt talk of distributive justice, ethics or morality.

35. See 'Save the planet plea to world leaders by Blair', *The Times*, Tuesday 24 June 1997, p. 1.
36. Beckett, 2003, p. 160.
37. Gummer observes that 'Climate change threatens our world and our children's future . . . If we act effectively we can confine the impact of climate change within a containable measure. If we do not, the effect could make the lives of our grandchildren immeasurably more difficult and perhaps threaten the future of the planet itself.' See Department of the Environment, 1997, p. 3.
38. See, for example, Pearce, 2005a. The EU ETS works by issuing businesses across the EU certificates that permit them to emit a certain amount of CO_2 into the atmosphere in a certain year. Companies that emit more than their initial allocation must then buy additional certificates from others that have emitted less. The scheme entered into force on 1 January 2005 and covers emissions until 2007.
39. Following Joseph Raz, I take humanism to be the view that 'the explanation and justification of the goodness or badness of anything derives ultimately from its contribution, actual or possible, to human life and its quality' (Raz, 1986, p. 194). The IPCC takes an explicitly humanist (or 'anthropocentric') view, according to which the effects of climate change 'are valued only in terms of their value for human recreation, medicine, and other aspects of human welfare' (IPCC, 1996c, p. 61).
40. The argument has been defended by numerous writers, albeit in different forms. See, for example, Shue, 2001, pp. 449ff; and Athanasiou and Baer, 2002, pp. 14ff.
41. See, for example, Arrow et al., 1996, pp. 125ff.
42. Michaels et al., 2000 and Michaels, 2004.
43. Lomborg, 2001, pp. 258ff.
44. See, for example, Fred Singer, 2000.
45. See, for example, T. Banuri et al., 1996, pp. 85ff; and Jamieson, 2001.
46. Onora O'Neill, 1996, p. 115; Jamieson, 2003, pp. 290–95.
47. Shue, 2001, pp. 450ff.
48. Jamieson, 2001, pp. 290–94.
49. Rawls, 1971, pp. 7ff.
50. As, for example, argued in Cohen, 2001, pp. 134ff.
51. Rawls, 1971, pp. 34ff. According to Rawls, intuitionism is the doctrine that 'there is an irreducible family of first principles which have to be weighed against one another by asking ourselves which balance, in our considered judgment, is the most just' (p. 34).
52. Bentham, 1962, Chapter 1.
53. A range of human-centred normative theories are discussed in Elliot, 2001, pp. 177ff.
54. Peter Singer, 1975; 1993; Regan, 2004.
55. Rolston III, 1989; Paul Taylor, 1986; Attfield, 2003.
56. Leopold, 1949; and Callicott, 1989.
57. John O'Neill, 2001, p. 163.
58. See, for example, Macklin, 1981; De George, 1979.
59. Nozick, 1974, p. 153.
60. See Griffin, 1996, pp. 3ff.
61. See Rawls, 1971, pp. 20ff and pp. 48ff; Daniels, 1996; Buchanan et al., 2002, pp. 371–8.
62. See Glover, 1977, pp. 26ff.
63. Hypothetical examples, by contrast, 'involve instances of situations or events that have occurred, or could occur without requiring us to rewrite physics or change our basic conception of how the world works' (Jamieson, 1993, p. 484).
64. Parfit, 1984, pp. 200ff.

2. Space, time and the science of climate change

> What is now plain is that the emission of greenhouse gases, associated with industrialisation and strong economic growth from a world population that has increased sixfold in 200 years, is causing global warming at a rate that began as significant, has become alarming and is simply unsustainable in the long-term.[1]

Tony Blair

> It is your human environment that makes climate.[2]

Mark Twain

2.1 INTRODUCTION

In this chapter, we shall take a closer look at the IPCC's main findings, set out in the Second and Third Assessment Reports (SAR and TAR). In particular, we shall examine the evidence for the IPCC's claim that climate change will impact significantly on the well-being of future generations.

The IPCC is not a traditional research grouping. It is an intergovernmental body charged with the responsibility of assembling and publishing peer-reviewed findings of scientists engaged in climate change research. The successive assessments of the IPCC represent years of protracted discussion and negotiation amongst thousands of scientists, as well as representatives of UN member states. As a result, the IPCC's findings do not always correspond to the views of individual researchers. As one critical evaluation has put it, 'the IPCC procedures are a cross between a scientific peer-review and an intergovernmental negotiation'.[3] Despite the presence of a certain amount of politicisation, however, and so long as its findings are viewed critically and rival sources considered, the IPCC's assessments provide the most authoritative picture of contemporary climate change research available at this time.

The IPCC's work is divided into three 'working groups.' Working Group 1 (WG1) is concerned with the science of climate change; Working Group 2 (WG2) is concerned with impacts and vulnerability; and Working Group 3 (WG3) is concerned with socio-economic issues. In the SAR and TAR, each group assembled research on the causes of climate change as well as its likely future impacts.

- WG1 report that global average temperature rose by 0.6°C in the 20th century as a result of human activities and claim that it will continue to rise on all models of the enhanced greenhouse effect.[4]
- WG2 report that climate change has already begun (and will continue) to affect the physical and biological systems that support human life, and, on balance, these systems will be affected adversely.[5]
- WG3 report that climate change will have long-term socio-economic impacts on all countries, and that the net global impacts are expected to be adverse, with developing countries suffering the most.[6]

In what follows, the greenhouse theory of climate change is explained in layman's terms, and some of the key, largely negative, impacts are discussed in relation to two components of human well-being (health and economic–social issues). For the purposes of simplicity, the discussion avoids endorsing a particular notion of human well-being. Rather, the focus will be on the vital physical, biological and socio-economic systems that provide the background for all views of well-being.

2.2 THE SCIENCE AND ORIGINS OF CLIMATE CHANGE

The idea of a 'natural greenhouse effect' appears to have been introduced by French mathematician Jean Baptiste Fourier (1768–1830). In a series of articles, Fourier observed that the atmosphere appeared to behave in a similar way to a giant 'hothouse', trapping heat that would otherwise escape into space.[7] Later, the British physicist John Tyndall (1820–93) recognised that small changes in the composition of the atmosphere could affect climate. In 1861, Tyndall published a paper that discussed the absorptive properties of carbon dioxide (CO_2) and water vapour and went on to hypothesise that changes in CO_2 concentrations may have been responsible for the timing of glacial and interglacial periods.[8] Later, in 1896, Svante Arrhenius (1859–1927), a Swedish chemist, estimated that a doubling of CO_2 in the atmosphere would result in a 5–6°C rise in global surface temperature.[9] The work of these 19th-century pioneers was developed in the 1930s by engineer and amateur climatologist Guy Callendar. Callendar claimed that only increased CO_2 emissions from fossil fuel combustion could explain the upward trend in temperature he observed during the first decades of the 20th century.[10]

A number of studies linking greenhouse gas concentrations to climate variables followed, but it seems that a 1957 paper by Roger Revelle and Hans

Suess was critical in the formation of opinion. The paper argued famously that, in contributing to CO_2 concentrations in the atmosphere, 'human beings are now carrying out a large-scale geophysical experiment of a kind that could not have happened in the past nor be reproduced in the future'.[11] However, it was not until the IPCC's First Assessment Report (FAR) in 1990 that anthropogenic climate change was acknowledged by the UN, and the majority of member states, as a major threat to the international community.[12]

While there remain numerous uncertainties associated with understanding global climate, the science behind the natural greenhouse effect is, in most respects, uncontroversial. Energy is radiated from the sun mainly in the visible, short-wave, part of the spectrum. Much of this energy reaches the Earth, with approximately 30 per cent or so being directly reflected back into space, either as a result of being scattered by clouds and microscopic airborne particles (called aerosols) or by being reflected from the land or oceans.[13] The remaining radiation warms the Earth's surface before being redistributed throughout the atmosphere by processes of atmospheric and oceanic circulation and ultimately much of it (around 70 per cent) is radiated back into space. In equilibrium, the amount of energy that the Earth's surface receives from the sun is balanced by the amount of energy radiated back into space, although this outgoing energy is radiated at a much lower temperature. Any disturbance in the amount of radiation received from the sun and/or the amount of energy that is retained in the Earth's atmosphere causes a change in the total energy available in the Earth's atmosphere. These are called 'radiative forcings'.[14]

One factor that has altered the balance of incoming and outgoing radiation in the past, and which has caused a positive forcing, is the accumulation of naturally occurring greenhouse gases in the atmosphere. When present in the atmosphere, greenhouse gases, such as CO_2 and water vapour, reduce the efficiency by which the Earth cools to space by absorbing outgoing radiation at certain wavelengths. The radiation trapped by the absorptive properties of greenhouse gases warms various parts of the atmosphere, notably the lower part of the Earth's atmosphere called the troposphere, and this air radiates energy in all directions, keeping the Earth warmer than otherwise would be the case (at present, about 15°C). In the absence of this effect, the Earth would have a similar surface temperature to the moon (approximately −18°C).

The science behind the 'enhanced greenhouse effect' is also relatively uncontroversial, although there is great disagreement as to its magnitude. Human activities (such as fossil fuel use) that increase atmospheric concentrations of naturally occurring greenhouse gases, or introduce new greenhouse gases that are not naturally occurring, act so as to reduce further the efficiency with which the Earth cools to space, upsetting the climate equilibrium established by the natural greenhouse effect. Recent research indicates that anthropogenic concentrations of greenhouse gases have been increasing in the atmosphere for at least 8000 years. The enhanced greenhouse effect, then, may have its origins much further back in time than many assume.[15] Nevertheless, the bulk of greenhouse emissions have been released in the last 200 years, mainly as a result of the use of fossil fuels, and it is the period from 1760 to the present that is the focus of most climatologists. The global emissions of the most important greenhouse gases in this period are given in Table 2.1. As the table shows, concentrations of CO_2 in the atmosphere increased from 280 000 parts per billion (ppb)[16] in pre-industrial times to 365 000 ppb in 1998. If we count more recent observations made by the Mauna Loa Observatory in Hawaii, which give a figure of 377 000 ppb for the end of 2003, then CO_2 has increased 19 per cent since 1959 and 35 per cent since the start of the industrial revolution.[17]

Table 2.1   Current and pre-industrial emissions[18]

Greenhouse gas	Pre-industrial atmospheric concentration (ppb)	1998 atmospheric concentration (ppb)	Lifespan (years)	Global warming potential (over 100 years)[19]
Carbon dioxide (CO_2)	280 000	365 000	50–200	1
Methane (CH_4)	700	1745	12–120	23
Nitrous oxide (N_2O)	≈270	314	50	296
Perfluoromethane (CF_4)	0.040	0.080	>50 000	5 700
Hydroflurocarbon 23 (CHF_3)	0	0.014	12	12 000
Sulphur hexafluoride (SF_6)	0	0.004	3 200	22 200

Increased CO_2 concentrations are believed to be responsible for the bulk of the anthropogenic warming witnessed over the course of the 20th century. Nevertheless, the IPCC observes that the importance of other greenhouse gases should not be underestimated – particularly since these gases are much more efficient at inducing climatic change than CO_2, and the combined climatic impact of these gases relative to CO_2 is increasing sharply.[20] According to recent estimates, for example, CO_2 is responsible for roughly 61 per cent of the enhanced greenhouse effect, methane for 19 per cent and the less common gases for 20 per cent.[21]

A key finding of the SAR was that the enhanced greenhouse effect has already caused a small warming of the Earth's atmosphere. The SAR observed that the warming witnessed in the 20th century was 'unlikely to be entirely natural in origin' and that 'the balance of evidence suggests that there is a discernible human influence on global climate'.[22] This finding was underlined by the TAR, which claimed that global temperature has risen by 0.6°C in the 20th century and that this was *likely* to have been the largest 100-year increase during the last 1000 years.[23]

2.3   FOUR IMPORTANT FINDINGS

The IPCC make four important claims relevant to intergenerational justice:

(a)   The climate is expected to change in the future even if existing and future governments adopt measures to reduce greenhouse emissions.

(b)   There are measures of mitigation and adaptation available through which the future costs of climate change could be reduced.

(c)   There are significant uncertainties associated with predicting climate change, such as the role of non-greenhouse influences on climate.

(d)   These uncertainties do not imply that nothing should be done to reduce the threat of future climate change.

(a)   In order to establish the magnitude of future climate changes, it is necessary to predict future atmospheric concentrations of both natural and anthropogenic greenhouse gases. This requires careful determination. Building on the SAR (which indicated a temperature increase of between 1 and 3.5°C, and a mean sea-level rise of between 13 and 94 cm, by 2010) the TAR developed a number of 'emissions scenarios' in order to estimate future levels of greenhouse emissions, and with them likely figures for global warming in the decades before 2100.[24] These scenarios covered all the major greenhouse gases, each being based on a different possible future that incorporates different assumptions about world population, economic growth, the success of existing attempts to limit greenhouse emissions by certain international agreements, and the sensitivity of climate variables to greenhouse gases (in particular, CO_2). For example, one such possible future 'describes a future world of very rapid economic growth' while another 'describes a world in which the emphasis is on local solutions to economic, social and environmental sustainability'.[25] As part of the TAR, each greenhouse scenario was fed into the most up-to-date computational models that simulate the response of the climate system to changes in the composition of the atmosphere. From the results of this modelling, the IPCC claimed that:

*   Atmospheric CO_2 concentrations will rise to between 650 and 970 ppm by 2100.

- global surface temperature will rise by between 1.4 and 5.8°C by 2100, and this rise is 'very likely' to be without precedent in the last 10 000 years'.[26]
- global average sea-level will rise by between 0.11 and 0.77 metres by 2100.[27]

From the ethical point of view, the IPCC's projections of future average temperature and sea-level rises on all scenarios fits well with the claim that climate change will alter the pattern of benefits and burdens across many generations. While greenhouse gas concentrations are evenly distributed throughout the globe, localised differences in the nature of climate processes mean that the effects of both global warming and sea-level rises will vary from region to region. Some developed countries, such as the UK, seem set to be moderate losers. Recent research suggests that, depending on region and scenario, average annual temperatures across the UK will increase between 2°C and 3.5°C by 2100; the frequency of very warm seasons will increase; and annual rainfall will increase by at least 10 per cent by 2080. Increases in extreme weather such as storms, flash floods and heatwaves would follow.[28]

Developing countries, especially those that are partly or entirely low-lying, as well as small-island states, are expected to be much more adversely affected. The Maldives, for example, which consists of 1200 islands lying, on average, two metres above sea-level, is an example of a country that could cease to exist in a hundred years on several of the IPCC's scenarios due to rising sea-levels. In fact, plans already exist to evacuate many of the island group's 360 000 inhabitants, although experts are hopeful that adaptation measures such as sea defences, reforestation and reparation of coral reefs may delay disaster.[29]

(b) There would, perhaps, be little point in considering climate change as raising important ethical questions if little could be done to offset or reverse the bad effects it threatens for future quality of life. It would appear from the IPCC's research, however, that there are several options available to governments to reduce the threat posed by these effects. There are, broadly speaking, two separate categories of measures that the IPCC suggest might be undertaken: measures of *mitigation* and measures of *adaptation*.

Measures of mitigation (defined as those that prevent avoidable climate change) can be divided into two categories: those that will increase the number or efficiency of greenhouse *sinks* and those that will reduce the number or efficiency of greenhouse *sources*. Greenhouse sources are processes or activities, such as fossil fuel combustion, that introduce greenhouse gases, or their precursors, into the atmosphere. Greenhouse sinks, such as plants or oceanic mechanisms, absorb certain greenhouse gases so they play no further warming role.[30]

The IPCC claims that reductions in atmospheric greenhouse concentrations could be achieved by both reducing the climate impact of sources, and increasing the impact of sinks. For example, measures could be adopted to increase energy efficiency in both the industrial and domestic sectors; transport practices might be altered; and more efficient land management practices could be adopted. Moreover, many of these measures, according to the IPCC, would have benefits that would equal or exceed their costs quite apart from the way in which they would be expected to mitigate the threat of climate change. That is, they would be 'no regrets' measures.[31]

The IPCC also outlines a range of adaptation measures that would modify human practices to fit in better with climate changes when and where they occur. These could be institutional, behavioural, technological or social by origin. Adaptive capacity across these sectors is considered a crucial part of future research into climate change since greenhouse emissions will not stabilise for many decades even if mitigation measures are pursued aggressively.[32] Water security could be maintained in many areas by improved flood defences, improved infrastructure for water storage, collection and distribution, and resettlement away from costal areas prone to flooding.[33] Human health impacts could be minimised by improved public health infrastructure in communities vulnerable to direct and indirect effects of climate change, such as extreme weather or increasing incidence of infectious diseases. Design of the urban environment will also be central to any adaptive response.[34] Finally, the socio-economic base of vulnerable countries and regions could be protected by improved infrastructural planning and the strategic (re)location of industrial buildings away from coastal areas or areas prone to extreme weather events.[35] Such proposals indicate that, for many countries, the most efficient mechanism of climate adaptation is socio-economic development.

(c)   The IPCC observes that there are numerous limits on their ability to predict the nature and scope of future climate change. The SAR and TAR mention the following four areas where future research is essential if the greatest uncertainties are to be addressed.

i.   Projections of future emissions of greenhouse gases, as well as other
     agents that determine global climate
The key problem, here, is the atmospheric role of aerosols. These are small atmospheric particles that have both natural and anthropogenic origins, such as the combustion of fossil fuels, forest fires, aeroplane jet trails, biomass burning and volcanic activity. Although they have a relatively short atmospheric lifetime (usually up to a few days), aerosols can have a significant effect on climate, directly, by 'backscattering' solar radiation into space that would otherwise reach the Earth's surface, and indirectly by modifying clouds

so that they are more reflective.[36] In fact, it has been shown that large accumulations of aerosols can lead to so much less sunlight hitting the Earth's surface that it can counteract greenhouse warming altogether in some regions. This has become known as 'global dimming'.

In many ways, the science behind global dimming is well-established. Research conducted by the IPCC as part of its SAR and TAR indicated that both natural and anthropogenic aerosols can have a significant dampening effect on global mean warming (reducing underlying 20th-century warming from 0.8°C to the observed 0.6°C), as well as completely offsetting current warming in some regions in the Northern Hemisphere.[37] In fact, analyses of the global cooling effects of the Mount Pinatubo volcano eruption of 15 June 1991, which released millions of tonnes of aerosols into the atmosphere, and led to a temporary cooling of the Earth, drove the science of climate modelling ahead in the 1990s.[38]

It is recent analyses of the *scale* of global dimming that has surprised climatologists. Scientists Shabati Cohen and Gerald Stanhill (who christened the phenomenon) claimed in 2001 that aerosol build up has been responsible for a 2.7 per cent drop in globally averaged solar radiation reaching the Earth per decade in the past 50 years, a figure that is compatible with other research on the topic.[39] This suggests that dimming is more important than the IPCC assume and has masked the fact that the Earth will warm more rapidly than standard models allow for as soon as aerosol concentrations reduce as a result of existing anti-pollution measures.[40] Crucially, if the more pessimistic analyses of global dimming prove correct, policymakers in the future may be faced by a stark choice: either continue to reduce emissions of aerosols to reduce air pollution and thereby miss out on the limited protection global dimming gives from the worst of global warming, or attenuate the attack on aerosol use for the sake of its indirect cooling role thereby missing out on further benefits of recent reductions in air pollution.[41]

ii.   The representation of 'feedback' processes that tend to add or subtract
      to an initial increase in anthropogenic greenhouse emissions

The problem here is that, although many scientists believe that feedback processes will bring about a net increase in global temperature, there exist both negative and positive feedbacks in the biosphere. The carbon dioxide fertilisation process is a good example of a negative feedback. Here, increases in CO_2 are accompanied by an increase in efficiency in the take up of CO_2 by plants and trees, with the result that the total amount of CO_2 in the atmosphere reduces and warming is reduced. An example of a positive feedback is the way in which global warming results in an increase in water vapour in the atmosphere that goes on to prompt more warming and so on.[42] Much research clearly needs to be done to understand these crucial processes.

iii.   The improvement of climate change data gathering techniques, such as
       measurements of solar radiation and oceans temperature

The main source of controversy here is the role of solar output. It has been
suggested by some scientists that much of the reported warming of the 20th
century comes as a result of natural variations in radiation from the sun (as
measured, for example, by sun spot activity) and not from the enhanced greenhouse effect.[43] However, it is more likely that the variable sun was a significant factor in climate change only during the early part of the 20th century.

Since changes in the amount of solar irradiance are too small to be the
culprit for recent climatic changes, other researchers have suggested a more
indirect connection between solar activity and climate. They claim that
reduced solar activity prevents fewer of the cosmic rays that help to form
clouds reach the Earth, with the overall effect that temperature falls at the
surface.[44] The solar output theory of climate change is controversial, however,
and few scientists believe that it accounts for more than a small proportion of
the 0.6°C global warming reported by the TAR.[45]

iv.   Low probability, high impact, climate effects

The IPCC note that 'future unexpected, and rapid climate system changes
(as have occurred in the past) are, by their nature, difficult to project', a
consideration which it observes gives rise to the possibility of 'surprises'.[46]
One such 'surprise' arises from the risk that increases in sea surface temperatures in the North Atlantic combined with the melting of the Greenland
Ice Sheet could lead to a slowing down – or re-positioning – of the thermo-
haline circulation (or 'gulf stream') process that transports heat throughout
the globe through movements of surface and deep-sea water. Such an event
would have large effects on climate in Europe and North America. However,
there are huge problems quantifying the probability of such events actually
occurring.

(d)   According to the IPCC's version of the much discussed *precautionary
principle*, 'actions giving rise to *possible* but quantifiably unknown and potentially very large risks [ought to be] avoided or corrected.'[47] This principle, in
one form or another, has a fairly long history in environment and public health
policy and research. Although it is unclear when the notion was first introduced, or by whom, Harremoës and colleagues report that medical authorities
in London invoked the principle in the 1850s in order to stop a major cholera
epidemic. In this case, a water pump suspected of being a vehicle for the
disease was taken out of service despite the fact that the causal link between
contaminated water and cholera had yet to be proven.[48] Many other docu-
mented cases of the principle's use, however, are more recent and are linked
to the principle's inclusion in a number of international legal documents, such

as the 1992 Rio Declaration on Environment and Development and the 1992 UN Framework Convention on Climate Change.

Despite its growing popularity, the precautionary principle is neither easy to interpret nor apply. Problems can be divided into those arising from its meaning or from the consequences of its use. One conceptual problem arises from the principle's complexity, which flows from the different emphasis that can be given to its three core elements:

- awareness (but not complete understanding) of some process or activity. This might constitute knowledge of a link between two variables (such as contaminated water and cholera) but not full understanding of this link;
- reasonable grounds on which to claim that the effects of the process or activity are harmful;
- reasonable grounds on which to claim that preventing the activity will be less costly to human well-being than the alternative.

In short, we might say that the precautionary principle applies when there is *limited awareness*, *high stakes*, and an *effective solution* to some social problem.

One problem with the principle so conceived, is that of balancing the level of proof needed to identify a given activity as a threat, and the quality and quantity of the threat as measured by its possible impact on human well-being – that is, the interplay between the *awareness* and *high stakes* components.[49] So, while some environmental groups have claimed a precautionary approach would involve the abandonment of new technologies that cannot be shown to be completely safe (such as genetic modification of plants or storing CO_2 underground), others argue that it implies only that scientific uncertainties should not be used to delay measures that would improve human well-being.

Another conceptual problem is that, quite aside from problems of interpretation, the notion seems inherently unscientific because it reverses the burden of proof that is normally assumed by 'sound science' according to which one does not act as if an activity is hazardous until one has hard evidence for this view.[50] The precautionary principle, it is argued, incorporates an unscientific conception of risk such that environmental activities can be defined as hazardous on purely subjective grounds: that is, if people think that an activity is harmful, then it *is* harmful. This approach means that the distinction between 'real' risks and 'perceived risks' is violated.[51]

Writers concerned about the consequences of the precautionary principle argue that it places undue pressure on scientists to avoid so-called 'false negatives' (that involve the underplaying of the harmful effects of an activity or product) but to ignore the dangers of so-called 'false positives' (that involve labelling a harmless activity or product as harmful). Another consequence, argue some, is that scientific research suggesting that there *may* be a link between some activity, *x*, and an adverse impact, *y*, is used by lobbyists to demand a moratorium or prohibition of this activity, rather than further research to establish the extent of the link.[52] This can, moreover, have the effect that consumers and policymakers can become distracted from significant, known, threats in favour of unproven, uncertain, threats. It is also claimed that the proponents of precaution overplay the potential long-term risks of new technologies, such as genetic modification, relative to their likely net benefits;[53] or encourage low, zero or negative growth policies that jeopardise the well-being of the present and future poor.[54]

But many of these objections are misguided, both in general terms and as criticisms of the IPCC. Few scholars concerned with the relations amongst science, society and environment now entertain such a strict, positivistic, understanding of natural science. It is widely accepted that perceptions of risks play some role in the construction of scientific research – for example, in the setting of the standards of statistical confidence used in research dealing with very serious health risks, as well as in the choice of hypotheses. Moreover, an increasing number of writers deny that risk can be established independently of social and historical norms.[55]

For all these reasons, the IPCC's research seems much better placed than its 'sound science' critics to make sense of recent developments in risk analysis, as well as the complexities and feedback mechanisms associated with climate change. It seeks to strike a balance between the search for undeniable proof of an activity's safety and the overplaying of threats that are not yet understood. As we have seen, the IPCC has constructed confidence scales to model scientific uncertainty in a way that can be useful to policymakers; it has also avoided applying the precautionary principle to the more 'conjectural' climate possibilities, such as shifts in global climate caused by changes in the directionality (or intensity) of the gulf-stream, that lie beyond the present limits of scientific understanding. Above all, it has embraced a spirit of humility about unknowns that is lacking in the work of the sceptics, who, in focusing only on what can be claimed about the climate system with 'certainty', underplay the importance of the enhanced greenhouse effect. In this sense, their insistence on sound science is similar to that of the critics of shutting down the water pump in the case discussed above, who apparently bemoaned the lack of a proven causal relationship between polluted water and infectious disease.[56]

2.4   CONTRARIAN CRITICS OF THE IPCC

The IPCC has come under attack from a number of quarters, for reasons quite apart from its endorsement of the precautionary principle. The main problem, argue the 'sceptics' or 'contrarians', is that the IPCC's climate models do not appear to explain why temperature increases at the Earth's surface in the past 25 years or so have not been accompanied by a similar warming of other parts of the atmosphere, or take into consideration the climatic effects of recent observed variations in solar radiation.[57] As we have seen, many scientists now believe that the disparities between such temperature records can be understood in terms of the temporary cooling effects that aerosols have on global climate; and changes in solar output are not thought to be large enough to explain the observed warming.

For the student of climate change ethics, however, much of this dispute is of limited relevance. Few sceptics deny the existence of climate change altogether, or that climate change will impact *to some extent* on the distribution of benefits and burdens across generations. Rather, they emphasize that the warming will be less marked than expected by the IPCC (with a doubling of CO_2 in the atmosphere raising average temperatures by around 1.5°C (a figure at the bottom end of the IPCC's predictions) and that climate change will bring about many more beneficial effects on future human populations than are currently admitted by the IPCC. Thus while Patrick Michaels (a leading sceptic) has remarked in an interview with *New Scientist* that 'you can't make a case for a global apocalypse out of a 1.5°C warming', even the modest changes in climate predicted by the sceptics will impact significantly on the well-being of future human populations, particularly in developing countries and small-island states.[58]

This point comes out even more clearly in the work of Bjørn Lomborg. Lomborg is highly critical of the IPCC's assessments of climate change, which he thinks provide an overly pessimistic picture of climate change and its likely impact on human well-being.[59] He states that 'present [IPCC] models seriously overestimate CO_2-induced warming', and goes on to claim that there are huge uncertainties associated with the climate system that the IPCC downplay. Critically, he argues that the cooling effects of aerosols and clouds, the role of water vapour and changes in solar activity are not yet fully understood; and changes in any of these variables could offset future warming completely under certain scenarios.[60]

The assumptions behind the IPCC models are also criticised as being pessimistic regarding the benefits of efficiency gains in the renewables sector, the control of population growth, and the rates of emissions in both methane and CO_2.[61] Finally, drawing on a range of sources, Lomborg argues that the IPCC is overly pessimistic about the negative impacts of climate change in terms of agriculture, human health, extreme weather events and sea-level rise even if we embrace a mid-range IPCC estimate of future climate change.[62]

Lomborg, however, at no stage denies the existence of the anthropogenic greenhouse effect, or that global warming will alter the pattern of benefits and burdens across generations and nations, (1) by reducing the quality of life of certain individuals and groups (for example through an increase in heat-related deaths in some developing countries); and (2) by influencing the distribution of resources (for example by improving the developed world's agricultural base relative to the developing world). Rather, he claims that many of the impacts will be positive, and that the negative impacts are best approached in terms of *adaptation* rather than *mitigation*. Thus, while Lomborg's analysis is important in the debate about the costs, and effectiveness, of measures designed to manage climate change such as the Kyoto Protocol, it is entirely consistent with climate change being an important ethical issue.

The critical error from the ethical point of view is that the sceptics assume conveniently that an environmental problem can be ignored if its net effect is not negative. This is quite clear in the work of Lomborg, who reduces global environmental change to one solely of managing resources for the sake of overall utility (or welfare) maximisation, and also in the work of Fred Singer who argues that 'if the net benefits of warming are indeed positive (adding also the appreciable benefits of a reduction in sea-level rise), then one should do nothing to oppose such a warming'.[63] But this *utilitarian* approach to climate change impacts is not the dominant view in philosophical circles. Typically, great value is placed on values such as individual rights, basic needs, human virtue, or some other ideal that cannot be reduced to human welfare maximisation.

This methodological bias is most clear when we consider health impacts. Lomborg, and other sceptics, provide no real explanation of how deaths and illnesses brought about by climate change can be assigned a monetary value that captures their true ethical costs. The IPCC, on the other hand, has consistently allowed room for the idea that mortality and morbidity impacts are not easily placed within a mainstream economic cost–benefit analysis. In this sense, even if there are large uncertainties built into its impact models, the IPCC's approach is more sophisticated than that of the sceptics.

To sum up, there are serious flaws in the natural science, social science and ethics of the sceptics, as well as the interactions amongst these alternative approaches. The IPCC is undoubtedly an imperfect source of information, but on every important level offers a more sophisticated and comprehensive attempt to relate natural science findings to considerations of human well-being.

2.5   SPACE, TIME AND CLIMATE CHANGE

What can we reasonably say about the spatial and temporal effects of climate change if our starting point is the SAR and TAR?

Spatial variations in climate change impacts – for example, flowing from temperature change, precipitation, extreme weather events and sea-level rises – will be a key element of the next 100 years and beyond, a consideration that is often overlooked as a result of the focus on global average changes in sea-level and temperature, and global economic impacts. One of the central claims of successive IPCC assessments has been that it will be the poorest countries,[64] as well as certain populations within developed countries,[65] that are most vulnerable to climatic change. Partly, this is because poorer countries have less capacity to adapt to climate change. The economies of poorer countries are generally more sensitive to climatic impacts as they are more reliant on the agriculture, forestry and fishing industries that are particularly vulnerable to coastal and water resource changes.[66] Their capability to handle climate changes is also hampered by often inefficient, or undeveloped, economic and social institutions such as insurance markets and healthcare systems.

Physical vulnerability factors are also important. Many developing countries are located in parts of the world – such as the tropics – that are expected to experience severe climate events (such as droughts, floods and windstorms) that will threaten water and food security.[67] Coastal zones and small islands, for example, are particularly vulnerable to sea-level rises as a result of their physical environment and location.

It is worth pointing out that, even if we assumed that the physical impacts of climate change were evenly distributed between states, the costs of adaptation would almost certainly exacerbate existing international inequalities.[68] Richer countries not only have superior adaptive capabilities due to highly developed industrial and commercial sectors, they also appear to have greater discretion in their consumption behaviour. That is, while a large proportion of the activities that require the emission of greenhouse gases in the developing world concern 'subsistence', emissions from the developed world often involve less essential activities, including use of cars and planes. This is the basis of the distinction made by developing country negotiators to the Kyoto Protocol between 'survival emissions' and 'luxury emissions'.[69] According to the TAR, global warming will 'increase the disparity of well-being between developed countries and developing countries, with disparity growing for higher projected temperature increases'.[70]

It is also worth repeating the fundamental asymmetry at the heart of the climate change phenomenon. Although *all* countries emit greenhouse gases, the responsibility for emissions are in no way evenly distributed throughout the world looked at on a country-by-country, or per capita, basis. Developing countries, who will be the worst affected on almost all models of impact and vulnerability, bear the least responsibility for the concentrations of greenhouse gases that have built up over the last 200 years. The SAR estimated that the industrialised world (North America, EU and other European countries, Russia, Japan and Oceania) accounted for around two-thirds of all anthropogenic CO_2 emissions to 1988,[71] a figure broadly compatible with more recent research into cumulative emissions by the World Resources Institute.[72] According to the US Carbon Dioxide Information Analysis Center (CDIAC) – which has analysed total CO_2 emissions from fossil-fuel burning, cement production and gas flaring – the USA emitted over 1500 million metric tonnes of carbon in 2000, or 5.40 tonnes per inhabitant. This equates to 24 per cent of global emissions, and is roughly the same amount as released by the whole of Europe and the Russian Federation combined. For the purposes of comparison, Bangladesh, which the IPCC singles out as a major victim of long-term impacts of climate change, was seventy-first out of 212 countries in terms of total fossil fuel emissions (8 million tonnes of carbon) and had per capita emissions of just 0.06 million tonnes in 2000, roughly 90 times less than the USA.[73]

Nevertheless, the picture is changing. Sustained economic growth, as well as other socio-economic drivers such as urbanisation and population growth, mean that China, India and other non-OECD countries will progressively increase their contribution to – and thus responsibility for – greenhouse gas build-up. Depending on the source, and how one defines 'developing' and 'developed', many projections see the developing world's total emissions surpassing the developed world by 2020.[74] This suggests that no effective approach to the stabilisation of greenhouse gases in the atmosphere can take place in the long term without the participation of the developing world. As the past and current big emitters, however, developed countries are under great ethical and political pressure to take the lead in the construction of a global climate regime.[75] As Singer notes, all models indicate that the per capita emissions of developing countries will lag behind developed countries for many decades, so it is unclear what ethical case for developed world inaction can be derived from total emissions figures.[76]

Temporal variations in climate impacts also pose great ethical and political problems. Spatial and temporal impacts are also related at a deeper level given that the most vulnerable of all to climate change will be *future* members of developing countries. There is, then, no clear-cut distinction between intergenerational and international climate injustices, or any obvious clash in climate policy between the plight of the present poor and the future rich. Moreover, a similar inequity arises in the attribution of responsibility for climate change. Future generations, who have as yet contributed nothing to the problem, will be forced to bear a more than proportionate share of its costs.

Nevertheless, climate change is a long-term process and many of the negative impacts that the IPCC discuss seem set to skip the present generation. This is because there are a number of time delays built into atmospheric processes.[77] There are, then, aspects of climate change that threaten only the not-yet-born. As the IPCC observe, some threats may be so grave that 'it may not be possible to compensate future generations for reductions in well-being caused by current policies, and, even if feasible, such compensation may not actually occur'.[78] Just a few examples of these very long-term changes are:

- rising sea levels as a consequence of thermal expansion of the oceans;
- changes in the composition of the ice sheets that will contribute to sea-level rise and temperature increases for thousands of years;
- the prospect of low-probability, high-cost impacts such as those resulting from a slowing (or re-positioning) of the gulf-stream process.

The diversity of these changes reveals that climate change will cause a 'complex network of changes' in the Earth's atmosphere and the human populations that depend upon it.[79] One aspect of this complexity is that climate changes will impact unevenly across the ecosystems and industries that prove vulnerable to climate changes. The consensus amongst climate researchers, however, is that the result of such large and complex modifications in the atmosphere will be, on the whole, *negative*. Partly, this is due to the direct affects on human health and well-being that individual events such as floods, droughts and wind storms will have on future populations. But it is also because human communities have adapted to their pre-climate change environments over thousands of years, and so atmospheric changes will tend to be disruptive and costly.[80]

2.6 FUTURE IMPACTS OF CLIMATE CHANGE: HUMAN POPULATION HEALTH

The health of human beings is intimately related to the integrity of a variety of physical systems (such as weather patterns) as well as that of ecosystems (such as coral reefs). Shifts in the conditions that determine the integrity of these systems brought about by climate change, therefore, pose a clear threat to the health of human populations. While there is a considerable amount of uncertainty associated with predicting the future human health implications of climate change – particularly in the longer-term – the SAR defended the following three claims.

- The cumulative impacts of climate change on human health will be, on balance, extensive and adverse.[81]
- Climate change will impact upon human health both directly and indirectly.[82]
- The indirect impacts of climate change will predominate over the direct impacts in the longer term.[83]

All three findings were confirmed by the TAR,[84] which developed and extended the earlier research on human health impacts, as well as by successive assessments conducted by the World Health Organisation, World Meterological Organisation and the United Nations Development Programme.[85]

Perhaps the most notable health effects discussed by the SAR and TAR were those that the IPCC predicted would occur with a *high degree of confidence*. According to the IPCC's definition, such findings were those denoted by a 'wide agreement, based on multiple findings through multiple lines of investigation.'[86] Three types of health impact were ascribed the highest degree of confidence:

- increases in mortality as a result of increases in frequency in *extreme* weather events;
- increases in mortality and illness following increases in long-term global warming and sea-level rises;
- increases in the transmission area of various biological disease agents.

Each of these health impacts is discussed in brief below. While I concentrate on the negative impacts of climate change on human health, it does seem likely that there will be a range of beneficial effects as well, one example being decreases in cold-related deaths in winter months and improved agricultural yields for some crops in some countries.[87] I assume that providing evidence of *negative* impacts is sufficient to demonstrate that important questions of intergenerational distribution are posed by climate change.

2.6.1   Floods and Other Extreme Weather Events

Extreme weather events can be defined as 'infrequent meteorological events that have a significant impact upon a society or ecosystem at a particular location'.[88] Such events can occur suddenly (as in the case of floods or cyclones) or more gradually (as in the case of droughts). There are two main categories of extreme weather events: *simple* and *complex*.[89] Simple events are those that involve unusually high or low values for a single climate variable at a given location such as air surface temperature. Good examples are heatwaves and cold snaps. Complex events, in contrast, are those that are associated with changes in a number of climate variables. A good example is that of droughts. Climate change is expected to lead to worldwide rise in the frequency of both sorts of event. Of particular concern, however, are floods, droughts, forest fires, wind storms and tropical cyclones.[90]

While it seems clear that certain populations will be particularly vulnerable to these phenomena – such as impoverished island-based societies and developing countries more generally – developed countries will also be at risk. The UK Department of Environment has argued that climate change will cause an increase in the frequency and intensity of storms, high winds and river flooding in Northern Europe and will have a variety of negative, although also some positive, impacts on morbidity and mortality levels in the United Kingdom.[91] Elsewhere, the IPCC use the case of the Central European floods of 1997 to emphasise the point that the physical and disease risks of flooding are not limited to developing countries.[92] This was further underlined by the impacts of the catastrophic floods across Europe in 2002 and 2003 that post-dated the TAR.[93]

Floods are caused by one or more key factors, three of which are particularly important.[94] First, sudden increases in rainfall in a vulnerable location. Second, sustained bouts of rainfall culminating in soil saturation. Third, rises in sea-levels in coastal areas unconnected to rainfall events. The IPCC suggest that climate change will increase the frequency of all three of these pathways. It will, for example, affect the distribution and intensity of rainfall, bringing about an increase in the frequency of days where heavy rainfall occurs. As noted above, it is also expected to bring about significant rises in global sea levels in the distant future as a result of oceanic thermal expansion and glacial melting.

It is the developing world that will bear the brunt of the negative effects of flooding. The IPCC notes, with high confidence, that flood events will increase mortality and morbidity in developing countries, particularly indirectly through diarrhoea, respiratory disease, hunger and malnutrition.[95] Developing countries with a history of flood damage are particularly at risk. Bangladesh, for example, has experienced a number of recent flood events and recent research indicates that flooding in the country will increase greatly as global sea levels rise.[96] The 1988 and 1998 floods killed 2400 and 1000 people respectively, and in each case led to over 1 000 000 people being displaced.[97] However, both events are dwarfed by the huge storm surge of 29 April 1991 that killed more than 130 000 people. This was arguably the largest natural disaster to date that may have its origins in climate change.[98]

Most of the fatalities of flood events occur within a short space of time as a result of people being drowned or being swept into large objects. However, floods take their toll on other aspects of human health.[99] First, due to the problems associated with maintaining sanitation facilities in the aftermath of flooding, the incidence of infectious diseases often increases. Second, the nutritional status of flood victims (particularly the young and the elderly) is vulnerable in the aftermath of flooding. Third, by damaging containment facilities of toxic substances, flooding can lead to environmental pollution and subsequent human health problems, for example related to the contamination of food supplies with pesticides. Fourth, studies have suggested that some of the most significant (and long-term) human health impacts of flooding relate to post-traumatic stress and other psychological disorders.

2.6.2 Heat Stress

One of the key features of climate change over the next century will be increases in global mean temperature at the Earth's surface. Increases in mean temperature will be accompanied by an increase in the frequency of very hot days in many regions, as well as warmer seasons, years and decades.

Extremes of heat, as well as cold spells, are a well-known cause of physiological stress and death.[100] They are known, for example, to cause damage to internal organs and exacerbate cardiorespiratory and cardiovascular diseases in humans, as well as causing accident rates to rise, albeit in a way that is modified by a range of other factors including socio-economic status and age.[101] The TAR observed that, 'global climate change is likely to be accompanied by an increase in the frequency and intensity of heat waves . . . there is a high level of certainty that an increase in the frequency and intensity of heat waves would increase the number of deaths from hot weather'.[102]

It has been argued by some that mean temperature rises in winter will lead to a large decline in cold-related illness and deaths during the winter months in many regions, more than offsetting deaths in summer.[103] It has also been suggested that, in the past, populations have adapted successfully to temperature changes even greater than those of the most pessimistic IPCC models, raising doubts about the IPCC's impact assessments.[104] However, the problem with such optimistic views is that the magnitude of these 'offsetting factors' is very difficult to establish;[105] and the tremendous population growth of modern times, urbanisation and the location of so much of the world's population in coastal areas calls into question the optimistic adaptation scenarios that underpin these claims.[106] Moreover, there are other problems intrinsic to the notion of offsetting, notably that some outcomes do not seem to be straightforwardly compared in the sense that they cannot be offset against one another. Should we assume, for example, that a climate change that benefits more persons than it harms is unproblematic from the *ethical* point of view? To put the point in a more direct way, it will, I assume, be of very little consolation to the families of the estimated 20 000-plus Europeans who lost their lives as a result of heat stress in the summer of 2003 that many other deaths were prevented by the warmer conditions later in the year brought about by the same climatic conditions.[107] Nor should the benefits of warmer conditions divert our attention from the possibility that tens of thousands of people will die as a result of global warming in the future who would otherwise not have died.[108]

2.6.3 Infectious Diseases

Infectious diseases can be divided into two main types, depending on the mode of transmission involved. *Directly contracted diseases*, such as tuberculosis, involve no intermediary mechanism and are often spread from person to person. *Indirectly contracted diseases* are spread through a 'vector' organism (such as a mosquito, in the case of malaria) or through a non-biological 'vehicle' (such as water, in the case of hepatitis). Biological organisms and processes linked to the spread of infectious disease are highly sensitive to changes in climate variables such as temperature and precipitation.[109] Climate change, therefore, is expected to cause widespread, if uncertain, changes in both the incidence and geographical distribution of indirect and direct infectious diseases.[110] In their analysis of the problem of greenhouse induced changes in the pattern of both vector- (and non vector-) borne diseases, McMichael et al. conclude that 'available evidence and climate change models indicate that climate change will alter the pattern of the world's infectious diseases',[111] and, according to some scientists, the spread of infectious diseases is the most important health risk of climate change.[112]

One cause for concern is the impact that climate change will have on *malarial transmission*, although there are a number of infectious diseases that could be affected. Infections of malaria are caused by several distinct species of parasite, each of which possesses different reproductive and physiological properties. There are also several different species of mosquito which act as vectors for the disease, many of which only flourish where air temperature exceeds 16°C. Above these levels, small increases in temperature accelerate parasitic development inside the mosquito.[113]

Recent research suggests that malarial infection affects far more people than was previously held, with over 500 million new cases arising annually of the most deadly form, *Plasmodium falciparum*.[114] According to the World Health Organization (WHO), the disease accounts for more than 1 million annual deaths worldwide, mainly in the developing world, and approximately 40 per cent of the world's population are at risk of exposure. It is also a major cause of international inequality, with the WHO estimating that substantial differences in GDP arise between countries with and without malaria as a result of contrasting health and economic impacts.[115] A global warming of just a couple of degrees could result in an increased survival rate in various species of mosquito in temperate areas. As a result, McMichael et al. conclude that it is 'highly likely' that the geographical distribution of malaria infection will be altered by climate change, and that the change would result in both a rise in annual malaria related deaths, and the widening of the potential malarial transmission zone.[116] This view was broadly shared by the TAR, although it went on to note that it is unclear whether total transmission rates will rise since regional increases and decreases may cancel each other out.[117] Again, unless we take a utilitarian view, the IPCC's research on infectious diseases raises deep ethical questions: different people will fall ill, and later die, as a result of human interventions in the climate system.

2.7   FUTURE IMPACTS OF CLIMATE CHANGE: SOCIAL, ECONOMIC AND CULTURAL IMPACTS

Estimating the social and economic impacts of climate change is a huge task. Not only must accurate models of climate change itself be constructed, but so must models of development, population growth, migration, and other human variables that are in constant flux.[118]

The IPCC's research on this issue is principally coordinated and conducted by Working Group III, the function of which is to 'assess cross-cutting economic and other issues related to climate change' and to conduct 'technical assessments of the socio-economics of impacts, adaptation, and mitigation of climate change over both the short and the long term and at the regional and global levels'.[119] Despite the many sources of uncertainty surrounding the assessment of the economic impacts of climate change, the SAR claimed that the costs associated with a doubling in CO_2 concentrations would be a net decline in global world product (GWP[120]) of between 1.5 and 2 per cent, which equates to a cost of between $500 and $650 billion per year, as measured by 1995 US$.[121] These figures are not uncontested. The research behind them has been criticised for underplaying the uncertainties of impacts further in the future, but also because it was based upon models of climate change that are now outdated.[122] Nevertheless, most studies support the view that anything other than a very modest rise in global temperature will lead to a net negative impact on global output.

All studies emphasise, however, that the economic costs of climate change will be unevenly dispersed. The burden will fall more heavily on the developing world. The IPCC estimates that the yearly costs of climate change following a doubling of CO_2 will be between 1 and 1.5 per cent of GDP for the developed world, but between 2 and 9 per cent of GDP for the developing world. Moreover, a greater economic impact is expected if CO_2 concentrations are not limited in the more distant future or if present models turn out to be too optimistic regarding the sensitivity of climate to greenhouse gas build-up. Subsequent research has provided broadly consistent figures, although it should be added that, in the TAR, the IPCC does not offer such precision. Even sceptics, such as Lomborg, accept that the total cost of global warming up to the year 2100 (assuming no substantial greenhouse policies are adopted) will be at least $5000 billion, as measured by 2000 US$.[123]

One problem with existing economic assessments of climate change is that few studies discuss the consequences of 'high impact, low probability' events, such as the melting of the West Atlantic Ice Sheet. In fact, many economists doubt if traditional cost–benefit analyses can be extended to deal with such events.[124]

A second problem is that there are large variations in damage figures between economic models. The IPCC note that 'attempts to quantify the costs associated with climate change involve inherently difficult and contentious value judgments, and different assumptions may greatly alter resulting conclusions'.[125]

A third problem is that even well-regarded assessments neglect the importance of a range of impacts that are not easily ascribed monetary values. Social and cultural 'bads' – for example relating to the disappearance of a culture as a result of climate changes or the social and political instabilities brought about by population displacement – all seem to have a non-economic dimension. A number of sources within the climate change community have also expressed doubts about the connection between the GDP per capita of a country and the quality of life enjoyed by its inhabitants. Much recent research has, for example, questioned the connection between wealth and quality of life after a certain level of prosperity has been reached. This is because non-economic goods, such as social capital or negative freedom, can be as important to a person's life prospects as their share of society's wealth. Social capital refers to the social relationships, institutions and collective social capacities that provide the background for individual well-being, whereas negative freedom refers to what a person can do without interference from others or the state.[126]

The above problems, as well as alternative approaches to them, have given rise to a fierce debate amongst sceptics and the IPCC regarding the impact of climate change on the further future. At one extreme, climate change is viewed as a global threat, second only in its possible effects to global nuclear war. Athanasiou and Baer, for example, have argued recently that 'the consequences of global warming will soon become quite severe, and even murderous, particularly for the poor and vulnerable'.[127] At the other extreme, climate change is seen as something that can be adapted to by most populations with little hardship as a result of inevitable improvements in technology and economic incentives, and which offers a range of possibilities and benefits.[128] For the latter camp, it is the international climate regime's attempts to mitigate climate change, as set out in the Kyoto Protocol, that are the biggest threats to global welfare.

In fact, for Lomborg and others inspired by his work, the priority for governments ought to be to promote projects that benefit the world's *current* poor that have little or nothing to do with the climate system, such as those that prevent the spread of AIDS and malnutrition in developing countries.[129] To give priority to climate policies that will have little if any long-run positive impact on future well-being, is, for Lomborg, not just inefficient but unethical.[130] But, as we have seen, this approach is flawed. In reducing environmental and inter-generational ethics to a problem solely of economic efficiency, the approach underestimates the long-run costs of climate change and neglects the likely increase in inequality between developed and developing world and the creation of large numbers of environmental refugees.

As to the issue of regional costs, the IPCC suggest that countries that possess a 'diversified industrial economy and an educated and flexible labour force' will suffer least from the effects of climate change, whereas countries which possess specialised economies and 'a poorly developed and land-tied labour force' will be expected to fare much worse.[131] The picture becomes even more complex when we look at particular sectors, and longer time frames. A doubling of CO_2, for example, could well benefit the agricultural sector in the developed world.[132] However, it would lead to much more seri-ous problems in the developing world, which lacks the same adaptive capac-ity.[133] It is this capacity to adapt, rather than the physical properties of the climate changes themselves, that will define the level of socio-economic damage a country sustains.[134]

There is, then, a certain amount of guesswork associated with attaching socio-economic costs and benefits to climate changes both in the context of countries and regions, or in particular areas of human activity. Nevertheless, it is worth discussing perhaps the most disturbing example of socio-economic vulnerability discussed by the IPCC – *small island states*. The fate of small islands, many of which lie less than three metres above sea level, has received a great deal of attention in the SAR and TAR, as well as in discussion of climate change more generally. While these states have contributed little to global climate change (with perhaps 1 per cent of all CO_2 emissions to date) they will be its greatest victims.[135]

Small islands are vulnerable to both the direct and indirect effects of climate change, but are limited in their capacity to adapt to these.[136] This is because:

- their geographical location and size prevents more than a limited inland retreat in the face of sea-level rises;
- their relative and absolute poverty means that they have limited ability to respond to environmental change;
- their inhabitants are dependent on coastally located resources, which are easily damaged by extreme weather events;
- they are often dependent on tourism, which is easily disrupted by extreme weather events.

Moreover, there are clear and present climate threats that will exploit these vulnerabilities. The increased variability to short-term climate events (such as floods and storms) projected by the IPCC will prove very costly for these states, for example in terms of agricultural yield. According to some researchers, these costs may be even harder to bear than those associated with sea-level rises.[137] In addition, gradual rises in sea level are expected to exacerbate water security (through salinisation of fresh water reserves) and food insecurity (through both coastal erosion and salinisation).[138] The IPCC observes that, 'in global terms the population of small islands is relatively small, but a number of distinct societies and cultures are threatened with drastic changes in lifestyle and possibly forced abandonment from ancestral homelands if sea-level rises significantly.'[139] The less vulnerable are expected to suffer from loss of tourism and recreation trade as a result of sea-level rises.[140] However, the more vulnerable small-island states (such as the Marshall Islands, Maldives, Kiribati and Tivalu) face the very real risk of complete destruction in the longer run.[141]

The plight of the small island states raises huge ethical questions concerning the allocation of costs, and compensation, associated with extreme climate impacts. Some of these relate to the emerging concept of 'cultural ethics' – the study of the duties that we might be said to have to protect and promote cultures – which can be approached in at least two different ways. The first approach is to claim that persons have a right to live in a particular settlement, region or state. If these rights exist, it is not clear that any amount of compensation can justify one population possessing a lifestyle that forces others, in the distant future, to become environmental refugees.

The second approach is to claim that climate change threatens the national sovereignty of small islands in a way that cannot be weighed against other sorts of climate cost and benefit. The idea is that the value of the group right of self-determination cannot be reduced to other values, and thus violations of this right cannot be waived aside by the costs of climate change mitigation for other states. Climate change, here, becomes a matter of *national security* and should be treated with the same gravity as other such threats, such as international terrorism.[142] A slightly different way to develop the approach is to argue that groups and cultures possess some inherent ethical status that is not reducible to the well-being of its citizen members or to the value of political sovereignty. Climate changes that lead to the destruction of communities, on this view, are seen as wrong in a similar way to acts or social policies that lead to the death of individual human beings.[143]

2.8 SUMMARY

In this chapter, we have seen that global climate change, in virtue of threatening to bring about a range of changes in the natural, economic, and cultural environment of human beings, will greatly influence the distribution of benefits and burdens across generations. We have also seen that the distributive consequences most relevant to discussions of climate change are those that involve countries, or populations, that are badly off already becoming even worse off in the future. Finally, we have seen that there are significant defects in the arguments of Lomborg and others who are sceptical of the IPCC on both natural- and social-scientific grounds. One key issue is that the sceptics ignore many of the negative impacts that climate change will have on individuals and the cultures they belong to as a consequence of their implicit endorsement of utilitarianism. This approach focuses on aggregate gains, or losses, of welfare that accompany changes in the environment that provide a context for human life. Yet, it is most people's view that it is not enough to establish whether the consequences of an activity is *net* positive or negative, but also to investigate its distributive effects and historical origins, or at the very least have an argument as to why these do not matter. In the next chapter, I want to explore in greater depth the reasons why climate change matters from the perspective of a number of theories of distributive justice.

NOTES

1. Speech delivered to mark the 10th Anniversary of His Royal Highness's Business and the Environment Programme, London, 15 September, 2004 (http://www.number-10.gov.uk/output/page6333.asp).
2. Twain, 1996, p. 109.
3. Bernstein et al., 2002, p.16.
4. See 'Summary for policymakers', Houghton et al., 2001, pp. 1–20 (hereafter IPCC, 2001a); and 'Summary for policymakers', Houghton et al., 1996, pp. 1–7 (hereafter IPCC, 1996a).
5. See 'Summary for policymakers', in McCarthy et al., 2001, pp. 1–18 (hereafter IPCC, 2001b); and 'Summary for policymakers', in Watson et al., 1996, pp. 1–18 (hereafter IPCC, 1996b).
6. See 'Summary for policymakers', in Bruce et al., 1996, pp. 1–16 (hereafter IPCC, 1996c); Metz et al., 2001, pp. 1–14 (hereafter IPCC, 2001c).
7. See, for example, Fourier, 1824.
8. Tyndall, 1861.
9. Arrhenius, 1896.
10. Callendar, 1938.
11. Revelle and Suess, 1955.
12. Houghton et al., 1990. A useful history of climate change is provided in Weart, 2003.
13. Trenberth et al., 1996, p. 57.
14. See Schimel et al., 1996, pp. 108–18.
15. See, for example, Ruddiman, 2003 and 2005.
16. Ppm (parts per million), ppb (parts per billion = 1000 million), and ppt (parts per trillion = 1000 billion) refer to the ratio of greenhouse gas molecules to the number of molecules of dry air in the atmosphere.
17. Keeling and Whorf, 2004.
18. Prather et al., 2001, pp. 244–5; Schimel et al., 1996, pp. 92–3.
19. The global warming potential (GWP) of a gas is the warming contribution of 1 kg of this gas relative to 1 kg of carbon dioxide (IPCC, 2001a, 'Technical summary', pp. 46ff).
20. IPPC, 1996a, 'Summary for policymakers', pp. 15–23.
21. European Environment Agency, 2004, p. 6.
22. IPCC, 1996a, 'Summary for policymakers', p. 6.

23. According to the IPCC, 'virtually certain' means that a given result has a greater than 99 per cent chance of being true; 'very likely' (90–99 per cent chance); 'likely' (66–90 per cent chance); 'medium likelihood' (33–66 per cent chance); 'unlikely' (10–33 per cent chance); 'very unlikely' (1–10 per cent chance); 'exceptionally unlikely' (less than 1 per cent chance). See IPCC, 2001a, 'Summary for policymakers', p. 2.

24. Figures for the SAR taken from IPCC, 1996a, 'Technical summary', pp. 39ff; for the TAR's discussion of projected climate change, see IPCC, 2001a 'Technical summary' (pp. 21ff) and Cabasch et al., 2001, pp. 527ff.

25. IPCC, 2001a, 'Technical summary', p. 63.

26. IPCC, 2001a, 'Technical summary', p. 69. These figures are broadly compatible with research undertaken since the publication of the TAR. See Stainforth et al., 2005.

27. IPCC, 2001a, 'Technical summary', p. 75.

28. See, for example, Hulme et al., 2002; Department of the Environment, 1996, p. 4.

29. The IPCC discusses the key threats to small island states, such as the Maldives, Bahamas, Kiribati, the Marshall Islands, in Leonard A. Nurse et al., 2001, pp. 843–75. See also, Barnett and Adger, 2003.

30. See United Nations, 1995, p. 5.

31. See Markandya et al., 2001, pp. 474–6.

32. IPCC, 2001b, pp. 6–9.

33. IPCC, 2001b, pp. 9–12.

34. IPCC, 2001b, p. 12.

35. IPCC, 2001b, pp. 12–14.

36. Cotton and Pielke, 1995, pp. 132ff.

37. See Penner et al., 2001, pp. 291ff; Houghton, 2004, pp. 48–51.

38. See, for example, Mitchell et al., 2001, pp. 705–12; McCormick et al., 1995.

39. Stanhill and Cohen, 2001; see also Liepert, 2002.

40. See Fred Pearce, 2003, p. 7.

41. This dilemma was explored in a recent edition of the BBC's *Horizon* Programme on 13 January 2005 (http://www.bbc.co.uk/sn/tvradio/programmes/horizon/dimming_trans.shtml).

42. Houghton, 2004, pp. 30ff; Cox et al., 2000, pp. 184–7.

43. Friis-Christensen and Lassen, 1991; Thjell and Lassen, 2000, pp. 1207–13.

44. Svenskmark, 1998.

45. See Laut, 2003.

46. IPCC, 1996a, 'Summary for policymakers', p. 7.

47. Pearce et al., 1996, p. 185, italics in original.

48. Harremoës et al., 2002, pp. 5ff.

49. Foster, 2000.

50. See, for example, Beckerman, 1995, pp. 88–103.

51. Miller and Conko, 2001.

52. See van den Belt, 2003.

53. Miller and Conko, 2001. This claim is challenged by C. Raffensperger et al., '. . . and can mean saying "yes" to innovation', 1999.

54. Lomborg, 'Global warming', in Lomborg, 2001, pp. 305ff.

55. John Barry, 1999, pp. 158–61; Beck, 1992, p. 62; Slovic, 2000.

56. Harremoës et al., 2002, p. 7.

57. See, for example, Michaels, 2000 and 2004.

58. Pearce, 1997.

59. Lomborg, 2001, pp. 258–324.

60. Lomborg, 2001, pp. 266ff.

61. Lomborg, 2001, pp. 278ff.

62. Lomborg, 2001, pp. 287ff.

63. Fred Singer, 2000, p. 25.

64. The TAR claims that Africa is particularly vulnerable to climate change, for example in terms of food and water security, health impacts, and desertification (IPCC, 2001b, 'Technical summary: impacts, adaptation and vulnerability', pp. 44ff). Elsewhere, the TAR

reports that the agricultural sector will be particularly hard hit in some developing countries (see, Gitay et al., 2001, p. 270).

65. The TAR mentions in particular the situation of the indigenous people of Australia and New Zealand in this regard (IPCC, 2001b, pp. 620–21) although poor communities in many developed countries, especially those in urban areas and coastal zones, would also be at risk.
66. See, for example, 'Summary for policymakers', IPCC, 2001b, pp. 9ff.
67. The IPCC go on to argue that people in developing countries are 'much more affected by extreme events' as a result of socioeconomic vulnerability and poor response mechanisms, and that weather-related disasters in these countries can be up to 30 times more costly in relative economic terms than in industrialized countries (McMichael et al., 2001, pp. 458–60).
68. Banuri et al., 1996, pp. 91ff.
69. Banuri et al., 1996, pp. 92–3. The distinction between 'subsistence' and 'luxury' emissions appears was introduced by Agarwal and Narain, 1991. See also Shue, 1993, pp. 39ff.
70. IPCC, 2001b, 'Summary for policymakers', p. 8.
71. Banuri et al., pp. 94–5.
72. World Resources Institute, 2003, pp. 258–9.
73. CDIAC 'National Fossil-Fuel CO_2 Emissions' (http://cdiac.esd.ornl.gov/trends/emis/tre_coun.htm). See also United Nations Economic Commission for Europe 2004.
74. The IPCC gives this figure (which refers to emissions equality between OECD and non-OECD countries) in Banuri et al., 1996, p. 97. Peter Singer, citing research by the World Resources Institute, puts the equalisation point as 2038 (Singer, 2002, p. 33).
75. Shue, 1999, pp. 533ff.
76. Singer, 2002, p. 33.
77. IPCC, 2001a, 'Summary for policymakers', p. 17.
78. Arrow et al., 1996, p. 130.
79. Houghton, 2004, p. 143.
80. Houghton, 2004, pp. 144–5.
81. See McMichael et al., 1996a, pp. 561–84.
82. According to the IPCC, 'direct' health impacts 'result from changes in climate characteristics or short-term weather extremes that impinge directly on human biology', such as deaths connected with extreme weather events. By contrast, 'indirect' impacts, such as illnesses connected with air pollution, 'do not entail a direct causal connection between a climatic factor (such as heat, humidity, or extreme weather event) and human biology' (see McMichael et al., 1996a, pp. 568ff).
83. McMichael et al., 1996a, p. 563.
84. McMichael and Githeko, 2001, pp. 451ff.
85. McMichael et al., 2003; McMichael et al., 1996b; Royal Society, 1999. See also Haines and Patz, 2004.
86. IPCC, 1996b, 'Preface', p. x.
87. See, for example, European Environment Agency, 2004, pp. 67–9.
88. McMichael et al., 1996b, p. 123.
89. Hales et al., 2003, p. 79.
90. McMichael et al., 1996a, pp. 570–71; and McMichael and Githeko, 2001, pp. 459–60.
91. Department of the Environment, 1996, pp. 192–3; and Department of Health, 2001, pp. 70ff.
92. McMichael and Githeko, 2001, p. 460.
93. European Environment Agency, 2004, pp. 75ff; Hardy, 2004, p. 181.
94. See McMichael et al., 1996b, pp. 129–32; and pp. 145ff.
95. IPCC, 2001b, 'Summary for policymakers', p. 12.
96. Mirza et al., 2003.
97. Del Ninno et al., 2001, pp. 5ff; Houghton, 2004, pp. 150ff.
98. Sattur, 1991.
99. McMichael et al., 1996b, pp. 130ff; Hales et al., 2003, pp. 93ff.
100. See, for example, Hardy, 2004, pp. 172–4.

101. Hales et al., 2003, p. 89.
102. McMichael et al., 2001, p. 457.
103. See Lomborg, 2001, pp. 297ff.
104. Fred Singer, 2000, pp. 21ff.
105. McMichael et al., 1996b, pp. 53–4; Hardy, 2004, p. 174; European Environment Agency, 2004, p. 74.
106. See IPCC, 2001b, 'Summary for policymakers', pp. 12–17.
107. European Environment Agency, 2004, p. 74.
108. One recent study has suggested that up to 20 000 people will die yearly as a result of climate change induced heatwaves in Europe during this century. See Schär et al., 2004.
109. McMichael et al., 1996b, pp. 71ff; Patz et al., 2003, pp. 103ff.
110. McMichael et al., 1996a, pp. 576–7; 1996b, pp. 96–104.
111. McMichael et al., 1996b, p. 105; Patz et al., 2003, pp. 114ff.
112. See Hardy, 2004, p. 175.
113. McMichael et al., 1996a, pp. 571–2.
114. Snow et al., 2005.
115. See the WHO's information resource on malaria <http://www.who.int/topics/malaria/en/>.
116. McMichael et al., 1996b, pp. 75ff; Patz et al., 2003, pp. 112–13.
117. McMichael and Githeko, 2001, p. 454
118. Tol, 2002, pp. 48ff.
119. IPCC, 1996c, 'Preface', p. ix and 'Summary for policymakers', p. 5.
120. Global World Product (GWP) refers to the aggregated Global Domestic Products (GDPs) of all countries. GDP is normally used with an individual country in mind, and refers to the total value of goods and services produced domestically by a country during a given year.
121. Pearce et al., 1996, pp. 214–5. See also Houghton, 2004, pp. 184ff.
122. See Tol, 2002, pp. 47–8.
123. Lomborg, 2001, p. 310.
124. See Azar and Lindgren, 2003, pp. 247ff; Tol, 2003.
125. Banuri et al., 1996, pp. 91ff.
126. The classic discussion of negative freedom is provided by Isaiah Berlin (see *Four Essays on Liberty*, 1969, pp. 121ff). The importance of social capital for human well-being is discussed by Dasgupta, 2001; Putnam, 1993.
127. Athanasiou and Baer, 2002, p. 10; Hardy, 2004, p. x.
128. Lomborg, 2001, pp. 300ff; Fred Singer, 2000, pp. 21ff.
129. See Lomborg, 2004, p. 23.
130. Lomborg argues that 'the present faces far more pressing issues than redistribution of wealth among far richer nations in a hundred years' time – such as securing access to clean water and sanitation for everyone on the planet' (2001, p. 312).
131. IPCC, 1996c, 'Summary for policymakers', p. 11.
132. The UK Department of Environment also note that there will be a range of beneficial effects for certain parts of the forestry, agricultural, and tourist industries (1996, pp. 67ff).
133. J.B. Smith et al., 2001, pp. 938–40.
134. Stott et al., 2001, p. 385.
135. Nurse et al., 2001, pp. 854–5.
136. Arnell et al., 2001, pp. 224–5; Commonwealth Secretariat, 1997, pp. 65ff.
137. Barnett and Adger, 2003, p. 325.
138. IPCC, 2001b, 'Small island states', p. 863.
139. Bijlsma et al., 1996, p. 310.
140. Bijlsma et al., 1996, p. 310; IPCC, 2001b, 'Technical summary: impacts, adaptation, and vulnerability', pp. 60–62.
141. Bijlsma et al., 1996, pp. 296–8; and Commonwealth Secretariat, 1997, pp. 67ff.
142. See Barnett and Adger, 2003, pp. 331ff; Stripple, 2002.
143. See Page, 1999, and Chapter 6 below.

3. Climate change, future generations and the currency of justice

Equality is a popular but mysterious ideal. People can become equal (or at least more equal) in one way with the consequence that they become unequal (or more unequal) in others.[1]

Ronald Dworkin

Two central issues for ethical analysis of equality are: (1) Why equality? (2) Equality of What? The two questions are distinct but thoroughly interdependent. We cannot begin to defend or criticize equality without knowing what on earth we are talking about.[2]

Amartya Sen

3.1 THE SCOPE, SHAPE AND CURRENCY OF JUSTICE

Preceding chapters have shown that climate change, even assuming that extensive measures of mitigation and adaptation are put into place, will alter the distribution of benefits and burdens both across space and time. It will further extend inequalities between developed and developing countries, and it will undermine the well-being of many who belong to future generations. In the following two chapters, we will be investigating the relevance of climate change for competing theories of distributive justice as well as asking which theories provide the most useful approach to climate change.

Theories of distributive justice can be analysed in terms of their approach to three issues: *scope*, *shape* and *currency*. The *scope* of justice concerns the entities we identify as the legitimate recipients of benefits and burdens in society. It concerns, for example, the question of which agents are bearers of value, and why, and what sorts of claims these agents hold against others. It also concerns the issue of the strength of this value, and these claims. There are, as such, a wide range of positions available to those exercised by the question of scope. We might apply our theory of distribution only to human beings; to human beings and non-human animals; to all living creatures; or to all living creatures, as well as certain physical structures or processes. Even within a strictly *humanist* paradigm, to which this book is a contribution, there are a number of additional issues of scope to be addressed, notably those that turn on the spatial and temporal limits of justice; that is, whether only compatriots living at the same time, persons belonging to all countries living at the same time, or all persons living at all times have distributive claims against others.[3] Finally, there is the question of which entities or institutions are responsible for providing the benefits outlined by any theory of distribution.

The *shape* of justice concerns the pattern of benefits that a theory of distribution recommends, in short, how much of a given measure of advantage (or benefit) people should receive. Popular answers to this question have been offered in terms of efficiency, equality, priority and sufficiency. That is, it has been suggested that we distribute benefits and burdens so that human (or possibly animal) well-being is thereby maximised, or so that all are equal, or so that the worst off group in society is as well-off as possible, or so that as many people as possible have enough to lead a good life.

The *currency* of justice concerns the aspect of well-being, or unit of benefit or advantage, on which our distributive concerns should focus. The idea is that a clear account of the entities that count for a theory of justice, as well as what the profile of benefits should be across these entities, must be attached to some further account of what it is that is shared between these entities. Popular suggestions for what we should seek to distribute across society have been *resources*,[4] *welfare*,[5] *opportunities for welfare*,[6] *basic capabilities to function*,[7] and *access to advantage*.[8]

To sum up the above, we might say that the three issues concern *who* should get *what* and *how much* under any suggested distributive scheme.

As with any division of a political or philosophical concept, there exists a certain amount of fuzziness at the boundaries of each component. It is, for example, very difficult at times to assign contributions to the literature exclusively to these three issues, or discuss the nature of one of the three without discussing the others. Nevertheless, the distinction between these aspects of justice is important as it reminds us that theories of distribution occupy a three-dimensional space that provides a diversity of possibilities that has not been hitherto exhausted.[9]

Many authors have taken it for granted that certain accounts of the scope of justice must accompany certain accounts of the shape, and currency, of justice. It is common, for example, to defend egalitarianism at the level of shape with universalism at the level of scope;[10] or welfarism at the level of currency with maximisation at the level of shape;[11] or resourcism at the level of currency with egalitarianism at the level of shape;[12] or capabilities and functionings at the level of currency with sufficiency at the level of shape.[13] My point is not that certain combinations are not more obvious, or defensible, than others. But rather that these connections are at a deeper level contingent in the sense that they need to be embedded within a wider explanation of how a given theory's approach to all three fits together.

3.2   CONSEQUENTIALIST AND PROCEDURAL JUSTICE

While the model offered above could be accepted by a large range of theorists of justice, it is not all encompassing. It is particularly useful for those who subscribe to what we might call *consequentialist justice*, of which the broad egalitarian views at the heart of this book are a species. Consequentialist justice assumes that there are certain desired outcomes of acts and social policies, such as that they promote social welfare or are beneficial to the worst off in society. It may be contrasted with *procedural justice* which assumes that acts or social policies should be chosen according to certain decisionmaking procedures, for example that they respect the equal status of persons and treat like cases alike. As we shall see, both consequentialist and procedural thinking are key elements of the debate about the equitable management of global climate change, as well as the concept of sustainable development in broader terms.[14] Nevertheless, there arise significant difficulties in harmonising the two approaches to justice as well as principles that they generate.

Robert Nozick has done much to bring these different approaches to justice to the attention of political theorists. According to his version of the consequentialist-procedural distinction, we can distinguish between *end result*, *patterned* and *historical* principles.[15] Historical principles explain how resources should be distributed in terms of how those resources came to be owned, and how they were later transferred amongst persons. End result principles, by contrast, urge us to distribute resources according to some ideal that is unconcerned with the prior claims that different persons may have. A good example is the utilitarian principle that resources should be distributed so that social welfare is maximised regardless of historical resource claims. Here, the procedures we adopt in our policymaking are wholly subservient to the goal of utility maximisation. Finally, patterned principles require that we distribute so that people's holdings vary according to some 'natural dimension', such as moral merit, social usefulness, intelligence, or personal need (or a weighted combination of these). Since some of these dimensions internalise information about past events and actions in order to establish present entitlements, patterned principles can be both historical and non-historical.

Libertarians, according to Nozick, embrace only historical principles.[16] Here, no goal, however positive, can justify us interfering with repeated acquisitions and transfers of resources so long as procedural justice has not been violated. We might say, then, that this view denies that there are any problems to be solved concerning the *shape* or *currency* of distributive justice. It holds instead that distributive justice has no 'shape' or, in other words, that there is no part of distributive justice concerned with the distribution of benefits and burdens to which people lack prior claims. Although it is still tempting to locate libertarianism within the above three dimensional model by indicating a 'zero value' for shape and currency, it seems that this theory generates a new type of model which is incompatible with those that describe theories of broad egalitarianism (which, to recap, are theories that distribute according to equality or some related ideal).

The distinctions between consequentialist and procedural justice, and amongst *historical*, *end result* and *patterned* principles, can help us understand the diversity of principles that have found their way into climate agreements. Prominent examples are the *polluter pays principle*, the *proportionate contribution principle* and the *sufficiency principle*.[17] The 'polluter pays' principle is well known. It holds that the perpetrators of some act of environmental damage ought to bear the costs of its bad effects. The 'proportionate contribution' principle holds that moral agents should contribute to the solution, or amelioration, of environmental problems in proportion to their ability, usually judged by income and wealth. The 'sufficiency' principle states that environmental policies should aim at bringing as many people as possible to the point where their basic needs are met. These principles, which are integral to Article 3 of the UN Framework Convention on Climate Change, often converge in requiring large sacrifices of present persons to protect the environment bequeathed to future generations, but are motivated by very different ethical positions.[18] Different combinations of principles can nonetheless have contrasting implications for climate policy.[19]

In this chapter, we will be focusing on recent attempts to spell out the largely consequentialist and end-result question of the appropriate currency of distributive justice and, with the aid of examples, relating these attempts to preceding debates about the impacts of global climate change. The motivation is that, while issues of historical wrongs and property rights are key parts of the debate, it seems that any equitable, and workable, approach to climate change must take into consideration the effects it will have on our successors. There are, in addition, reasons for thinking that historical approaches may never emerge from conceptual puzzles concerning the rectification of inequities brought about by previous generations who had no knowledge of the enhanced greenhouse effect, as well as the problem of holding individuals responsible for the diffuse effects of their emitting behaviour. Focusing on the effects themselves, and theories designed to limit the inequities that they bring about, seems much more straightforward.

As in previous chapters, the discussion focuses primarily on duties to remote future persons (or generations), whom are defined as those that will come into existence after all those now living have ceased to exist. At this point, we assume that there is no theoretical implausibility associated with the idea that members of future generations *can* have claims on social resources in roughly the same fashion as existing persons, even if, all things considered, these claims may turn out to have less weight than those possessed by our contemporaries.

3.3   EQUALITY AND JUSTICE OF WHAT? EQUALITY OF WELFARE?

What is it that broad egalitarians should seek to equalise across society? What measure or currency of advantage? This important issue, known in the literature as 'equality of what?',[20] or the 'problem of distributive equality',[21] has generated a host of contrasting attempts to spell out what an egalitarian society would look like, and has clear relevance for environmental and intergenerational justice. Following the humanist approach of the book, it seems clear that the appropriate currency of advantage will be linked, albeit more subtly than might initially be assumed, to the concept of human well-being, or what it is for a person to lead a good life *from that person's perspective*.

One theory that argues that well-being should be equally distributed across society is *welfare egalitarianism*. The idea, as Dworkin has put it, is that 'a distributional scheme treats people as equals when it distributes or transfers resources amongst them until no further transfer would leave them more equal in welfare.'[22] One writer who has embraced welfare equality, at least temporarily, is Ted Honderich. Honderich suggests that resources should be distributed such that 'we approach as close as we can, which may not be all that close, equality in satisfaction and distress.'[23] Another is Richard Layard. Layard argues that public policies should be adopted that will bring about equality of welfare (or in his terms 'happiness').[24] The notion of welfare to which Honderich, Layard and other welfarists[25] adopt requires some clarification. This is because there are a number of alternative accounts of what welfare itself consists of, two of the most popular accounts being *success* or *conscious-states*.

Conscious-state (or mental-state) theories of welfare – such as those proposed by Layard and Honderich – hold that welfare consists in the presence of certain desirable conscious states. The relevant states can be 'simple', as in the case of the pleasure a person derives from eating an ice-cream, or 'complex', as in the case of the enjoyment a person derives from a tragic novel or romantic cruise. Equality of welfare as conscious-states requires that 'distribution should attempt to leave people as equal as possible in some aspect or quality of their conscious life.'[26]

Success-based theories of welfare, in contrast, hold that a person's welfare is some function of their success in fulfilling their goals and preferences. These goals and preferences might concern how benefits and burdens should be distributed amongst other persons in society ('political preferences'), how they themselves are faring ('personal preferences'), or the promotion of their values ('impersonal preferences'). Moreover, more or less restricted versions of the success theory can be constructed depending on whether only personal; personal and impersonal; or personal, impersonal and political preferences are counted. We might refer to these possibilities as restricted, *part*-restricted and unrestricted welfarism respectively. Adopting welfare as success as the currency of egalitarian justice requires that 'distribution and transfer of resources until no further transfer can decrease the extent to which people differ in their success'.[27]

Success-based theories of welfare are generally viewed as superior to conscious-state theories. This is because they can account for the idea that a person can be low in welfare even if they experience pleasurable conscious states, for example because a number of their strongest desires have been thwarted without them knowing, and without them experiencing any conscious disappointment. They can also explain how people can be well off even if they are in temporary pain, such as where a person gives birth or experiences a painful, though nevertheless subjectively worthwhile, love affair. In the following, when I refer to equality of welfare I mean by this equality of welfare *as success*.

On first inspection, equality of welfare would seem well suited to issues of intergenerational and global justice. All beings capable of entertaining preferences will be covered by the theory, no matter when or where they live, and no one person's preferences will be viewed as having more weight than any other. The theory, then, seems to be both inclusive and egalitarian. Acts or policies that impact upon the integrity and health of the natural, economic, and cultural environments, for example, will clearly impact upon the desire-satisfaction of future human beings (as well as many non-human animals) and so equality of welfare seems broadly applicable to the sorts of climate impacts discussed earlier.

The idea that distributive justice should be neutral to considerations of both time and space is deeply ingrained in welfarist thinking. In an early contribution to the literature on welfarism and future generations, Frank Ramsey argues that we should not 'discount later enjoyments in comparison with earlier ones, a practice which is ethically indefensible and arises from the weakness of the imagination'.[28] Ramsey's articulation of the impartiality and universalism underpinning welfarism is echoed by Peter Singer, who writes that 'it makes no moral difference whether the person I help is a neighbour's child ten yards from me or a Bengali whose name I shall never know, ten thousand miles away.'[29]

One problem with extending equality of welfare across generations, however, is that acts and social policies will affect not merely future persons' possession of resources such as income and wealth, but also their preferences. Let us take as a starting point the broad range of climate impacts discussed in the previous chapter. Adaptations in the preference base of future persons that mitigate the possible negative impact of climate change on the welfare of future persons, and thus nullify any prima facie welfare inequality injustice, could be brought about in at least two ways. First, members of earlier generations might manipulate the genetic make-up of their offspring in order that the latter are better able to flourish (in the sense of fulfilling desires and preferences) in an environment affected by climate change. This might seem far-fetched, but there is increasing research being conducted by scientists who hope to offer parents not just the possibility of screening for severe diseases in the future, but also the ability to modify their offspring so that they are well adjusted to changes in the environment.[30] Second, members of later generations might adapt to their degraded surroundings by learning not to desire so intensely access to clean air, or by learning to exploit the possibilities offered by a warmer, or wetter, climate. This might seem implausible, but research suggests that human society has adapted constantly to changes in climate over the last 20 000 years.[31]

Since the desires of many, if not all, future persons will be shaped so that their welfare is less compromised by the effects of climate change than is commonly surmised, it would seem that, on the welfare egalitarian view, far fewer persons in the remote future will be disadvantaged than is often held. Consequently, even if equality of welfare could be extended to cover dealings between different generations in principle, recent findings on the impacts of climate change would not necessarily be of import for this distributive theory in practice.

As it transpires, even the most plausible interpretations of welfarism as a theory of justice or equality are flawed, so such disquieting conclusions are not forced upon us. The main problem is that welfare egalitarianism has wildly counter-intuitive implications for our dealings with contemporaries and compatriots, as is demonstrated by a brief analysis of the following two hypothetical examples. As we shall see, the source of these counter-intuitions is to be found in the jump from using welfare as a theory of the quality of life of a single person, to its being used to determine what a person deserves from the standpoint of justice.

The first problem is that distributing resources in order to equalise welfare across a given domain without taking into consideration the different tastes and preferences people have, and the way these were acquired, risks indulging people who experience less welfare than others because their tastes are costly to satisfy. Consider the case of Louis, who quite deliberately cultivates a preference for expensive food and wine.[32] It seems inappropriate for an egalitarian society to compensate people such as Louis who have acquired such tastes through elitist aspirations or lack of self-discipline. Welfare egalitarianism, however, would have us give extra resources to those, such as Louis, who possess expensive tastes until their welfare is equal to others even if they (a) acquired their expensive preferences voluntarily and (b) do not regret that they acquired them.[33] This has been called the *expensive tastes* problem.[34]

A second example indicates that welfare equality cannot explain why people should be compensated for disabilities that do not prevent their owners from enjoying an average, or higher than average, level of welfare. Consider the case of the Dickensian character Tiny Tim.[35] Tim's legs are paralysed, so, if he is to gain any degree of personal mobility, he requires a wheelchair. Unfortunately, Tim has not got the resources at present to purchase one. Fortunately, he is a very cheerful fellow – so much so that, despite his disadvantage, he maintains a high level of well-being. Like many people who live in dire circumstances, either due to personal handicaps, poverty or environmental degradation, he has, we might say, *adapted* his desires in order to make the most of his life prospects; he has 'psychologically adjusted to persistent deprivation', as Sen has put it.[36] Should Tim, in spite of his cheerfulness, receive compensation in order to purchase a wheelchair? Should not his adaptiveness be ignored by distributive justice?[37] We might call this the *cheap tastes* problem.

Many, if not all, of the philosophers who have analysed similar cases hold that people in Tim's situation have at the very least a *prima facie* claim to compensation (a prima facie claim is one that generates an obligation on the part of others as long as no lexically prior, or morally weighty, obligation overrides it). The problem is that equality of welfare seems badly suited to explain this belief. Welfare egalitarians seek to view Tim's situation as being of distributive significance only to the extent that his disability means he experiences less welfare than others, something that is ruled out by his cheerful disposition. In fact, if Tim's disposition is 'too sunny' he might be in danger of forfeiting some resources back to the rest of society in order to maintain equality of welfare! But, for many, this seems absurd. As G.A. Cohen has put it, Tim's capacity for happiness in the face of adversity would not normally lead egalitarians to 'strike him off the list of free wheelchair receivers' for they believe that the physically handicapped should be 'adequately resourced, whether or not they also need them to be, or to be capable of being, happy'.[38]

The cheap tastes (or adaptation) problem is an important addition to the armoury of the non-welfarist as it is equally damaging to a popular reformulation of equality of welfare. The reformulated theory argues that we should abandon the idea of equalising interpersonal welfare in favour of equalising interpersonal *opportunities for welfare*. The idea is that, in most circumstances, people should be held responsible for the preferences that they possess, and also for the amount of effort they put into their attempts to satisfy these preferences.

According to Richard Arneson, for example, equality of opportunity for welfare consists in each person facing equivalent ranges of options in terms of how well their lives *could* turn out. That is, the sum of all of the expected levels of welfare associated with each possible life a person could live must be equal for equality of opportunity for welfare to obtain. The idea is that it is not a person's actual low welfare level that indicates his relative disadvantage, but that the welfare sum of all of his possible lives is lower than others. The reformulated theory, then, gives little solace to those that are born healthy, and enjoy a good start to life, but subsequently enjoy a low level of welfare due to their own negligence or fecklessness. Deserved interpersonal inequalities in welfare, here, are seen as 'nonproblematic from the standpoint of distributive equality'.[39]

On first inspection, the reformulated view seems readily extendible to issues of intergenerational distribution for more or less the same reasons as the unmodified view: that is, it is blind to considerations of space and time, and treats all people (as bearers of preferences) equally. Thus, while this account is motivated at its core by an abstract notion of equality according to which 'other things being equal, it is bad if some people are worse off than others through no voluntary choice or fault of their own',[40] there seems to be little reason to think that these people must be members of the present generation.

Climate change provides an apposite example. The extent to which people of different generations will enjoy lives of equal quality in the sense that they enjoy 'equivalent arrays of options'[41] will be determined in part by their health, as well as that of their contemporaries. But the increased instances of extreme weather events, rises in sea levels and generally warmer weather will impact upon the health of future persons, and in turn on their opportunity to realise various life plans. It can be predicted, for example, that in many countries climate change will limit the options people have to pursue activities in the open air at certain times of the year, as well as during heatwaves and other extreme weather events. It will also, more critically, lead to many more people dying than would have been the case, thus reducing the amount of welfare they might have achieved. Obviously, the presence of such inequality is susceptible to other developments, such as the fact that the existing generation may create and bequeath additional technology to their successors in order to compensate for the lost welfare opportunities brought about by certain impacts of climate change. Nevertheless, climate change seems a clear source of intergenerational inequality of opportunity.

One problem with this line of thought has already been discussed above – namely, the prospect of adaptations in the preference base of future persons.

Suppose that the policymakers in charge of climate policy decide to invest a large amount of money in a programme of re-education which has the aim of ensuring that people coming into existence in the future will be much better adapted than they are today to a world changed by climate change (the alternative, let us assume, would have been to invest much larger sums on measures to avoid the worst aspects of climate change altogether). Would the policymakers' actions violate the norm of equality of opportunity for welfare? The future persons concerned, let us imagine, would have access to far fewer natural resources than present persons, and those which they do have access to, such as clean air and water, would be of a lower quality.

By re-educating people to accept the new environmental conditions, however, the programme would enable the creation of subsequent generations who have adapted their preferences to a more polluted environment – in a sense creating generations of persons who look on their environment in a similar way to which Tiny Tim views his disability.[42] The result would be that the sum of the expected utilities of many future persons' life plans might be at least as great as those enjoyed by members of the present generation. These people would enjoy neither less welfare, nor less equality opportunity for welfare, than their ancestors despite enjoying a worsened natural resource base. They will consequently have no complaint at the bar of welfare egalitarianism.

The above discussion suggests that, when we are concerned to equalise people's life-prospects, this equalising cannot be fully expressed in terms of equalising welfare, either absolutely or relative to opportunities. Rather it must be expressed in terms of a different currency of advantage.

3.4   INTERGENERATIONAL EQUALITY OF RESOURCES

One alternative to equality of welfare is *equality of resources*, of which there are two main variants: *equality of impersonal resources* and *equality of impersonal and personal resources*. In the following, it is argued that, although both variants can be adjusted to cover dealings between generations, neither is defensible.

3.4.1   Equality of Impersonal Resources

Perhaps the most influential theory of equality of impersonal resources has been proposed by John Rawls. In *A Theory of Justice*, Rawls argues that the problems that afflict welfarist theories of distribution, such as utilitarianism, can be avoided if we seek to distribute what he calls *primary goods* so that, unless the worst off in society gain from their unequal distribution, these goods are dispersed evenly. Primary goods are in effect 'generalised resources' that serve as all-purpose means for people's pursuit of what they want out of life (whatever this might be) and according to Rawls they fall under five main categories: [43]

1. 'the basic liberties as given by a list';
2. 'freedom of movement and choice of occupation against a background of diverse opportunities';
3. 'powers and prerogatives of offices and positions of responsibility';
4. 'income and wealth';
5. 'the social bases of self-respect.'[44]

Rawls's theory of distributive justice proceeds as follows. Social and political principles required as rules for the design of just institutions are those that would be chosen by rational, self-interested persons in a hypothetical contractual situation (*the original position*) behind a *veil of ignorance* that precludes the contracting parties certain types of knowledge (such as their talents) so that they can negotiate freely and fairly. The idea is that, as there are no known preferences in the original position, the contracting parties define social outcomes in terms of the *social primary goods* that are needed for persons to pursue their individual life plans and function as citizens within a just society. The social primary goods, Rawls argued, should be distributed equally unless an unequal distribution would be in the interests of the worst off.[45]

Although Rawls did not apply his primary goods egalitarianism to future generations in any direct sense, he did embrace extensive obligations not to damage the environment bequeathed to future persons. In *A Theory of Justice*, he argued that the contracting parties, who were defined as 'heads of family lines', could be seen as sharing a sentimental concern for their nearest descendants such that this well-being can be treated as a public good. The principle of fairness will then require that all persons who are capable play their part in contributing to the cost of its upkeep. Rawls in this way achieved a measure of intergenerational justice by treating the well-being of future persons as a primary good of present persons, rather than making future persons subjects of justice that possess their own primary goods (we return to this argument in Chapter 5).

Another author who defends a theory of intergenerational resourcism, while retaining a broadly Rawlsian framework, is Brian Barry. Barry argues that the consumption of non-renewable natural resources over time 'should be compensated for in the sense that later generations should be left no worse off (in terms of productive capacity) than they would have been without the depletion'.[46] A key issue for any theory of equality, Barry thinks, is the appropriate consumption of non-renewable natural resources across time. When reserves of non-renewable resources (such as oil or natural gas) are depleted, the costs to our successors of extracting and then using these resources are increased. There are also costs imposed upon our successors as a consequence of the *side effects* of depleting these resources, such as global climate change, air pollution and destruction of the ozone layer. As a consequence of these costs, it is crucial to establish how much existing generations may deplete stocks of non-renewable resources without violating the requirements of intergenerational justice.

It would be unfair, Barry thinks, to require existing generations to leave *all* non-renewable resources untouched for the sake of future generations (that is, to consume nothing). Neither would it be possible for each generation to replicate in every detail the non-renewable resources it uses. However, it would appear to be a sound principle that existing generations ought not worsen the opportunities available to future generations by depleting non-renewable resources with no compensatory action or recompense. Indeed, such a requirement would seem to cohere with a number of articulations of the idea of sustainable development according to which development is a matter of balancing the claims of different generations.[47] It is also a view favoured by a number of economists and other theorists concerned with intergenerational justice and international law.[48]

The idea of making recompense, of course, typically leaves it open for a given compensation for a depleted resource, X, to be compensated by the provision of a given commensurable resource, Y – so long as this compensation enables the recipient to be no worse off than they would have been had the original resource, X, not been used up. Intergenerational resourcism, then, need not preclude the consumption of any exhaustible resources, but that any consumption is offset in some way. Perhaps the most obvious example of such compensation in the intergenerational context would be the way in which improvements in technology (e.g. energy saving techniques) appear to compensate for losses of natural non-renewable resources (eg coal, oil or natural gas). Because it will not be possible, or required, to set the level of compensation so high that it can deal with any future world population, Barry sums up his view as follows:

> Sustainability requires at any point in time that the value of [equal opportunity] per head of population should be capable of being maintained into the indefinite future, on the assumption that the size of the future population is not greater than the size of the present population.[49]

In more recent work, Barry has argued that resource equality demands that we regard the climate system as a 'global commons', the use of which must be allocated according to principles of equal distribution such that all persons have an equal right to emit greenhouse gases.[50] The main policy implication of this view is taken to be the endorsement of the 'Contraction and Convergence' model popularised by the Global Commons Institute, according to which all countries converge over the course of the next century on some per capita greenhouse emissions level that is consistent with sustainable development.[51]

3.4.2   Intergenerational Equality of Impersonal and Personal Resources

One problem with equality of resources has prompted some to amend, but not abandon, the theory. The problem is that some people, despite having the same bundle of impersonal resources as others, might not enjoy equal life chances as others because they experience some 'personal' disadvantage. Consider those who are born hard of hearing. Bringing it about that they have the same shares of impersonal resources as everybody else might still not remedy the relative lack of life chances that they experience as a result of their disability. Consider the case of Tiny Tim. According to equality of impersonal resources, Tim should get the same resource share as others, despite his sunny disposition. However, no claim for compensation will arise if an equal share of impersonal resources is insufficient for Tim to purchase a wheelchair.

There are clear analogies between the case of Tim and the case of the future victims of climate change. Not all of the negative impacts of climate change can be readily explained in terms of deficits in transferable resources, neither can they be easily offset by extra allocations of these, for example by increased savings and investment. Climate change will increase, and alter the spread of, a range of infectious and non-infectious diseases, and increase mortality and morbidity in many regions as a result of heat events, storms, floods and forest fires. Even if some of the health impacts of climate change can be framed in impersonal terms, the complexity of the health impacts indicates that most cannot. A simple resourcism of social primary goods, productive capacity or some other conception of impersonal resources, then, seems an inadequate approach to intergenerational justice.

The amendment to resourcism that might overcome these problems is to widen the account of the currency of distribution to include *personal resources*, such as talents or handicaps. So in our example of the person who is hard of hearing, or in the case of Tiny Tim, the disability concerned would be viewed as a personal resource deficit that is (other things being equal) deserving of compensation. The idea, as Ronald Dworkin has put it, is that resourcism must not only seek to eradicate undeserved inequalities in holdings of impersonal resources (such as income, wealth and legal and social opportunities) but also those that result from people's undeserved differential holdings of personal resources (such as strengths, talents and personal health). It is only in this way, Dworkin thinks, we can respect the liberal egalitarian norm of respecting the integrity of persons (and the choices they make) while recti-fying injustices arising from chance.[52]

Part of the reason that Rawls and other resource egalitarians have stepped back from this more radical understanding of resource equality is that natural endowments are not easily transferred from person to person, and it is unclear how a liberal society that believes in personal freedom and dignity could put an egalitarianism of both personal and impersonal resources into effect. Could it not involve, in the final analysis, violations of personal freedom similar to those parodied in the Monty Python film *The Meaning of Life*, where agents of the state carried out policies of forced organ donation? Moreover, would not even the paternalistic approach fail in its own terms since the nature of some handicaps is such that complete equality would not prevail if we transferred literally *all* available personal and impersonal resources to the very worst off?[53]

The problem that exercises Dworkin, and other proponents of the extended resourcist view, is not how to transfer personal resources across fellow citizens to bring about equality, but how to define a distribution of transferable resources that would best approximate the situation where all undeserved interpersonal inequalities were removed. Moreover, it is important to note that Dworkin does not think that all deserve to have an equal bundle of impersonal and personal resources throughout their lives. For him, a theory of distribution should treat all members of society with equal concern and respect, and this means that they should be held accountable for the pursuit of their life plans. What distributive justice can do is to neutralise the effects of fortune and contingency on people's lives so that there exists a 'level playing field' of opportunity for all to make the most of the resources at their disposal.[54]

Dworkin develops his theory of equality of resources in terms of two hypo-thetical situations that utilise economic market ideas to model an equal distrib-ution of resources within society. In the first, the hypothetical auction, shipwreck survivors agree to divide up the unowned resources of an hitherto uninhabited island by bidding, from a position of parity, for the resources they want.[55] The resulting distribution is held to be equal so long as none of the islanders prefers the bundle of resources obtained by another bidder. This test of egalitarian distribution has become known as the 'envy test', and distribu-tions of resources that meet this test are called *envy-free distributions*. Although Dworkin holds that the auction device offers an illuminating model of resource equality, he notes that the envy test will only hold for a short time after the initial auction. This is because people will be free to consume, produce and trade with the result that inequalities in resource bundles, and thus envy, will arise. In order to maintain resource equality over time, Dworkin argues, it would be necessary for people to agree to invest in a certain amount of insur-ance to compensate those who become worse off through circumstances beyond their control (bad 'brute luck') but which is blind to inequalities that are within people's control (bad 'option luck').[56]

According to the second hypothetical market situation, the hypothetical insurance device, we imagine what insurance premium people in our society would have purchased against the risk of being someone who is unlucky in life if they had the chance.[57] The level of cover that an average person of normal prudence would chose in circumstances of equal terms, and in the context of a competitive insurance market, is then translated into a social welfare system funded by social taxation. Although the determination of the level of insurance cover is abstracted from human behaviour in the real world, the idea is that we 'give people who have been unlucky the compensation that they very probably would have bargained to receive if they had had the opportunity they should have had.'[58] The insurance device, then, shows how a society that takes the freedom of its members seriously could provide all of its members with health care and welfare provision as determined by the amount people would be hypothetically willing to pay in terms of insurance, but leaves it open that some people will lead better lives than others if they make better use out of the resources at their disposal.

At bottom, the auction and insurance devices establish a sort of balance between helping those who have impoverished resource bundles (such as the handicapped and untalented) and not penalising those (such as the healthy and talented) that freely chose to develop their powers and increase their well-being through their exercise. As such, while it includes within its scope redistribution designed to rectify inequalities of personal resources (such as talents) and impersonal resources (such as personal wealth), it is unconcerned with inequalities arising from people's different personality traits (such as their tastes).[59]

Dworkin's theory has attracted a large critical literature, for the most part focusing on questions of domestic justice. However, it also has interesting implications for climate change that have been largely ignored. Recall that, to the extent that future generations will inherit through no fault of their own a damaged context within which to pursue their life plans, intergenerational equality of impersonal resources regards these people as deserving of compensation. This is because such people – or at least many of them – will have access to a less than abundant bundle of impersonal resources, and hence opportunities, than were available to earlier generations. We could say that this theory endorses the test that no generation should *envy* the impersonal resources enjoyed by predecessor generations.

However, climate change will also have effects that undermine intergenerational equality of personal resources by increasing rates of physical and mental disease amongst both adults and young children.[60] The IPCC's successive assessments indicate all too clearly that the quality of life of many millions of our successors will be irrevocably shaped by the decisions that are taken in the following decades about how to respond to climate change. These successors, on Dworkin's view, have ample reason to envy the personal and impersonal resource allocation enjoyed by previous generations. We might call this the *extended* envy test.

Because their envy is not grounded in life decisions that they can be held accountable for (for the most part, their disadvantage flows as a result of brute, rather than option, luck), and they have reasonable grounds to regret their disadvantage, they will have a claim to a greater share of the social welfare net. The idea is that, for the insurance device is to be truly insensitive to chance, but sensitive to choice, the coverage chosen by the average, prudent, person should be much greater (and the social welfare system subsequently much more extensive) for all generations to be covered by the theory. If it were not, then members of future generations would be in a similar position to impoverished contemporaries who live in a society that set the average level of cover too low because it focused on the level of cover the average risk-prone, rather than prudent, person would select in the context of a competitive market for insurance. The thought is that we extend the scope of the theory to include the insurance requirements of present and future persons.

Of course, if future generations go on to worsen the problem of climate change by their own actions, intergenerational resource equality will not come to their rescue. They would, like their predecessors, have to bear the costs of their life choices. But to ignore the special claims of future people when we know that changes in the environment they face will almost certainly worsen their resource endowments would seem to deny members of future generations their due under Dworkin's resourcism. The theory, as extended, seems to coincide greatly with Barry's notion that each generation should pass on to the next at least as good a material resource base as it inherited, but adds that extra investments must be made by each generation to make sure that the extended envy test is met.

A number of objections have been raised to Dworkin's theory of justice. Many of these concern the workings of the hypothetical insurance idea, and can be seen as a debate internal to resource egalitarianism.[61] I put these to one side. There are, however, more fundamental objections that ground their own answers to the 'equality of what?' problem. The first of these maintains that the measure of advantage embraced by Dworkin is too narrow to capture what it is that people should have equal shares of. In short, it is argued that the account underplays the heterogeneity of what makes a life go well, as well as the importance of making sure that all people have the substantive freedom to achieve this. The second line of attack claims that resourcism is blind to many important inequalities because it insists that only *repudiated* expensive tastes deserve compensation. I turn to a more detailed consideration of these contrasting critiques in the next two sections. At this point, I want to prepare the ground for them by showing the ambiguities of the Dworkinian view in the light of an interesting hypothetical case.[62]

Jade, whose arms are otherwise healthy and in working order, suffers from a rare condition which causes her great pain whenever she moves her arms. This 'non-disabling' pain can be prevented if she takes an expensive drug, and does not affect her ability to move her hands, or function normally in any other sense. All other things being equal, Cohen asks, does Jade deserve (as a matter of justice) extra resources so that she can acquire this drug? If we think that she does, it seems that we are forced to abandon resourcism since Jade's disadvantage cannot be explained as either a personal or impersonal resource deficiency. It seems, instead, to be some kind of welfare deficiency, or a deficiency in some other currency of well-being that we have yet to discuss. The conclusion seems to be that if we want to compensate people in such cases we must seek to equalise a conception of interpersonal advantage that recognises not just the importance of some more sophisticated currency of advantage that shares features of both welfare and resources.

We might, of course, think that the example is bizarre, and a long way from the reality of climate change. It is worth noting, however, that a number of disadvantages are not easily framed in terms of resources. Chronic pain, generalised anxiety, depression, panic disorder, and post-traumatic stress disorder all remain controversial topics of debate from an aetiological point of view, but have profound effects on a person's quality of life despite not being easily explainable as a negative resource endowment. It is estimated that up to one in seven people suffer from chronic pain, which is defined as continuous pain for three months or more, although it is not always possible to find the true cause since pain is felt even when no damage is present.[63] Moreover, at least some of the above conditions are sensitive to changes in climate variables such as air temperature and air pressure, and there is evidence that the incidence of these conditions will increase as a result of climate impacts, in particular those causing demographic and economic disruption.[64]

It is worth noting that Dworkin, in *Sovereign Virtue*, argues that equality of resources is fully compatible with the thought that non-disabling pain, if sufficiently debilitating, is deserving of compensation so long as its victim regrets his disability. He writes that:

> almost everyone would agree that a decent life, whatever its other features, is one that is free from serious and enduring physical or mental pain or discomfort, and having a physical or mental infirmity or condition that makes pain or depression or discomfort inescapable without expensive medication or clothing is therefore an evident and straightforward handicap . . . A pain-producing infirmity is a canonical example of a lack of personal resources for which equality of resources would, in principle provide compensation.[65]

The problem with this response, however, is that it does not fully address the implications of the chronic pain example, which is not to merely to show that sufferers of chronic pain deserve compensation at the bar of egalitarian justice, but that the normative basis of this compensation is some feature of their well-being that is anterior to their resource endowment: their *welfare*. Suppose Jade suffered from a relapsing and remitting case of chronic fatigue syndrome – she feels fine at the moment, but knows that she can relapse at any time. The condition, and thus resource deficiency on Dworkin's view, is still present in the strict sense, but it has no real impact on Jade's level of welfare. It seems that Dworkin must choose between the view that there is an equally strong case for compensation both during and outside remission (which is implausible) and the view that there are grounds for compensation only outside remission (a view that can only be explained by an appeal to Jade's welfare). Put a different way, Dworkin may have shown us that Jade's welfare deficit comes as a consequence of having an ailment, but he hasn't explained how the reason for being concerned from the point of view of justice can be anything other than the welfare loss associated with it.[66]

3.5   EQUALITY OF BASIC CAPABILITIES

According to basic capability egalitarianism, we should seek to equalise the 'substantive freedoms' (or *'capabilities'*) that people have to achieve the life that they have reason to value. This theory of justice, as others we have looked at, has both a well-being and an egalitarian component. According to the well-being component, the things people have reason to value are held to be partic-ularly important *functionings* – that is, abilities or states of mind – that are related to, but at a deeper level separate from, the means that make them achievable and their impact on a person's welfare.

Amartya Sen, who, along with Martha Nussbaum, is the most prominent holder of the view, argues that there are two main categories of functioning: elementary and complex.[67] Elementary functionings are those 'doings' and 'beings', such as being well nourished or having access to adequate clothing and shelter, that can be secured by income, wealth and personal liberty. Complex functionings, on the other hand, such as self-respect and the ability to take part in the life of one's political community, depend, at least in part, on factors independent of resource possession, including the attitudes of others in society. Both types of functioning, according to Sen, pick out features of a person's life that are essential to their leading a decent life and can be contrasted with trivial functionings (and the capabilities to achieve these), such as jumping on the spot.[68]

The egalitarian component is the simple idea that each person should enjoy an equivalent array, or set, of capabilities to achieve valuable functionings, both simple and complex. To the extent that poverty, poor environmental conditions, physical handicap or inequitable social arrangements prevent a person having the capability to achieve the same functionings as others in society, then they have a prima facie claim at the bar of distributive justice.

The theory, as outlined, marks a significant step away from both welfarism and resourcism. Consider the paradigm example of an elementary, or basic, capability: that of being well nourished. The distributive importance of food for welfarists lies in terms of the way in which their consumption satisfies preferences, and for resourcists it is the possession of the food itself. But, as Sen notes, having access to a regular supply of food gives people much more than just a regular supply of welfare, and what it does for them cannot be explained solely in terms of resource possession. Rather, such access facilitates 'the capability of functioning in a particular way, e.g. without nutritional deficiencies of particular types'.[69]

Basic capability egalitarianism, Sen argues, would require differential distributions of resources even if it can sometimes be hard to distinguish a capability inequality from a resource inequality. A person with a lower metabolic rate, for example, requires less food in order to become, and continue to be, well nourished than a person with a higher metabolic rate. All other things being equal, the former will have a superior capability set, and so will have no complaint if more resources are allocated to the latter to maintain equality.[70] Sen writes that, 'what people get out of goods depends on a variety of factors, and judging personal advantage just by the size of personal ownership of goods and services can be very misleading.'[71]

On the other hand, equalising capabilities will not always mean equalising welfare. Although it is far from straightforward to compare the welfare levels of different people, it seems clear that different people derive different amounts of welfare from a given amount of food. The clearest case of this is when one person's favourite food is another's object of hatred. Moreover, some capability inequalities are not experienced as subjectively bad, or regrettable, by those they penalise. One example of this discussed by Martha Nussbaum is the case of women who do not experience gender injustices as painful because they have adapted their preferences to suit their life situation.[72] The idea then is that there are some human capabilities whose loss, or absence, does not reduce a person's welfare, but should nevertheless be seen as distributively significant.

Sen's capability egalitarianism has been developed further by Nussbaum. More explicitly than Sen, Nussbaum holds that it is the *capabilities* that people have to achieve valuable functionings, and not the *achievements* of the functionings, that should be the focus of egalitarians.[73] Nussbaum seeks to entrench the notion of basic capability equality into the constitutional framework of a liberal society, rather than merely use it as a currency for comparisons of interpersonal well-being. Further, it is important that capability egalitarianism does not violate the basic liberal ideas of tolerance and respect for the choices people make and the diverging conceptions of the good life that they entertain. The scope of this subtly adjusted version of capability equality is limited to helping persons reach the point where they have 'a realistic option of exercising the most valuable functions.'[74] Whether they choose to take these options is left to their own conscience.

Nussbaum lists a number of 'central human capabilities' that she holds to be integral features of a life that is 'truly human', but which must also be viewed as revisable according to public discussion and debate. The functionings and capabilities that comprise a life of high quality are not, then, derived from an account of human good that is historically and spatially unchanging, but represents an 'overlapping consensus' amongst people who think very differently about the good life. They are divided into three groups: *basic capabilities*, such as hearing and sight, are innate talents that enable people to develop more advanced capabilities; *internal capabilities* are developed states of the person, such as sexual functioning, which may or may not be realised depending on environmental and other factors; and *combined capabilities* are internal capabilities that are facilitated by suitable external conditions, such as the capability of religious expression in a society tolerant of religious diversity.[75] The list of 'central human functional capabilities' is as follows:[76]

1. life;
2. bodily health;
3. bodily integrity;
4. senses, imagination, thought;
5. emotions;
6. practical reason;
7. affiliation;
8. a relationship with other species;
9. play;
10. control over one's environment.

Nussbaum holds that a person who lacks any of these capabilities falls short of leading a decent life, and that deficiencies in a given capability cannot be offset by the provision of more of the others. Consequently, her view is that a just distribution of wealth would bring each and every person up to the point where they have sufficient of each capability, and where this is not possible as many people as possible should be so benefited. Inequalities above the point where all have enough of all capabilities are not dealt with and in this sense Nussbaum's theory is a hybrid of equality and sufficiency.[77]

The basic capability theory appears well suited to the context of both international and intergenerational distribution. Both Nussbaum and Sen argue that the capability metric gives rise to useful cross-country comparisons of well-being that can be of assistance to policymakers and practitioners concerned with international poverty. Although the approach is located within a politically liberal scheme that defines capabilities and functionings in terms of public debate and deliberation, it is also an expressly universalist theory in terms of the scope of its application. It is designed, then, to be of use when analysing the distribution of wealth in non-liberal societies and, potentially, amongst different generations.

I have not the space to give justice to the application of basic capability equality to questions of global poverty, except to note that it has attracted broad support in the arena of international politics. *Inter*generationally, the theory appears to require that present persons, and the states they belong to, should not act so as to undermine the possibility that members of future generations will enjoy their basic capabilities to function. To the extent that global environmental problems make it impossible for future people to enjoy either equal capability sets (Sen) or sufficient levels of capabilities considered one-by-one (Nussbaum), these problems (and the actions and policies that caused them) involve great injustice. Our concerns here will certainly be different from either the resourcist or the welfarist. It will not be the aim of distributive justice to secure a resource base for future generations which is equal to that enjoyed by previous generations, or a non-diminishing social welfare function, but rather to preserve an environment that enables future persons to retain the same substantive freedoms to be healthy, well fed, and well clothed that their ancestors possessed.

Consider the way in which climate change is expected to impact upon food production and food security both within and between future generations. Reliable sources of good quality food are crucial for the development and health of existing and future human populations and recent research suggests that a number of changes in climate variables will alter the total amount, and nutritional quality, of the food that will be available to future populations.[78] Sea-level rises, for example, are expected to bring about loss of land, soil infertility and loss of fresh water for irrigation projects. As a result, food production and nutrition in many coastal regions is expected to be undermined. However, food production may also be threatened in the future in semi-arid areas as a result of global warming as well.

In fact, when all the changes in climate variables are taken into consideration, the IPCC claims that many more people belonging to future generations are at risk from hunger and malnutrition as a result of climate change. A central finding in the SAR was that 'an extra 40–300 m people will be at risk of hunger in the year 2060 because of the impact of climate change on top of a predicted 640 m people at risk of hunger by that date in the absence of climate change'.[79] The TAR added that 'degradation of oil and water resources is one of the major future challenges for global agriculture. These processes are likely to be intensified by adverse change in temperature and precipitation'.[80] Taking nutritional status as a key example of a basic capability, then, the IPCC's research indicates that climate change will influence the distribution of basic capabilities across generations.

Climate change will also impact upon the distribution of basic capabilities *within* the generations to come. This is because changes in climate variables will impact more adversely upon people's basic capabilities in some regions than others in line with variations in adaptive capacity. The application of the view will differ somewhat depending on the exact specification of the lists of basic capabilities and whether the view takes an egalitarian or satisficing form. Nevertheless, both interpretations suggest strong climate justice since climate change is a clear and present threat to individual capabilities (control over ones environment, bodily health and bodily integrity) as well as the broader capability to construct a life plan and execute it.

3.6   INTERGENERATIONAL EQUALITY OF 'MIDFARE'

Capability egalitarianism appears to avoid many of the problems that plague rival theories. However, it also has certain drawbacks. I have space to mention two: the 'indexing' and 'access' problems.

The indexing problem has two aspects. As we have seen, Sen's answer to the 'equality of what?' problem is a measure of personal well-being that lies somewhere between the competing metrics of resources and welfare. It is neither the 'cause' (resources) or the 'effect' (welfare) of a person's life going well, as Cohen has put it.[81] To assess whether two persons, Smith and Jones, are equal we must be able to determine that they enjoy the same capabilities to function. The problem is that there are a number of different *basic* functionings that we might want to isolate, so unless Smith has all of the capabilities that Jones has and at least one more (or vice versa) their sets of capabilities do not overlap and thus it is impossible to say which is better off.[82] Imagine, for example, that Smith and Jones are adequately nourished, but Smith is susceptible to various diseases while Jones has a severe learning disorder. In such circumstances, people's basic capability sets seem non-comparable.

Nussbaum's account of the basic capabilities, because of its specificity and insistence that each person requires each of the capabilities on the list to lead a satisfactory (and 'equal') life, can avoid the first version of the indexing problem.[83] The second version of the problem is less tractable, however, and arises when everyone is above the level where their basic needs are met. At this level of well-being, people diverge not in terms of their capability to meet a restricted number of universal needs (such as clothing, shelter or nutrition) but in terms of more complex capabilities (such as higher education or leisure time).[84] That some sense of welfare, or a closely related metric, is needed to make sense of people's relative well-being in such contexts is underlined by the fact that different people value different capabilities to different degrees. How, for example, can we say that Smith is worse off than Jones if both have the capability to meet their basic needs, but differ in terms of their capabilities to meet their non-basic needs?

A more complicated version of the indexing problem will emerge at the intergenerational level given that human needs, capabilities and functionings are in constant flux, even if some core needs (such as nutrition and respiration) are universal. In response to these issues, capability egalitarians tend to emphasise that the question of what a basic capability is, and what weight it should have relative to other capabilities, is an inherently political matter. The idea is that, just as the capability to express one's ideas takes different forms (and has different limits) in different countries, different capabilities related to how people enjoy the natural environment will change over time. The problem is that it seems a fetishism of democratic deliberation to leave the resolution of clashes between different capabilities in the hands of public debate if the stakes are so high that a global environmental catastrophe might be involved.

The *access problem* is more difficult to explain, and leads us in the direction of a fairly serious revision of the capability view. Sen argues that the more extensive a person's substantive freedom to achieve valuable states of mind and body, the better his life is going. The strong element of freedom brought into the theory by the notion of capability is important for Sen as he seeks to construct a theory of equality that gives a central role to human autonomy and the importance that this has to people's well-being. The result is that the emphasis is very much on *capabilities* rather than functionings or achieved welfare. The problem with this approach, however, is that it plays down the relevance of states of the mind and body that are (a) important to how we judge the quality of a person's life, yet (b) not under the control of their bearers.

Consider, once again, the capability to be well nourished. Sen's view is that the substantive freedom to nourish oneself (or not) is a paradigm basic capability. The model here is that adults, through one means or another, secure foodstuffs and then exercise the capability of feeding themselves. The fact that this is best seen in terms of capability, and not functioning, can be shown by the fact that in some instances people refuse to nourish themselves, for example if they believe they are unjustly imprisoned, or as a consequence of religious belief, or for health reasons. Sen holds that only the capability theory of equality can distinguish between those who choose to fast, and those that starve as a result of poverty.[85] But, as G.A. Cohen has argued, the connection between the well-being conferred by food is only contingently connected to the freedom, or capability, to feed oneself. Very young children, the sick, and the elderly also require food (the resource) in order to achieve the valuable state of being well nourished (the functioning) with the effect that they experience happiness (the welfare). The fact that they are not in a position to self-nourish, or indeed refuse to nourish themselves, seems irrelevant from the point of view of equality.[86] Those who fast may have more options than those who starve, but this does not seem to be relevant to the question of which dimension of human well-being should be adopted as the currency of distribution.

The same holds for other subjects of justice, in particular members of future generations. Future persons do not possess the capability of determining, or controlling, the environment bequeathed to them by their predecessors. The extent to which they will be able to fulfil their wants is shaped by the activities of third parties in more or less the same way as the well-being of functionally incapacitated members of the present generation. But we still want to say that present policies on climate change will affect the well-being of our successors for better or worse even if they will not affect their freedom, or capability, to inherit a biosphere that provides access to clean air, water and so on (they have no such freedom: either it is bequeathed or not – we cannot choose whether we inherit an undamaged environment in the same way that we cannot choose to be born).

It seems that the Sen and Nussbaum have overplayed the active side of well-being (concerned with what people do and become) at the cost of the more receptive side of well-being (concerned with physical and mental states of a person). That is, they have focused on what we extract from resources in an active way, and neglected what we receive from resources more passively. This distinction is subtle, and often not so critical when the persons in question are fully competent, autonomous and contemporaneous. But it is important when the focus is widened to those whose well-being is largely determined by events beyond their control.

Moreover, and this is the key point, the general thrust of Sen's view does not require that we talk about human freedom or capabilities as being at the heart of our egalitarian thinking, only that there exists a currency of advantage that takes up the conceptual space between welfare and resources. Cohen has described this currency as *midfare* and his proposal is that egalitarians should seek to equalise *access to advantage*, where 'advantage' is interpreted as midfare, and 'access' is interpreted in a broader way than 'capability'.

According to midfare equality, people have access to the 'midfare' associated with good quality food and nutrition even if they are not actively exercising their capability to achieve the functioning of nutrition. Put simply, while Cohen agrees with opportunity welfarism that people are responsible for the consequences of their actions, but not for the opportunities they face, he proposes that egalitarians should adopt a broader, more heterogeneous, understanding of social and economic advantage. Crucially, the importance of people's substantive freedom to achieve valued functionings is downplayed. Cohen, then, is offering us a sort of hybrid theory incorporating both capabilities and welfare.

Recall that all welfarist views experience difficulties in the light of examples of undeserved handicap. You will recall that Tiny Tim was paralysed, though because of his sunny disposition he experiences more welfare than most others in society. Moreover, because of this disposition, Tim also possesses a 'life-plan tree' that is superior to others in the sense that the sum of all the expected levels of welfare of each of his possible life plans is greater than that of many of his contemporaries. We have seen that equality of opportunity for welfare will not only refuse to allocate Tim extra resources so that he can purchase a wheelchair, but will also require that some resources be taken from him. According to equal access to advantage, distributive equality at least recognises Tim's prima facie claim to receive the wheelchair, for midfare egalitarians seek to equalise a conception of advantage that recognises the importance of resources and functionings, as well as welfare.

So much for the superiority of midfare over welfare. Next, we return to the case of the arthritic person, Jade.[87] Recall that Jade, whose arms are otherwise healthy and in working order, suffers from a condition which causes her great pain whenever she moves her arms. This pain, however, can be prevented if she takes an expensive drug, and does not affect her ability to move her hands normally. Midfare egalitarianism seems well placed to explain why Jade deserves compensation. This is because, through no fault of her own, Jade experiences a midfare deficiency that is not reducible to her resources, welfare, or capability to function.

Midfare egalitarianism, like its rivals, can be usefully applied to issues of intergenerational and climate justice. Since the majority of adverse future impacts of climate change will be registered as impairments in the part of well-being singled out by all of the common approaches to the 'equality of what?' problem, there exists a great deal of convergence in this aspect of distributive justice. However, midfare egalitarianism, as a consequence of its heterogeneity, will identify certain changes in people's fortunes as a result of climate change that other theories cannot. Recall the case of the policymakers who adopted a programme of re-education in order to finesse the requirements of intergenerational equality of opportunity. On Cohen's view, their actions would violate the requirements of midfare equality. This is because the future persons it brings into existence will be disadvantaged, if not in terms of opportunities for *welfare*, then in terms of midfare components such as psychological and physical health, nutrition and education. They will experience their dignity and equal worth as being violated by the destructive behaviour of previous generations.

While there remains a great deal more work to be done to clarify the notion of midfare, justice as equal access to advantage seems to provide us with not merely a promising approach to the 'equality of what?' problem, but also to international and intergenerational justice. The approach is at least as useful in practical terms as welfarist currencies that are dogged by problems of inter-personal comparison arising from a focus on conscious states; superior to resourcist currencies that tend to overplay the importance of income and wealth in the well-being of an individual or community; and finesses problems of indexing and access that trouble capability egalitarianism. Finally, it is reconcilable with the thought that what constitutes valuable human function-ing is at least partly determined by normative-political factors that are only understandable though public discussion and debate.[88]

NOTES

1. Dworkin, 1981a, p. 185.
2. Sen, 1992, p. 12.
3. The spatial scope of justice is discussed by numerous authors, including O'Neill, 2000, pp. 186–202, and Caney, 2005, pp. 102–47. The temporal scope of justice is discussed by Heyd, 1992 and de Shalit, 1995. Larry Temkin provides an excellent summary of both issues in Temkin, 1995.
4. Dworkin, 1981b.
5. Layard, 2005.
6. Arneson, 1989.
7. Sen, 1985.
8. Cohen, 1989.
9. I do not rule out at this point, and think it likely, that there are other important dimensions of justice that should receive our attention. But my view at this point is that the scope, currency, and profile dimensions are the most important of these.
10. See Sidgwick, 1981, p. 381.
11. Bentham, 1962, Chapter 1; see also J.J.C. Smart's contribution to Smart and Williams, 1973.
12. Dworkin, 1981b.
13. Nussbaum, 1999.
14. See, for example, Banuri et al., 1996, pp. 85ff.
15. Nozick, 1974, pp. 153ff.
16. See Nozick, 1974, pp. 149–64.
17. These principles, and their application to the climate change debate, are usefully discussed in Singer, 2002, pp. 26ff, and Shue, 1999.
18. See United Nations, 1995, pp. 5–6.
19. See, for example, Singer, 2002, pp. 27–34.
20. Sen, 1982, p. 353.
21. Dworkin, 2000, p. 11.
22. Dworkin, 2000, p. 12.
23. Honderich, 1976, p. 4. In later work, Honderich endorsed a theory of giving priority to the worst off, rather than of equalising people's fortunes. See Honderich, 1989, p. 47.
24. Layard, 2005, pp. 111ff.

25. *Welfarism* is the view that 'welfare is the only value which an ethical theory need take seriously, ultimately and for its own sake' (Sumner, 1996, p. 3).
26. Dworkin, 1981a, pp. 191–2; 2000, p. 18.
27. Dworkin, 1981a, pp. 191–2.
28. See Ramsey, 1928, p. 543; and Arrow et al., 1996, pp. 136ff. See also Sidgwick, 1981, p. 381.
29. Peter Singer, 1972, pp. 231–2; see also Singer, 2002, pp. 150ff.
30. There are, of course, two key questions here: first, will such techniques be available to large enough numbers of people in the foreseeable future to render a generation tolerant to a range of climate change impacts; second, should such techniques be permitted in a liberal egalitarian society? Lee M. Silver, a renowned geneticist, has responded in the affirmative to both questions in Silver, 1999, pp. 266ff. Philip Kitcher defends a more sceptical approach in Kitcher, 2002.
31. See, for example, Fagan, 2004.
32. Dworkin, 1981a, p. 230; 2000, pp. 49ff.
33. See Dworkin, 1981a, pp. 229ff, and 2000, pp. 48ff. See also Rawls, 1993, pp. 185–6.
34. Note that the objection is not that *no* expensive tastes are worthy of compensation. Some people may develop such tastes through circumstances entirely beyond their control, in which case they may (according to welfarism or some other account) deserve compensation. The claim is rather that equality of welfare cannot explain why we should not compensate people, such as Louis, who cultivate expensive tastes quite deliberately. For two different explanations of why *some* expensive tastes are compensable, see Cohen, 1989, pp. 922ff and Dworkin, 2000, pp. 287ff.
35. See Dworkin, 1981a, pp. 241–2, and 2000, pp. 60ff; and Cohen, 1989, pp. 917ff.
36. Sen, 1999, p. 67.
37. The issue of adaptation as a problem for all welfarist views is taken up by Sen (*Development as Freedom*, 1999) who argues that 'the mental nature of pleasure or desire is just too malleable to be a firm guide to deprivation or disadvantage' (p. 63).
38. Cohen, 1989, p. 918.
39. Arneson, 1989, p. 86. It is worth noting that Arneson has, in more recent articles, repudiated equality of opportunity for welfare, preferring an account based on basic capability achievement in the context of a view that gives priority to the worst off. See, for example, Arneson, 2000b.
40. Arneson, 1989, p. 85.
41. Arneson, 1989, p. 86.
42. Perhaps, as Brian Barry suggests, our descendants will 'learn to find satisfaction in totally artificial landscapes, walking on the Astroturf amid the plastic trees while the electronic birds sing overhead' (Barry, 1999, p. 102).
43. Rawls, 1971, pp. 90–95; 1993, pp. 178ff; 307ff. Rawls further distinguishes between 'natural' and 'social' primary goods. The possession of natural primary goods (such as personality or physical health), for Rawls, is influenced, but not wholly determined, by the structure of society and its distributive scheme, whereas the possession of social primary goods (such as income) is wholly determined by this (1971, p. 62).
44. The list in the text is taken from Rawls, 1982, p. 162.
45. Rawls, 1971, p. 302.
46. Brian Barry, 1989b, p. 519. See also Page, 1983, p. 58. The view is developed, with few fundamental changes, in Barry, 1999. Barry leaves the notion of 'productive capacity' unspecified, but he means by this the opportunities that each generation enjoy as a result of the renewable and non-renewable resources at their disposal.
47. See, for example, World Commission on Environment and Development, 1987, p. 43.
48. See Arrow et al., 1996, pp. 140–41; and Brown Weiss, 1992.
49. Barry, 1999, p. 109.
50. Barry, 2005, pp. 266–8.
51. See example, Meyer, 2000.
52. Dworkin, 1981b, pp. 284ff; 2000, pp. 79ff.
53. Kymlicka, 1990a, pp. 78ff.

54. Dworkin, 2000, pp. 88–9.
55. Dworkin, 1981b, pp. 284ff; 2000, pp. 68ff.
56. Dworkin writes: 'Option luck is a matter of how deliberate and calculated gambles turn out – whether someone gains or loses through accepting an isolated risk he or she should have anticipated and might have declined. Brute luck is a matter of how risks fall out that are not in that sense deliberate gambles' (2000, p. 73).
57. Dworkin, 2000, pp. 73ff.
58. Dworkin, 2002, p. 108.
59. Dworkin, 2000, pp. 285–6.
60. See McMichael et al., 'Heat, cold and air pollution', in McMichael et al., 1996b, pp. 43ff.
61. A number of these are raised in a special edition of the Journal *Ethics* devoted to *Sovereign Virtue* (*Ethics* **113** (October 2002), pp. 1–105) and the companion volume edited by Justine Burley (Burley, 2004). See also Arneson, 2002, pp. 367–7.
62. Cohen, 1989, p. 918; 2004, pp. 9ff.
63. The British Pain Society has published a manual for sufferers and carers concerned about chronic pain: 'Understanding and managing pain' (London, British Pain Society, 2004), pp. 1–20. It is available online (http://www.britishpainsociety.org/pdf/info_patients.pdf).
64. See McMichael and Githeko, 2001, pp. 473–4.
65. Dworkin, 2000, p. 297. See also, 'Ronald Dworkin replies', in Burley, 2004, pp. 349–50.
66. See, for discussion, Cohen, 2004, 'Expensive taste rides again', pp. 9–10.
67. Sen, 1999, p. 75.
68. It is worth noting that some deny that Sen's view counts as a genuinely distinct conception of equality. Dworkin, for example, has claimed that the view will collapse into welfarism if it defines complex functions specifically enough to avoid them being representable in terms of the resource metric, or resourcism if these functions are conceived generally enough to escape being framed in terms of welfare (see Dworkin, 2000, pp. 299–303; and 2002, pp. 136–40).
69. Sen, 1984, p. 316.
70. Sen, 1984, pp. 307ff.
71. Sen, 1984, p. 29.
72. See Nussbaum, 2001.
73. Nussbaum, 1999, pp. 29–54; and 2000b.
74. Nussbaum, 1999, p. 46.
75. Nussbaum, 2000b, pp. 84ff
76. Nussbaum, 1999, pp. 41–2; 2000b, pp. 78–81.
77. See Arneson, 2000b, pp. 47ff.
78. McMichael et al., 'Climate, food production and nutrition', in McMichael et al., 1996b, pp. 107ff; IPCC, 2001b, 'Technical summary: impacts, adaptation and vulnerability', pp. 44ff; Gitay et al., 2001, pp. 270ff.
79. McMichael et al., 1996a, p. 577.
80. Gitay et al., 2001, p. 238.
81. Cohen, 1993.
82. Arneson, 1995, pp. 495–6ff; Cohen, 1993, pp. 26–7.
83. See, for example, Brighouse, 2004, pp. 73ff.
84. Cohen, 1993, pp. 26–7; Arneson, 1989, pp. 92ff.
85. Sen, 1999, p. 75; 2004, pp. 333–4; Nussbaum, 2000a, pp. 129–30.
86. Cohen, 1993, pp. 20–21.
87. Cohen, 1989, p. 918.
88. Sen explores the advantages of views that embrace transparency and public scrutiny of what makes up individual well-being in Sen, 2004, (pp. 333ff) and 1999, (pp. 76ff).

4. Climate change, future generations and the profile of justice

4.1 INTRODUCTION

In this chapter, we look at the profile of distributive justice. As we shall see, there is as much diversity within the debate as to how much people should receive under a just distribution as there is to what their shares should be calculated in terms of. In fact, apparently subtle differences in the justification of different theories of the profile of justice can motivate substantially different approaches to both intra- and intergenerational justice.

The simplest approach to the profile of egalitarian justice might be called intrinsic equality. While theories of intrinsic equality differ according to the view they take of the appropriate *currency* of advantage by which distributive outcomes should be evaluated, they share the view that the task of distributive justice is to secure equality of well-being across some given population even if this involves sacrificing other values, such as economic efficiency. As Temkin has put it, the essence of intrinsic equality is that 'it is bad for some to be worse off than others through no fault of their own'.[3] Intrinsic egalitarians hold that equality is intrinsically valuable in the sense that it does not derive its value from its relation to other values, so while departures from equality might be justified within a wider ethical context, they are always bad in one respect.[4]

It is worth contrasting intrinsic equality with other, apparently related, views. Utilitarians, for example, hold that acts and social policies should be evaluated only in terms of their consequences, and that these consequences ought to be maximal in the sense that they promote the maximum amount of welfare possible. Depending on the circumstances, the utilitarian may prefer an equal distribution of income and wealth because this coincides with the desire to maximise welfare. The reason for this is that the worse off people are the more welfare they tend to derive from the resources at their disposal.

Utilitarians support public policies that benefit poorer segments in the population until further redistribution would be counter-productive from the point of view of realising maximal utility. This point will always be reached before all unavoidable inequality is realised, however, since incentive effects that encourage the well off to work harder are a key ingredient in maximising utility.[5] Utilitarians, then, hold that we should help the worse off because it is generally easier to help them than others – one only has to give them a little for their welfare level to improve a lot. In this sense, they are 'accidental', rather than intrinsic, egalitarians.

Utilitarianism has been widely discredited in moral and political philosophy for a number of reasons, some of which have been discussed earlier in terms of the related theory of equality of welfare. However, there are other 'accidental' egalitarian theories that are much more persuasive. In this chapter, I analyse the strengths and weaknesses of competing theories of the profile of equality and justice, and go on to apply them to intergenerational and climate issues.

4.2   EQUALITY OR PRIORITY?

Proponents of strict equality typically appeal to the lack of life chances that the worst-off experience in order to gain intuitive support for their view. However, the strict egalitarian seeks to reduce inequality even if this does not also involve the worst off being benefited. This might seem difficult to accept. Surely, reducing inequality always means raising the prospects of the worst off? The problem is that, as an *intrinsically* comparative view, concerned with relative differences in life prospects, strict egalitarianism views a situation where there is less inequality but many people who are badly off, as preferable to one where there is great inequality but where the worst off are much better off.[6]

Consider the following example, which relies on us being able to make rough comparisons of well-being between persons, and which involves different possible distributions of well-being in a simplified world where no person is more deserving of their well-being level. Jim and Jane enjoy 99 and 100 units of well-being respectively. Their parents have just bought them both an ice-cream, but due to differences in their tastes and physiologies, the ice-creams bring about different changes in their respective well-being levels such that Jim would gain five units and Jane two units. If we give the children the ice-cream, then Jim will enjoy 104 and Jane 102 units of well-being. Both children will be better off in absolute terms, but the price of this is greater *inequality*. This example may seem superficial. But it reveals a structural distinction between two superficially similar views: giving priority to the worst off can mean more inequality whereas reducing inequality can mean withholding benefits to the worst off.

The distinction between the ideals of equality and priority is a subtle one, and easy to overlook. But it seems to have important implications for our theory of distribution beyond the simplified case of Jim and Jane. One writer who is sensitive to these implications is Derek Parfit. Parfit clarifies and taxonomises the debate between those who seek to equalise the fortunes of persons according to some metric and those who seek to give priority to the worst off. The remainder of this section examines some of Parfit's claims and relates them to issues of intergenerational distribution.

In 'Equality or priority?', Parfit suggests that theories of equality can be divided into two groups, that is, those that assume that inequality is always in itself bad (*telic egalitarians*) and those that assume that inequality is bad only if it has certain origins – for example, it having arisen from wrong-doing (*deontic egalitarians*).[7] There are a number of interesting differences between these two views. One is that they part company over the relation between the amount of inequality and the badness of the inequality of any given situation. Thus, the telic view assumes that the more inequality that exists the worse the outcome. The deontic view, though, cuts the link between the amount of inequality and the badness of the outcome; one can have more inequality, but this might not mean we have a worse outcome. It all depends on how this inequality came about. One might say, then, that deontic egalitarians are not much concerned with outcomes and their comparison at all. They are nevertheless intrinsic egalitarians since they ascribe equality intrinsic value, and not merely because it is instrumental to other goals.

There are, as it turns out, several ways in which we might attribute intrinsic value to equality. *Absolute egalitarianism*, is the idea that no gain in any other value can outweigh the smallest loss of equality. Other, less extreme, forms of egalitarianism are more flexible. These guide us to balance equality against other values in line with alternative views on the weight we should give to equality. *Strong egalitarianism*, for example, claims that only large gains in other values can override the disvalue of inequality. *Moderate egalitarianism* holds that there is only a weak presumption to bring about equal outcomes; that quite small gains in other values can override large inequalities. Finally, *weak egalitarianism* holds that the presence of inequality only provides an ethical reason to disfavour an outcome if all other factors are equal.[8]

Endorsing any variant of intrinsic egalitarianism has important consequences. Consider a version of what has become known as the *levelling down problem.* Here, half of some population are blind while the other half is sighted, and this is the only relevant difference between the two groups. Strict egalitarianism would view a move to an *entirely* blind world as a good, or *just*, outcome in at least one respect, namely, that inequality has been reduced (for the purposes of simplicity, in this chapter *goodness* and *justness* are used interchangeably). Such a conclusion, argues Parfit, demonstrates the implausibility of telic egalitarianism – for how can a lowering of the well-being of some, with no corresponding rise in the well-being of others, be a good thing?[9]

The levelling down problem suggests that we must either reject the view that it is good in one respect to bring some down to the level of others even if no one benefits, or reject the view that inequality is always to some extent bad. The problem seems to apply to all obvious formulations of the telic view, but is arguably avoided by the some obvious interpretations of the deontic view. This is because the deontic view is limited in scope in that it condemns outcomes only if they arise from actions that involve injustice or wrongdoing of some kind. The sighted in our divided world case might be viewed as entirely innocent of the misfortune of their blind compatriots, so the inequality between these groups may not be regrettable from the deontic egalitarian point of view. Nevertheless, in theory, the deontic view could also require that we level down for the sake of no one if the original disadvantage was unjustly produced and some course of action could remove this disadvantage.

The levelling down problem can be reformulated to cover dealings between different generations and nations. Suppose that, following the research of Lomborg and other climate sceptics, we believed that future generations would all be better off than the present generation despite the environmental and social problems they will inherit. According to the telic view, it would be better in one respect if the present generation destroy a certain amount of resources so that our descendants will not be any better off than us! According to the deontic view, this argument appears to fall away as it does not seem reasonable to argue that the intergenerational inequality brought about by the actions of earlier generations to save for the benefit of later generations has unjust origins.[10]

Because it rests on our intuitions about the relative badness of unequal and equal outcomes, and the examples discussed are rather abstract, it is not obvious how egalitarians should respond to the levelling down problem. Some, such as Larry Temkin, have argued that the problem is illusory. Temkin holds that the levelling down problem merely shows us a consequence of egalitarianism, not a reason to reject it. Given that we believe in a number of ideals, including but not merely equality, Temkin's thought is that it is perfectly reasonable to claim that levelled down outcomes are always desirable *in one respect* even if they are never desirable *all things considered*.[11] Nevertheless, it is a powerful result in normative ethics to force a proponent of a rival view into the stance Temkin takes – which might be called 'biting the bullet' – as it puts a great deal of pressure on the other elements of the theory they defend.

Temkin's defence of telic equality raises a number of interesting questions about both the nature of distributive justice, as well as the appropriate method-ology adopted to analyse it. To some, Temkin is merely attempting to defend the indefensible.[12] The problem is that there is no agreed methodological procedure that enables us to separate an 'absurd' position from a radical state-ment of a new ethical theory that has yet to develop strong intuitive backing. Since the new theory may cohere better with beliefs people later come to hold, or with advances in our understanding of human psychology and well-being, it is not obvious that we should reject it on the grounds that it does not fit well with our current intuitions.

I return to this issue later, but it is worth noting that a different response to save egalitarianism in the face of the levelling down problem is to appeal to some version of the deontic view. The problem with the deontic view, which really adds force to Parfit's critique of strict egalitarianism as a whole, is that it cannot explain what is wrong with inequalities between individuals or groups that do not reciprocate with one another. Suppose two populations A and B exist, but have little or no mutual dealings because they are based in countries that have never before interacted. It is possible for each to benefit or harm the other, but they have decided not to interact up to this point. One day a member of population A decides to visit population B out of curiosity, and finds to his horror that the people in country B are very badly off compared with those in country A, although well-being in both societies is evenly distributed. On the telic view, the inequality between A and B is regrettable – and all things being equal, should be removed as a matter of justice – even if it was not brought about by wrongdoing. It makes no differ-ence, for the telic egalitarian, that the unequal populations reside in different countries or that equality prevails in each country considered in isolation of the other. The deontic egalitarian, on the other hand, will regard such inequal-ities as trivial from the point of view of equality and justice for the inequal-ity does not arise from wrongdoing. Granted that the deontic egalitarian might recognise other non justice-based or equity-based reasons to remove the inequality between A and B, such as compassion or charity, is the deontic egalitarian's position plausible? Can the origins of a situation's inequality be so important from the perspective of just entitlements? In what follows, I concentrate on telic equality and leave further evaluation of deontic equality to a future occasion.

Parfit suggests that one way in which those who are broadly sympathetic to the aims of egalitarianism might attempt to avoid the levelling down and divided world problems is to embrace the ideal of *priority*. According to this view, the worse off people are the more it matters from the ethical point of view that they be benefited. Parfit calls this the *priority view,* and those holding it *prioritarians.*[13] Prioritarians reject the basis of both telic and deontic egalitarianism, namely, that it is bad that some people are worse off than others though no fault of their own. This is because they are unconcerned with the comparative properties of distributions of well-being as such. Instead, they think it bad that people are badly off regardless of the position of others, and the lower the level of a person's well-being the stronger our duty is to help them. On this view, Parfit writes:

> ... benefits to the worst off matter more, but that is only because these people are at a lower absolute level. It is irrelevant that these people are worse off than others. Benefits to them would matter just as much even if there were no others who were better off.[14]

For illustration, consider the following hypothetical example that rests on our imagining that choices between competing social policies alter the distribution of well-being in a hypothetical country X.[15] For simplicity, I assume that the policy choices discussed, although they may alter the amount and distribution of well-being, will not alter the total number of persons who exist. We are to suppose that two sets of mutually exclusive environmental programmes are possible such that immediately after implementation people would derive the following levels of well-being.

Distribution 1
(1) all at 50   (2) half at 40, half at 70   (3) half at 20, half at 80

Distribution 2
(1) half at 49, half at 46   (2) half at 60, half at 45   (3) all at 40

In the case of Distribution 1, the requirements of equality and priority are the same. Other things being equal, they guide us to choose outcome (1), either because all are equal with respect to well-being (the equality view); or that the worst off are better off under (1) than they are under (2) and (3) (the priority view). However, in the case of Distribution 2, the equality and priority views do not require the same distributive profile since equality recommends that we choose outcome (3), whereas the priority view recommends that we choose outcome (1). It appears, at least in theory, that there are cases in which theories of equality and priority conflict.[16]

Two lines of thought suggest that the distinction between equality and priority matters from the point of view of intergenerational and climate justice. First, equality and priority diverge in what they require of us in relation to our successors. Second, climate change poses different sorts of challenge to egalitarianism and prioritarianism when they are applied across time and space.

Regarding the first issue, suppose that the populations experiencing different levels of well-being each belonged to a different generation (one of the 21st century and one of the 22nd century) and the lives of none of the members of these populations overlap. Suppose next that the differential prospects of the populations in the Distribution 2 example arise as a consequence of the different environmental policy choices adopted by previous generations (the population halves representing the earlier and the later generation respectively). For simplicity, we might say that option (1) equates to a moderate conservation stance, (2) to no conservation at all, and (3) to a quite radical conservationist stance. A spatial version of the example might look like this:

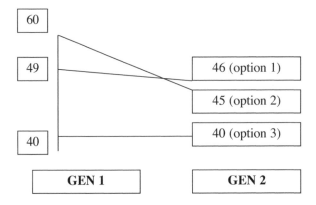

In this simple, two-generation model, intergenerational egalitarians would have at least some reason to prefer (3). That is, they would have an egalitarian objection to the other two divisions that does not arise with this distribution. Utilitarians, on the other hand, would favour (2). Finally, the outcome that would be best for the worst-off generation would seem to be (1). The picture would change, of course, as we include more generations in the analysis, but this example provides yet more support for the conclusion that it can matter that we are prioritarians, rather than egalitarians or utilitarians, from the intergenerational point of view.

Turning to the second issue, it seems that the research on climate change is highly relevant for any practical application of the priority view since climate impacts will undoubtedly influence the well-being of the worst-off members of future generations. As we have seen, it will impact upon the issue of which regions, and populations, of the world will be worst off in the future and to what extent. One example is the way in which global sea-level rises and climate induced reductions in food production and quality are expected to exacerbate inequalities between countries. It will also impact upon the issue of which generations taken as a whole will be worst off in the future and to what extent. Of great relevance, here, are the problems posed by climate induced air pollution and consequent cardiovascular disorders which are expected to plague developing and developed nations alike.

There is one problem with the claim that climate change will have effects that will engage prioritarians. This is that, barring what the IPCC calls catastrophic 'surprises', it is possible that climate change will not reduce the quality of life of future generations to that, or less than that, enjoyed by most members of prior generations. Sceptics such as Beckerman and Lomborg, for example, hold that even if no attempts are made to stabilise or reduce emissions of greenhouse gases in the near future, citizens of both developing and developed countries will be able to adapt relatively easily to rising sea levels and surface air temperatures because they will also inherit the resources to adapt to climate change. They think that it would be unfair to the worst-off members of the present generation to invest a great deal of energy and resources on the climate change problem which could otherwise be spent on alleviating present suffering.[17] As we have seen, however, the empirical evidence for this view is at best shaky. Much turns on the available evidence about long-term climate impacts, as well as the extent to which new technologies, such as underground carbon storage and clean energy sources, emerge to reduce the build-up of greenhouse gases in the atmosphere.

4.3   EQUALITY, PRIORITY, OR SUFFICIENCY?

In contrast to egalitarians and prioritarians, some philosophers, such as Harry Frankfurt, hold that social and economic benefits should be distributed in line with the ideal of *sufficiency*. The idea is that as many people as possible should have enough to pursue the aims and aspirations they affirm.[18] Attaining what we really care about, for Frankfurt, requires a certain level of well-being, but once this level is reached there is no further relationship between how well-off a person is, and whether they discover and fulfil what it is that they really care about. In this way, Frankfurt holds that above the level of sufficiency, it is not reasonable to seek more income and wealth even if this would mean that a person would increase their well-being. 'Having enough', however, is not the same as living a bearable life in the sense that one does not *regret* one's existence. Rather it involves a person leading a life that contains no substantial distress or dissatisfaction.

There are three main sufficiency-based objections to thinking in terms of equality or priority. First, that neither of these ideals has value independently of their contribution to the goal of bringing as many people as possible up to the point where they have enough. Second, that the concerns which lead many writers to endorse what they think are egalitarian positions are actually grounded, at a deeper level, in considerations of sufficiency.[19] Third, that these ideals are less easily operationalised or attained than the ideal of sufficiency.[20] After a brief review of the first objection, I turn to the intergenerational application of the sufficiency. Whereas the second objection is largely rhetorical and need not concern us here,[21] the third objection is more interesting, and I will return to it in later remarks on the fit between distributive theories and broader issues of fairness and practicability.

According to Frankfurt, the flaw in theories of distributive equality 'lies in supposing that it is morally important whether one person has less than another regardless of how much either of them has.'[22] What matters, Frankfurt argues, 'is not that everyone should have *the same* but that each should have *enough*. If everyone had enough it would be of no moral consequence whether some had more than others'.[23] This does not mean, however, that a concern to equalise people's holdings of resources, say, will always frustrate sufficiency. If this egalitarian concern has the result that more people are brought up to the point where they have enough, then the values of equality and sufficiency will converge. In this sense, an equal distribution may be a valuable means to the end of sufficiency.

Recall the case of *Distribution 1*. Here the outcomes were as follows:

---

(1) all at 50   (2) half at 40, half at 70   (3) half at 20, half at 80

Suppose that advances in the human and natural sciences furnished us with an answer to the question of what level of well-being constituted the level where a person has 'enough', and that this turned out to be 50 units. Then equality, priority, and sufficiency favour the same distribution: option (1). In such circumstances, Frankfurt observes, 'even if equality is not as such morally important, a commitment to an egalitarian social policy may be indispensable to promoting the enjoyment of significant goods besides equality or to avoiding their impairment'.[24] As in the case of priority and utility, then, the sufficiency view can provide a *non*-egalitarian reason to favour an equal distribution.

The differences between the three views only become manifest when we turn to the case of *Distribution 2*. Recall that the outcomes here were the following:

---

(1) half at 49, half at 46   (2) half at 60, half at 45   (3) all at 40

Suppose, again, that the sufficiency level for all was 50. Strict egalitarianism seems, other things being equal, appears to favour allocation (3) and the priority view would favour allocation (1), but the sufficiency view would favour allocation (2) since this would be the only allocation where *at least some people* had enough. For the sufficientarian, the distribution of benefits and burdens to achieve equality or priority in such cases is indefensible. It would be analogous to the tragedy involved in a famine situation of giving food to those who cannot possibly survive at the cost of those that *could* survive if they received extra rations. In this sense, the sufficiency theory is related to the medical concept of 'triage', according to which, when faced with more people requiring care than can be treated, medical resources should be rationed so that the most needy receive attention first. However, because the category of 'most needy' is defined in terms of the overarching aim that as many people as possible should survive a given emergency, triage protocols often lead to the very worst off being denied treatment in disaster situations in favour of those who can be helped to survive.

Frankfurt's view is that all distributive claims arise in some way from an analysis of where people stand relative to the threshold of sufficiency. Egalitarianism, by contrast, posits a relationship between the urgency of a person's claims and their *comparative* well-being without reference to the level at which they would have enough. Sufficientarianism, however, gives no special weight to the differences between people's level of well-being. Since bringing people to the sufficiency level exhausts our duties of distribution, Frankfurt thinks, egalitarianism urges us to recognise duties that do not exist. In linking ethical obligations and the idea of envy, egalitarianism contributes 'to the moral disorientation and shallowness of our time'.[25] In short, by encouraging the better off to pity the worse off, and the worse off to envy the better off, it encourages complacency and arrogance in some and a lack of self-esteem and respect in others.[26]

Although Frankfurt offers little concrete evidence for his social-psychological critique of egalitarianism, recent literature on trends in psychological health and well-being in industrialised societies does seem to support his suspicion of social comparisons and resource fetishism. Psychologists, such as Oliver James, increasingly link the preoccupation with comparative economic wealth and status with the rising incidence in mental illnesses (such as depression, anxiety, and panic disorder) observed in industrialised countries. The key to James's analysis is that a preoccupation with comparative wealth has encouraged people to compare continually their situation with the better off, rather than with those who are less fortunate. The result is a perpetual spiral of self-blame, depression and resentment termed 'relative deprivation' that reflects the belief of many that they are undervalued by others.[27] This increase in relative deprivation, it is argued, is exacerbated by a further phenomenon characteristic of modern societies called 'progressive deprivation'. This is where persons already suffering from relative deprivation succeed in raising their quality of life or standard of living only to become more miserable as a consequence of raising their expectations further.

Richard Layard, an economist, has assembled a wealth of data on inter-temperol comparisons of well-being, as defined as welfare, that support the central message of James's work. Layard found that levels of well-being, as measured by very large social surveys, had stayed constant, or in some cases declined, in many industrialised countries in the post-war era despite huge increases in total and per capita income and wealth.[28] Such findings raise what Layard calls the 'happiness paradox': 'when people become richer compared with other people, they become happier. But when whole societies have become richer, they have not become happier'.[29] Layard's explanation, which mirrors James's closely, is that the intrinsic connection between happiness and income exists only at relatively low levels of income and that other factors (notably upwards interpersonal comparisons of income and rising expecta-tions) adversely affect mental health in societies where income maximisation ('reoptimisation') is adopted as a key goal. He remarks that, 'the evidence shows that continuous reoptimisation is not the best route to happiness: you are more likely to be happy if you settle for what is "good enough" than if you feel you must always have the most'.[30]

Despite possessing distinguished origins in the work of Jean-Jacques Rousseau and William James, the literature on relative deprivation and the psychological impacts of income distribution is, in a number of respects, in its infancy. It is also, at best, indirectly linked to the 'profile of justice' debate as it concerns the empirical problem of explaining why the present inhabitants of industrial nations are no happier than many of their near ancestors despite enjoying both greater equality and greater absolute wealth rather than the *normative* question of what distributive entitlements these people have. In many respects, then, a range of positions on the one question could be compat-ible with a range of positions on the other.

Nevertheless, key aspects of this literature appear to give indirect support to the sufficiency view. This theory of distribution can accommodate quite nicely the thought that subjective well-being is unconnected to wealth above a certain point, as well as the thought that the individualism and consumerism characteristic of market economies is self-defeating from the point of view of raising societal well-being. Income and wealth, in particular, are unimportant for the sufficientarian above the point where a person has the wherewithal to lead a decent life, and the distribution of benefits is always subservient, on this theory, to the aim of enabling each person to pursue the life and values they care about. Finally, the sufficiency view echoes the relative deprivation litera-ture in regarding social comparisons as a key cause of human misery, even if it is not necessarily committed to the view that such comparisons are unavoid-able features of human nature.

Although the priority view is grounded in the badness of absolute (rather than relative) disadvantage, it also seems prone to the consequences of the spread of envy and pity mentioned above. This is because prioritarians hold that we should divert resources to the worst off group even if this will not lead to anyone leading a decent life that would not otherwise, or if this would mean sacrificing substantial benefits to persons who could be helped to lead a decent life if they happen to be slightly better off than others. The problem with prioritarianism is not that it separates people into distinct groups that are divided by their relative advantage (the 'have mores' and 'have lesses'), but rather that it separates people by their absolute advantage (the 'badly off' and 'the well off'). Such a division will encourage us to interfere constantly in people's lives in order to benefit the worst off. It is thereby inclined to produce the same sorts of envy and pity as egalitarianism, even if at a lower intensity.

Consider, next, the following example. A small developing country faces a choice of two climate adaptation policies. One involves investment to protect the agricultural sector from soil erosion and salt water intrusion, the other to protect the population from extreme heat events. The choice of policy is estimated to involve the population of 100 000 enjoying the following relative well-being levels after 10 years:

Table 4.1

	Before	**After**
Agriculture mitigation	Half at 10, half at 11	Half at 10, half at 25
Heat stress mitigation	Half at 10, half at 11	Half at 10.1, half at 11

It would seem that, if the policymakers in this country were consistent prioritarians, they would adopt the heat stress policy since this would benefit the worst off more. But this seems implausible. Assume, next, that the sufficiency level for all was 25. Prioritarians would still view the heat stress policy as involving the least injustice. Again, a prioritarian approach to this case now appears even more implausible. It seeks to give too much priority to the worst off; it would sacrifice the sufficiency of many thousands of people for the sake of 'trivial' benefits to those under the sufficiency level.

A third example that explains what sufficientarians believe is the following. Imagine that there are two groups, where one enjoys a considerably lower level of well-being than the other, where both groups enjoy a far better than sufficient life, and where the inequalities are undeserved. We can call these groups the *very happy* and the *extremely happy*. Egalitarians will claim that, if we could do something about it, the *very happy* group should be compensated for their relative well-being deficit. Why? Because this theory regards undeserved inequality as bad even if everyone is at least very happy; that is, it makes no ethical difference that the inequality is between groups, or persons, who are very well off. Even if they are pluralists, then, egalitarians will argue that the case for compensation in this case will *in one respect* be as strong as some other case for compensation grounded in some proportionate inequality between a moderately well-off and a very poor population. The sufficientarian, on the other hand, holds that the case to equalise in a world of very happy and extremely happy is not merely weak, but non-existent.

Next, consider the prioritarian approach to this case. Prioritarians regard the very happy in isolation of their relative happiness as they are only interested in absolute levels of well-being. Nonetheless, the very happy, as the worst off, deserve the attention of prioritarians even if they live so well they want for nothing. If we are able to help them become happier, that is, we ought to do so. But can this be right? Is there a duty to aid the worst off when they lead lives of a very high quality, and where they have more than enough to pursue the values they affirm?

We now have two objections to the priority view. First, the egalitarian's claim that prioritarianism is insensitive to the relative fates of people, however big the gap is between them. Second, the sufficientarian's claim that it makes no sense to claim that we have obligations to those who live well above the sufficiency level. One cannot, in good conscience, appeal to both of these objections at the same time, as the sufficiency and equality views are themselves incompatible, at least in their pure forms. What we can say is that the sufficiency view can explain how we can reject prioritarianism without embracing egalitarianism. This is because the case for compensating the very happy for their relative impoverishment falls away under sufficiency since this will not bring it about that anyone who did not have enough *before* will have enough *after* compensation is awarded.

4.4   SUFFICIENCY, FUTURE GENERATIONS AND CLIMATE CHANGE

We have seen that, at any point in time, the ideals of equality, priority and sufficiency may converge in the profile of benefits that they recommend. They will also converge in viewing as unjust human activities that predictably result in adverse climate impacts. However, over time, conflicts between these distributive theories will emerge since the composition of the worst off group, comparative fortunes, and people's positions relative to the sufficiency threshold are constantly changing.

As we saw in Chapter 2, two examples of climate impacts that look certain to influence the profile of well-being across time and space concern human health and food security.[31] All human beings require a certain level of health, as well as food security, in order to pursue whatever it is they really care about. It seems fair to say that there are limits to the level of general health and nutrition that is necessary for a person to have enough to pursue the life plan they endorse. However, to the extent that the actions of earlier generations damage the health of their successors with the result that the latter cannot pursue their life plans, then this would seem to violate the principle of sufficiency. Once again, we need not resort to the doomsday scenarios of rapid climactic change to claim that present environmental behaviour is putting at risk the entitlements of our successors.

The sufficiency view has attracted considerable support in environmental circles in the guise of the pre-eminent understanding of sustainable development as 'development that meets the needs of the present generation without compromising the ability of future generations to meet their own needs'.[32] Although this definition seems to have been deliberately left open to interpretation to be attractive to a wide range of ethical positions, the core idea is that each generation should refrain from activities that leave members of later generations without enough, but that this does not mean that a generation behaves unjustly if they make it difficult for their successors to enjoy exactly the same, or an improved, level of well-being unless this compromises the ability of their successors to lead decent lives. As such, the sufficiency version of sustainable development will result in a different set of requirements than alternatives based on priority or equality, such as that 'each generation is entitled to inherit a planet and cultural resource base *at least as good* as that of previous generations'[33] or that 'welfare per head of the population must never decline'.[34] Though the requirements of sufficiency may be stringent, requiring a generation to sacrifice a significant amount of well-being for the sake of its successors, they are in a deeper sense limited in a way that the requirements of rival theories are not. That is, the sufficientarian ceases to be concerned about the exact profile of benefits that pertains once everyone has enough.

As the duties of sufficiency are exhausted once all have reached the point where they have enough, the theory appears to avoid a classic objection to theories of broad egalitarianism that they demand too much both in terms of self-sacrifice as well as involve constant interference in people's lives to maintain a certain profile of benefits and burdens. In this sense, the ideal of sufficiency can be viewed as a potentially powerful mobilising force. It seems attractive, for example, on a wide range of ethical standpoints and ideologies, and not easily paced on the traditional left–right spectrum. This could be expected to make the theory easier to implement than its rivals since a larger range of groups in society may be more inclined to support it.[35] Moreover, a number of problems associated with equalising any preferred currency of advantage would be avoided, since achieving sufficiency for all will not require a precise distributive profile either within (or between) generations, only that all have enough.

Perhaps the central difficulty with the sufficiency theory is that the distributions it recommends are so sensitive to the initial profile of well-being in any given state of affairs. As applied to climate change, for example, a great deal depends on our view of the present, and likely future, condition of the natural environment, something that has both scientific and normative components. Whereas many are concerned that climate change will bring about a net worsening in the state of the natural environment and increase human morbidity and mortality, others argue that future generations will, despite climate change, enjoy a higher quality of life than that enjoyed at present as a result of economic development. The sufficiency view, as opposed to the equality and priority views, is very sensitive to our interpretation of how well off people are (and will be) relative to the sufficiency threshold and craves accurate information about well-being distribution as well as the nature of the threshold itself that is difficult to obtain.

Take the following three background scenarios where all persons currently lie below the point where they have enough. In a 'no scarcity' situation, we can help all above the threshold, although this would involve creating large inequalities. In a 'moderate scarcity' situation, we can help some, but not all, to reach the sufficiency threshold although, again, this would involve creating large inequalities and would not help the situation of the worst off. In a 'large scarcity' situation, we can improve the situation of many people, but not so many that any of these people will reach the sufficiency threshold.

The appeal of the sufficiency in 'no scarcity' and 'moderate scarcity' situations is fairly clear, if not uncontroversial. This is that its rivals seem to condemn interventions that result in all, or at least some, people leading a decent life for the sake of ethical goals that are unimportant in such circumstances, namely, the minimisation of inequality or the maximisation of the position of the worst off. The sufficiency view, however, cannot explain why we should intervene in order to improve human well-being in 'large scarcity' cases without the addition of further premises. This might seem counterintuitive.

The sufficientarian has at least two responses to this problem, one defensive and one offensive. Defensively, one could argue that it is too much to ask of one theory that it provide us with an intuitive approach to all possible scenarios. People's intuitions about what is right or wrong in particular cases, even when purged of obvious biases and prejudices, seem so diversely motivated that no theory of justice will cohere with all of them. Offensively, it could be claimed that sufficiency offers a genuinely distinctive approach to distributive justice in 'no scarcity' and 'moderate scarcity' situations, and 'large scarcity' situations are rare enough to be ignored. Evidence presented in previous chapters, for example, suggests that existing and future people can be helped greatly by mitigation and adaptation measures, and that climate change will reduce the numbers of people living above the threshold where they lead a decent life.

There are four further issues that need to be addressed before sufficiency can be declared the superior theory of distribution within, or between, generations. The most critical of these turn on the determination of the sufficiency threshold, as well as what should be done when either all, or none, have enough.

First, then, we must address the potential counter-intuitions with there being no further issues of justice, or injustice, when all have enough. The problem is obscured when the distributive context involves hundreds of millions of people in our own generation that live below the point where they have enough. But it is at least possible to imagine all having enough in the future, or at the very least that those not leading decent lives cannot trace their lack of sufficiency to human action. Can it be the case that, in such circumstances, there is no injustice that needs rectifying?

Consider the following example, where the sufficiency level has been set at 100:

---

(1) 99 per cent of persons at 100, 1 per cent of persons at 10 000

(2) 99 per cent of persons at 200, 1 per cent of persons at 1000

It seems that the sufficiency theory cannot distinguish between these scenarios, even though (2) would be preferable to (1) both in terms of equality and priority. That is, (2) would be much more equal and much better for the worst off.

One way of responding to this counter-intuition would be to embrace a pluralist distributive theory. Pluralism, in this context, means that we would appeal to different distributive principles, as well as different conceptions of advantage, in different contexts.[36] This could work in at least three ways. (i) the different principles could operate in different *domains*. For example, while we might appeal to the principle of giving priority to the worst off in contexts of distributions of resources within countries, we might appeal to the principle of giving as many people as possible enough resources to enable them to pursue their life plans in the context of distribution between countries. Or, we might apply equality principles within generations and sufficiency principles between generations.

(ii) different principles could apply in different distributive *circumstances*. For example, we might give absolute, or weighted, priority to a sufficiency principle when at least some can be brought up to the threshold, but apply equality, priority or utility principles when all are above the threshold.

(iii) we might subsume one principle under another while retaining the idea that the subsumed principle has some degree of intrinsic, and not merely instrumental, value. One way of doing this would be to argue that gross inequalities might be thought to undermine the possibility of achieving sufficiency because a person cannot possibly lead a decent life when many others have a much higher level of well-being, particularly if these persons are compatriots.[37] Against the undiluted sufficientarianism of Frankfurt, the idea is that the extent to which people can pursue that which they care about, and thereby lead a decent life, is determined partly by the way their lives compare to others. A measure of egalitarianism, here, far from being an irrelevant and potentially damaging pursuit, is 'an essential ingredient of the general concern with people's needs'.[38]

Such pluralist theories of distribution trade on the fact that the different ideals match our intuitions in different contexts, so any reflective equilibrium of principles, intuitions and background considerations will have to endorse principles that seem, on the surface, to be mutually exclusive. Constructing a defensible theory, however, requires much more than tinkering with different principles, and their weighting, in order to fit with our intuitions. It must also involve a careful consideration of the principles, and the connections between them, that is independent of intuitions about particular examples of their use. To miss this second step out would be to invite the criticism that the new theory is parochial in the sense that it 'merely systematises and renders coherent the particular beliefs of the cultural or ideological group among whose members the practitioner of the method happens to be.'[39] The problem is that it is not clear how any particular pluralist approach to the shape of justice could avoid this charge. The sufficiency theory, in particular, derives at least some of its plausibility from a radical critique of theories that urge re-distribution even above the point where all are content with their lives and would seem to be an uneasy partner in any pluralism. Egalitarian principles are singled out for particular criticism by sufficientarians because they encourage envy and pity.'[40]

Returning to the undiluted theory of sufficiency, the second problem to be overcome concerns the determination of the threshold where a person has enough and has no reason to seek more of what it is that makes life go well. Suppose we accepted that there was indeed a point that marks out the boundary between a life that has enough, and a life that does not have enough. As mentioned above, Frankfurt views 'having enough' as much more than having enough to make life bearable. The idea is that we give great marginal value to the gain in well-being that takes a person from just below to just above the point where they are content. But why should we weigh this positive change so heavily? Wouldn't the positive change to a person's well-being conferred by a life-saving operation that prolonged the life of a person who was under the threshold, but nevertheless glad to be alive, be a more appropriate focus for our distributive concerns?

Further difficulties arise in relation to the spatial and temporal definition of the sufficiency threshold. I have assumed up to now that the threshold must be to some extent determined independently of a person's view of how well their life is going. Theorists of need, however, have encountered great problems with establishing standards of need satisfaction that apply across countries and generations beyond some very basic needs, such as nutrition and personal health, and it seems that sufficiency theorists will encounter the same problems.[41] One problem is that the material and non-material conditions for a life of decent quality seem to vary greatly from region to region. How might we compare, for example, the need of people in developed countries to have mobile phones with the need of many in the developing world to feel the security of a culture that encourages social solidarity? Note that this is not merely a question of the availability and market penetration of goods, but that some goods make such an impression on the communities where they are introduced that they change the nature of what it means to function at a high level in that community.

Further problems with the specification of the threshold turn on the inherently social components of well-being which tend to be downplayed by the literature on the profile and currency of justice. The idea is that some well-being components, such as trust and solidarity, are neither easily quantified nor easily individuated. The idea is that a person's 'social capital' can be as important to their living a decent life as their possession of resources, basic capabilities or access to advantage.'[42] Until a reliable method of measuring people's possession of social capital or of controlling for the obvious differences in basic needs in different countries can be found, it is unclear how a theoretically sound, and practically useful, threshold could be established.

4.5 CHAPTER SUMMARY

It seems that we have reached something of an impasse. Proponents of each distributive theory continue to engage in argument and counter-argument in the hope of gaining a larger following, but there seems unlikely to be a breakthrough that will persuade large numbers of prioritarians, egalitarians or sufficientarians to break ranks.[43] Nevertheless, we can say a few things about the debate thus far. First, each of the distributive theories we have looked at can be reconciled with the very widely held conviction, as displayed in various opinion polls and social surveys, that activities predictably resulting in dangerous climate change are unjust, at least in part because they threaten the well-being of non-contemporaries as well as contemporaries. No broad egalitarian theory presented so far, however, can explain all of our distributive intuitions.

Second, each of the theories is vulnerable to objections from different directions. This is important to remember if we wish to avoid the simple, but widespread, error of defending one theory by criticising a second with counter-examples that favour a third, inconsistent with both!

Third, each of the views can be amended from their 'undiluted' forms in order to generate an increasing fit between distributive principles and considered convictions in the light of hypothetical examples. In fact, this is precisely the direction in which the discussion is heading.[44]

It is clear that much work still needs to be done to clarify and evaluate competing theories of the profile of justice if we are to establish the exact profile of benefits and burdens that we should aim for in our dealings with contemporaries and future generations. In advance of this, the main finding of the chapter is that there is a significant degree of convergence between the theories on the existence of stringent norms of intergenerational justice; and these norms of justice will be predictably violated by acts and policies that bring about the sorts of climate impacts outlined in Chapter 2.

NOTES

1. Maugham, 1971, Chapter 51.
2. http://www.quotationspage.com
3. Temkin, 2003b, p. 62.
4. A useful discussion of the theoretical assumptions and underpinnings of this view is provided in Temkin, 1993a, pp. 6–18.
5. See Mirrlees, 1980; Layard, 1980 and 2005, pp. 127ff.
6. A theory is 'intrinsically' comparative if it views the gap between how people fare according to some currency of advantage as important from the point of view of determining just entitlements. Strict egalitarians, for example, want to minimise the gap between the worse and better off. A theory is 'instrumentally' comparative if it uses information about how people fare relative to one another to determine just entitlements, but does not view the gap itself as relevant from the point of view of justice. Prioritarians, for example, might compare one person's situation with another in order to establish who, as the worst off, has the greatest claim to resources but they do not view the gap between the worse and better off as significant from the point of view of justice.
7. Parfit, 'Lindley literature: equality or priority?' 1995, pp. 1–43. Alternative versions of this paper are also published as 'Equality and priority' (Parift, 1998), pp. 1–20 and 'Equality or priority?' (Parfit, 2000). Note that, as Parfit describes them, both telic and deontic equality are *incomplete* theories of distribution in the sense that other values must be added in order for the complete range of possible distributive outcomes to be evaluated.
8. For a discussion of strong, weak and moderate egalitarianism, see Parfit, 1998, pp. 17ff.
9. Parfit, 1995, pp. 17ff; 1998, pp. 16–18. A version of the objection is also discussed in Raz, 1986, pp. 230–31, p. 235; and Nagel, 1979, pp. 106–122.

10. Actually, we have a slightly paradoxical situation here that may reveal a problem for the deontic view. The not yet born have no direct control over the behaviour of their predecessors, so they cannot be viewed as responsible for the positive or negative consequences of the social policies of earlier generations. On the other hand, it could be argued that policies that favour future generations unjustly bring about inequality to the disadvantage of present persons, particularly those living in developing countries. Such an argument has been defended by Beckerman, for example Beckerman, 1995, pp. 96ff.

11. See Temkin, 2003b, pp. 61–87 (especially p. 68); 2000 and 2003c.

12. See Crisp, 2003b, pp. 758ff.

13. Parfit, 1995, pp. 17ff; 1998, pp. 19ff.

14. Parfit, 1995, p. 23.

15. As explained in the last chapter, I favour the conception of well-being known as midfare (or achieved functionings) as the appropriate answer to the 'equality of what?' problem. Note, however, that the distinction between midfare, capabilities and resources is not critical in this context; all are essentially compatible with the following discussion. What is crucial to the discussion is the thought that rough interpersonal comparisons of well-being (however defined) are possible such that different policies can be associated with different sets of 'winners' and 'losers.' Note also that the numerical values used in the example have been pre-adjusted to cater for the diminishing marginal value of well-being. A gain of one unit to a person enjoying ten units of well-being is to be seen as an equal jump in life chances as that of a one unit gain to a person initially enjoying 100 units.

16. Some might claim that such exact measurements of well-being are impossible, or more strongly that it makes sense to use figures to express the fact that one person can be viewed as better off than another. This might seem an especially strong objection where 50 per cent of people are stipulated to enjoy 49, while the other 50 per cent enjoy 46, units of well-being. My response is that we do not normally object when someone observes in non-hypothetical conversation that one person can be higher in terms of what makes life go well than another when the differences between these persons are sufficiently great. If rough interpersonal comparisons of well-being are appropriate in such cases, why, we might ask, can they not be appropriate in more marginal cases? Since much of what I want to say concerns the hidden *theoretical* differences between different articulations of equality and the moral reasoning that lies behind them, however, I take the liberty of stretching the notion of well-being commensurability a little beyond that which is common in practice.

17. See Beckerman, 1999, pp. 85ff; Lomborg, 2001, pp. 305ff.

18. Frankfurt, 1987 and 1997. See also Rosenburg, 1995, and Arneson, 1995, pp. 496–500.

19. See Frankfurt, 1987, pp. 32–4.

20. See Rosenburg, 1995, pp. 66–70.

21. It is interesting, nevertheless, to point out a few passages where well known egalitarians reveal themselves as, at least in part, sufficientarians. Ronald Dworkin, in responding to the claim that resource egalitarianism will not compensate those who suffer nondisabling pain, argues that 'everyone would agree that a decent life, whatever its other features, is one that is free from serious and enduring physical or mental pain or discomfort, and having a physical or mental infirmity or condition that makes pain or depression or discomfort inescapable without expensive medicine or clothing is therefore an evident and straightforward handicap' (Dworkin, 2000, p. 297). John Rawls has also endorsed a sufficiency principle of distribution which takes precedence over other principles of justice when persons fall under the threshold where they are free and equal in the sense that they have 'to the essential minimum degree the moral powers necessary to engage in social cooperation and to take part in society as equal citizens' (Rawls, 2001, p. 20). Finally, Martha Nussbaum, in developing her capability approach, argues that all should enjoy a threshold level of each of the basic capabilities. She claims in *Women and Human Development* that: 'the notion of a threshold is more important in my account than the notion of capability equality ... my proposal is intended to be compatible with several different accounts of distribution above the threshold' (Nussbaum, 2000b, p. 12). While these passages do not prove Frankfurt's claim that egalitarian positions actually reflect, at a deeper level, a belief in sufficiency, it does suggest that its key proponents give weight to both values.

22. Frankfurt, 1987, p. 34.
23. Frankfurt, 1987, p. 21, original emphasis.
24. Frankfurt, 1987, p. 22.
25. Frankfurt, 1987, pp. 22–3, and 1997, pp. 3ff.
26. See Anderson, 1999; and Arneson, 2000a.
27. James, 1997, pp. 29ff.
28. Layard, 2005, pp. 29ff.
29. Layard, 2005, p. 31.
30. Layard, 2005, pp. 226–7.
31. For the human health impacts of climate change, see McMichael et al., 1996a, and McMichael and Githeko, 2001. For the food security impacts of climate change, see 'Fisheries' (pp. 511–38) and 'Agriculture in a changing climate: impacts and adaptations' (pp. 427–68) in McCarthy et al., 2001.
32. World Commission on Environment and Development, 1987, p. 43.
33. Arrow et al., 1996, p. 140.
34. Beckerman, 1999, p. 72.
35. See Rosenburg, 1995, pp. 66–8.
36. See, for example, Daniels, 1996, p. 208.
37. Marmor, 2003.
38. Marmor, 2003, p. 139.
39. Buchanan et al., 2002, p. 372.
40. Frankfurt, 1987, pp. 22–3, and 1997, pp. 3ff.
41. For an excellent critique of theories of need within the context of climate change, see Douglas et al., 1998.
42. Putnam, 1993, p. 113ff; see also Douglas et al., 1998, pp. 245ff;
43. Perhaps the best example of this 'deadlock' is the recent exchange of views of Roger Crisp and Larry Temkin. See Crisp, 2003b and 2003a; and Temkin, 2003a.
44. See Tungodden, 2003; Temkin, 2003b; and Brown, 2003.

5. The non-reciprocity problem

'We are always doing', says he, 'something for Posterity, but I would fain see Posterity doing something for us.'[1]

Joseph Addison

Action that has a meaning for the living has value only for the dead, completion only in the minds that inherit and question it.[2]

Hannah Arendt

5.1 INTRODUCTION

In previous chapters, we have assumed that distributive justice is inherently insensitive to considerations of space and time. Distributive entitlements, on this view, are determined independently of the issue of when or where their owners live. We have seen that, even if distributive theories are in this sense *universal* in scope, and *broadly egalitarian* in content, there exists significant disagreement as to what would be a just distribution of benefits and burdens.

In this and the next chapter, we investigate two arguments for thinking that the scope of our distributive obligations may be far narrower than is often supposed. The arguments that we will be looking at are located around two key concepts: *non-identity* and *reciprocity*. Non-identity refers to the fact that, on all respectable theories of what it is to be a person, each human being's personal identity is remarkably sensitive to events that pre-date their birth. We might say that each person would not in fact have come into existence if a woman had not conceived at the precise time that they did (if, that is, a particular sperm and egg had not been combined at that moment, either with or without medical intervention), and this was in turn affected by countless prior events, both large and small. The upshot of this empirical fact, as we shall see, is that the intergenerational application of a range of harm-based ethical theories is rendered questionable since even negligent actions and social policies will, thanks to non-identity, be responsible for creating the people that they are often held to harm. Non-identity is a problem for all of the theories we have looked at hitherto so long as they are formulated (a) to evaluate acts and policies by their effects on the well-being of particular people and (b) to apply to the further future.

Reciprocity, the notion that the presence of mutually beneficial interaction specifies in some way the duties we have to others, is another idea whose specification, as well as ethical significance, is central to how we deal with future generations. This is because the reciprocity that characterises dealings between generations is qualitatively different, and apparently much weaker, than that which holds between contemporaries. Reciprocity is, in addition, relevant to the question of how members of different countries belonging to the same generation should treat each other since compatriots tend to interact, and benefit from, each other to a greater degree than non-compatriots.

In what follows, an overview is provided of some influential 'reciprocity-based' theories of distribution and their application to the intergenerational context. I then go on to investigate some ways in which these theories might be modified so that they recognise the claims of those that cannot benefit others directly.

5.2   JUSTICE AS RECIPROCITY

The central premise of justice as reciprocity is that only individuals who contribute to the well-being of others are owed the full range of ethical duties. We might call this the *contribution requirement*. Here, the fact that a person is especially needy, or would benefit greatly from receiving certain benefits, does not mean that they are entitled to them. The contribution requirement can be used to specify both the scope and the profile of distributive justice. That is, it can be used to determine *who* has entitlements to social benefits as well as *what* these people are entitled in terms of shares of some currency of advantage.

Although there are countless ways in which a principle of reciprocity can be incorporated into a wider theory of justice, two main understandings of reciprocity have emerged in the literature that takes contributiveness as a foundational principle of justice. The first proposes that the requirements of justice are determined by considerations of *self-interest*; the second proposes that these requirements are determined by considerations of *fairness*.

5.2.1   Reciprocity as Self-Interest

According to this view, requirements of justice must be consistent with the pursuit of advantage of the individuals who are bound by them. The contributive model, here, is that entitlements to social benefits are distributed in strict proportion to people's contributions and/or their bargaining position relative to others (these two formulations can diverge, but I put this possibility aside). The resulting distribution of benefits may be egalitarian in profile. But, given the huge inequalities of power and productiveness amongst people, it is unlikely that self-interested reciprocity will coincide with any of the broad egalitarian theories discussed in Chapter 4.

According to David Gauthier's well-known derivation of self-interested reciprocity, norms of distributive justice are generated as 'a rational constraint from the non-moral premises of rational choice'.[3] Such norms are defensible only insofar as they can be shown to be *rational*, and they are rational only if they are conducive to the interests of rational individuals whose overriding goal is to pursue their own good. As 'constrained utility maximisers', persons will agree upon, and comply with, ethical requirements so long as (1) it is in their own interest to do so and (2) the selection of these requirements is the outcome of a rational bargaining situation which reflects relative bargaining powers. Where these two conditions are satisfied, norms of reciprocity will emerge to generate cooperation and ethical compliance amongst otherwise self-interested individuals.

Gauthier's account owes much to the writings of Thomas Hobbes. Hobbes famously grounded political obligation on the thought that individuals naturally seek their own advantage such that, in the absence of higher power to police disputes, there would result a war of 'every man against every man'.[4] Here we have the Hobbesian perspective of a state of nature where people's lives would be 'solitary, poore, nasty, brutish, and short'.[5] The solution, Hobbes argued, was that rational persons would agree to restrain their pursuit of self-interest and acquiesce to an absolute state authority and certain rules of social cooperation.[6]

Neither Hobbes nor Gauthier has a large following amongst the contemporary philosophical community, either in North America or Europe. Their writings, however, continue to attract a large critical literature, and have inspired libertarian political theorists such as Jan Narveson[7] as well as game theorists concerned with the question of how norms of justice emerge in populations of rational egoists.[8]

5.2.2 Reciprocity as Fairness

Suppose Fred promises Sid that he will give him a lift to the airport. Sid, in return, has promised that he will wash Fred's car when the latter returns from his trip. Some time later while Sid washes Fred's car as promised, the two friends discuss the connection between the notions of justice and reciprocity. Sid suggests that he is returning the favour so that both will continue to do each other favours in the future, and in so doing will better pursue their respective individual self-interests. But if one of them could somehow avoid doing the favour without being detected, or punished, by the other, then it would be both rational and ethical to do so. Fred suggests, however, that when he returns his favours he does this, not merely out of calculated self-interest, but out of a more intrinsic sense of fair play. Fred suggests further that he feels bound to keep the promises he makes even when this does not obviously maximise his self-interest. Finally, Fred claims that if Sid reneged on a duty of reciprocity in order to gain in terms of self-interest, he would let Sid know how disappointed he was even if it would risk their otherwise mutually beneficial relationship. It would be a matter of self-respect to respond!

Anyone sympathetic to Fred's view understands well the ethos of reciprocity-based theories that appeal to the notion of fairness in order to specify ethical requirements. Here, it is a particular notion of fair play, and not merely prudence, which lies at the heart of the justification of our obligations to others. Of course, acting fairly in such instances will often be prudential (there is evidence, for example, that people who are judged as reliable and honest by others tend to have higher status and higher incomes than others[9]). But 'functional' explanations of the value of fair play do not capture the key idea behind justice as fair reciprocity, namely, that behaving fairly is the right thing to do regardless of its consequences.

While, for the most part, we are concerned in this book with the status and application of alternative ethical concepts and theories abstracted from how far they are rooted in human and social psychology, it is worth noting that motivations of fair reciprocity are at least as widespread as those of self-interest. Recent psychological studies have shown, for example, that acting fairly stimulates the part of the brain that reflects positive affect.[10] Moreover, research by Herbert Gintis and others has suggested that human behaviour in general terms conforms to models of 'guarded cooperation' rather than 'unrestricted self-interest', even where these motivations conflict.[11]

Rawls captured the philosophical ethos of justice as fair reciprocity as the thought that 'we are not to gain from the co-operative labours of others without doing our fair share'.[12] There are, in fact, a number of ways in which we might develop this useful statement since the act of 'doing our fair share' is open to wide interpretation.[13] In the case of Fred and Sid, for example, the benefits to be exchanged are 'equivalent' in the sense that the duties concerned involve the creation of benefits of roughly equal magnitude. We might call this *benefit reciprocity*. This is an important category, but not exhaustive of what fair reciprocity has to offer. Some theorists have emphasised an understanding of reciprocity that involves equal sacrifices (or costs) in contrast to equal benefits as the key to fair reciprocity. The idea is that the costs of performing some reciprocal duties are much higher for some people than the cost of the action that gave rise to these duties, and it would not be fair to require equivalent exchanges in these circumstances. It would not be fair, for example, to expect Sid to wash Fred's car in return for a ride to the airport if, other things being equal, Sid has a physical disability that makes outdoor exercise very painful, whereas Fred very much enjoys driving. Rather, it would be appropriate only to require a contribution from Sid that reflects his individual abilities. We might call this *cost reciprocity*.[14]

Benefit and cost reciprocity are most usefully applied in the context of transactions between individuals that are both bilateral and uncoerced. However, they are much harder to apply to the relationship between individual and state, or between persons who lack contemporaneity. It seems difficult, for example, to compare the costs of citizenship with many of the benefits (such as national security or free speech) provided by the state; and even harder, as the quote from Addison suggests, to see how later generations can repay their dead ancestors for their sacrifices. A third version of fair reciprocity is more applicable to such cases because it assumes that reciprocal duties can be discharged both by providing benefits for those that have made sacrifices for us and, in addition, by providing benefits to others if the former is not possible. We might call this *indirect reciprocity*. In the example above, the idea would be that Sid could either discharge his duty to Fred by benefiting him directly (*direct reciprocity*), or by benefiting a 'substitute' (*indirect reciprocity*). Arneson usefully points out that indirect reciprocity is most powerful as an approach to distributive justice when it is proposed as the idea that each and every person cultivates a disposition to act in accordance with principles of fair play such that they benefit others continuously throughout their lives without stopping to count particular instances of benefit or cost (*generalised reciprocity*).[15] Public services, such as bloodbanks and organ donation schemes, are good examples of this sort of reciprocity since they are not premised on the idea that donors will necessarily benefit from the scheme directly.

5.3 CLIMATE CHANGE AND THE NON-RECIPROCITY PROBLEM

As we have seen, research conducted under the direction of the IPCC indicates that climate change will have grave consequences both for the integrity of the biosphere, and for the well-being of its future inhabitants. The IPCC's assessments have inspired international negotiations on adopting a coherent and binding regime of climate change mitigation and adaptation, the first output of which has been the Kyoto Protocol on Climate Change. The Protocol requires that the developed countries party to it reduce their greenhouse emissions by an average of 5.2 per cent from their 1990 levels by the end of 2012. The Protocol, which had at the time of writing been ratified by 141 countries, is viewed by many – though not all – as a useful and equitable step in the fight against climate change.[16] Enthusiasts emphasised that it will save significant numbers of existing and future persons from adverse environmental impacts while imposing only modest sacrifices on their predecessors. Moreover, its limitations, it is suggested, should be viewed within the context of it installing a 'prototype' climate regime that will be replaced at a later date by deeper cuts by a wider spectrum of parties.[17]

Critics, on the other hand, argue that the Protocol is flawed both in terms of its objectives and the mechanisms designed to meet them. It has been claimed, for example, that the Protocol will do little to prevent dangerous climate change[18] and that it will be very costly relative to the small beneficial effect it might have.[19] There are some grounds for this pessimism. A number of recent studies suggest that extending the Protocol beyond 2012 without strengthening, and widening, the Kyoto architecture would merely slow the rate of climate change. Wigley, for example, reports that global temperature would rise roughly 0.15°C less under an extended Kyoto scenario by 2100 relative to a business-as-usual scenario (that is if no international regime existed to combat climate change). Put differently, this would mean that the world would warm up by roughly 2.5°C by 2100, roughly 6 per cent less than could be expected by mid-range IPCC models.[20]

While the above doubts pertain to the efficacy of the Kyoto regime, there also arise more *intrinsically* ethical concerns about climate policy even if we supposed that Kyoto and its successors would protect future generations from dangerous climate change. Suppose, for example, that the Protocol is fully complied with. The vast majority of persons that will be the main beneficiaries of the modest greenhouse reductions involved will never be in a position to repay their predecessors for their compliance since these predecessors will be dead before the beneficial impacts of their restraint have materialised. On the other hand, justice as reciprocity assumes that requirements of distributive justice oblige us to act so as to provide benefits for others, including members of different nations or generations, only if these persons are in a position to reciprocate. But the only reciprocation that could be assumed on the part of future beneficiaries would seem to involve a potential improvement in the posthumous reputations of earlier generations, which would seem not to have any tangible effects on our present well-being. It would not seem just either on grounds of prudence or fairness, then, for earlier generations to sacrifice their well-being for the sake of later generations whom they will never meet and who cannot contribute to their lives. Let us call this the *non-reciprocity problem*.[21]

The non-reciprocity problem reflects the fact that dealings between persons whose lives at no stage overlap are characterised by a peculiarly intractable co-ordination problem. Here, reciprocal behaviour cannot apparently emerge in order to solve 'global commons' problems that turn on the equitable distribution of rights to, and usage of, global resources such as the atmosphere. Unlike members of different countries, for example, the parties cannot interact and cooperate for conceptual, rather than contingent, reasons; and, as a result, earlier generations have no reasons of fair play or prudence to save for their successors since their efforts cannot be returned by the beneficiaries.[22] Members of earlier generations seem, in this sense, to be in a similar situation to those living in an upstream community who have just realised that their industrial and agricultural sectors are polluting the environment of many distant communities living downstream without having to bear any costs themselves. The upshot of this line of thought is that, if reciprocity determines the scope of justice, as writers such as Rawls and Gauthier believe, there seems to be no room for future persons having claims to resources from their ancestors – they get what they inherit, and should count themselves lucky to get it!

5.3.1   Reciprocity as Self-Interest and the Non-Reciprocity Problem

Recall that Gauthier attempts to ground 'impartial constraints on the maximisation of individual utility by appealing to the benefits of co-operation'.[23] The problem for the intergenerational application of this view is clear: social cooperation requires the existence of mutual interaction, but mutual interaction only takes place between contemporaries, so a present individual, group or generation accepting a constraint on their respective self-interests in order to benefit future persons would amount to an unrequitable, and therefore irrational, transfer of benefit. Moreover, Gauthieran contractual parties must be aware of this, for Gauthier does not make use of a veil of ignorance device to shield the knowledge of his individual utility maximisers' invulnerability to future persons. For Gauthier, principles of distributive justice are to be selected from an initial situation characterised by fair bargaining between persons who have full knowledge of their situation. This is important because, according to Gauthier, theories of justice should explain why people will accept principles of justice in their actual lives assuming a prudential, rather than idealised, account of ethical motivation and compliance.[24]

It is perhaps surprising, then, that Gauthier attempts to defend a much more positive application of his theory to issues of intergenerational justice by arguing that 'each person interacts with others both older and younger than himself, and enters thereby into a continuous thread of interaction extending from the most remote human past to the farthest future of our kind' with the result that 'mutually beneficial co-operation directly involves persons of different but overlapping generations'.[25] The idea is that the potential benefits reaped by any generation refusing to abide by certain norms of conservation and investment will be outweighed by the gains of prolonging an agreement with overlapping successor generations. In this way, earlier generations, far from being in the situation of upstream polluters who cannot be punished for their behaviour, will be forced to bear the cost of their behaviour by members of later generations who also operate in the knowledge that they themselves will need to cooperate with their successors and so on. Intergenerational dealings, then, take on an *iterative* dimension according to this argument that a more static model of cooperation across time cannot explain. The result is that there are prudential reasons why 'the exhaustion of the world's resources does not present itself as an option'.[26] This has been called the *continuing contract argument*.[27]

The continuing contract argument is a member of a larger group of theories of intergenerational justice that generate obligations on the grounds that generations of humans do not simply come in and out of existence independently but rather overlap greatly with their precursors and successors. This overlap means that, far from being a merely altruistic activity, intergenerational cooperation can benefit existing persons as well as the not-yet-born. The continuing contract argument, however, is ultimately a flawed model of intergenerational justice, not because it fails to generate some reciprocity-based reasons for conserving resources, but that these reasons are rather weak. Crucially, they are too weak to outweigh the counterveiling benefits that any generation will enjoy by choosing to ignore them. There could never be any 'all things considered' prudential reason for a generation to establish and comply with a climate agreement for the sake of future generations, for example, since it would have already benefited (or not) by the previous generation's compliance (or non-compliance) and the sanctions that proximate future generations can bring to bear seem no match for the gains made by ignoring them.[28]

5.3.2 Reciprocity as Fairness and the Non-Reciprocity Problem

Given the above problems, self-interested reciprocity appears to be untenable as a constitutive, rather than sceptical, approach to intergenerational distributive justice. Can the same be said about fair reciprocity? If bonds of fairness are viewed as binding only those who cooperate directly, then the export of this approach to the intergenerational context appears equally limited. This is because the conditions for cooperation seem absent in dealings between generations that do not overlap. Rawls, for example, remarks that a situation of reciprocity exists only 'when there is an exchange of advantages and each party gives something as a fair return to the other'.[29] But, as he goes on to argue, over the course of history:

> no generation gives to the preceding generations, the benefits of whose saving it has received . . . each generation makes a contribution to later generations and receives from its predecessors. The first generation may benefit hardly at all, whereas the last generations, those living when no further saving is required, gain the most and give the least.[30]

In this passage, Rawls is emphasising the 'chronological unfairness' at the heart of intergenerational relations that involves earlier generations making endless sacrifices on behalf of successor generations. This unfairness, combined with an optimistic view of human progress and capital accumulation, led Rawls to abandon the application of principles of justice to the intergenerational context. To require earlier generations to sacrifice for the sake of their richer successors without possibility of requital would, he thought, have been a clear violation of the norm of fair reciprocity.

To the extent that members of remote generations cannot engage directly in the fair exchange of benefits, Rawls's theory seems an unlikely basis for stringent duties of intergenerational justice. Similar problems face those, such as Stuart White, who defend theories of justice focused on the fair exchange of costs, as well as benefits. According to White's theory of 'justice as fair reciprocity':

> where others bear some cost in order to contribute to a scheme of cooperation, then it is unfair for one to enjoy the intended benefits of their cooperative efforts (to a non trivial degree) unless one is willing to bear the cost of making a relevantly proportionate contribution to this scheme of cooperation in return.[31]

Suppose, for the sake of argument, that members of remote generations could affect each other's lives in some direct fashion. The problem is that no generation could establish whether a later generation intended to reciprocate an earlier sacrifice either through the production of an equivalent benefit, or through an effort matching their abilities. The fact that remote generations cannot interact in principle just underlines the weakness of all theories of justice as fair reciprocity in the light of the non-reciprocity problem.

5.3.3 Four Beliefs

The non-reciprocity problem arises when four beliefs are held at the same time.

1. Performing acts, or adopting social policies, that threaten the well-being of members of future generations violates certain requirements of justice.
2. The requirements of justice are owed only to those who can reciprocate with those who are bound by those requirements.
3. Reciprocity exists only between those persons who can interact with each other through some direct causal pathway.
4. Members of future generations cannot engage in activities that will have a direct, causal impact on members of the present generation.

It seems that proponents of justice as reciprocity have three options when faced with these incompatible beliefs. First, they could abandon the thought that justice can be extended in time beyond the nearest of generations (belief 1). Second, they could abandon their commitment to some aspect of justice as reciprocity (beliefs 2 and 3). Third, they could abandon the view that present persons are invulnerable to the actions of their distant successors (belief 4). The problem is that beliefs 2, 3 and 4 are hard to resist for theorists of reciprocity, and, as we saw in Chapter 1, belief (1) is very widely held. It seems that, if the notion of intergenerational justice is to be defended, the idea that justice is reciprocity-based must be dropped; or if justice as reciprocity is to be defended then the idea of strong norms of intergenerational justice must be dropped.

Can proponents of justice as reciprocity offer some response to the non-reciprocity problem? There are a number of possible responses, of which the most interesting turn on revising belief (3) in order to retain beliefs (1), (2), and (4).

The first response builds upon a version of indirect reciprocity, according to which a person, *A*, can engage in dealings of reciprocity with another person, *C*, even if there is no possibility of any bilateral interaction between *A* and *C*. The idea is that *A* engages in mutual interaction with a 'substitute', *B*, who in turn interacts with *C* according to *A*'s bidding or replaces *C* entirely as a beneficiary. Where *A* and *C* are members of different generations, the relation between them becomes one of *indirect intergenerational reciprocity*. The appeal to indirect reciprocity involves revising belief (3) so that it becomes:

3A.　Reciprocity exists only between those persons who can interact with each other through some *direct* or *indirect* causal pathway.

Two models of indirect reciprocity have been explored in the literature on intergenerational justice. The first assumes that a measure of reciprocity arises when existing persons provide benefits for the sake of members of future generations in return for the benefits inherited from past generations. I call this the *trusteeship model*. The second assumes that a measure of reciprocity arises from the fact that existing persons owe it to each other to provide various benefits for the sake of the well-being of their nearest descendants, which is treated as a collective good. I call this the *chain of concern model*.

According to the second response to the non-reciprocity problem, it is argued that agents can engage in dealings of direct reciprocity, even if they at no stage share contemporaneity. This is because *A* might be able to affect *C*'s well-being by bringing about changes in *C*'s 'relational' properties (these are changes that do not involve changes in a person's body or mind, such as their reputation or features of their relationship with other persons). We might refer to the distinctive category of reciprocity evident between *A* and *C* in such cases as *relational reciprocity*; and where *A* and *C* turn out to be members of different generations, the relation between them might be termed one of *posthumous intergenerational reciprocity*. In effect, the second approach recommends we revise belief (3) to claim that:

3B.   Reciprocity exists only between those persons who can interact with each other through some *relational* or *intrinsic* pathway.[32]

The most obvious way to make sense of the notion of posthumous inter-generational reciprocity is to suppose that members of later generations can harm (or benefit) their ancestors by thwarting (or furthering) the projects and goals of their ancestors, an idea that has a sounder basis in philosophical thought than one might suppose.

After some remarks about the limits of the non-reciprocity problem, it is argued that each of the above approaches offers some defence to non-reciprocity considerations, particularly when they are viewed in conjunction.

5.4   THE LIMITS OF THE NON-RECIPROCITY PROBLEM

5.4.1   Negative Versus Positive Duties

The first limitation of the non-reciprocity problem is that it only seems relevant to the scope of 'positive', rather than 'negative', duties of justice (to recap, negative duties prohibit the infliction of suffering, whereas positive duties require contributions to the well-being, of others) so it cannot be used as a complete objection to policies, or acts, that aim to protect future well-being. The lack of reciprocity between generations that the non-reciprocity problem trades on, then, need not worry those who hold that we have negative duties to our distant successors.

The inapplicability of reciprocity concerns to the specification of negative duties, such as the duty not to kill or harm others, is especially important in the context of climate change as a line of impact studies has emphasised the negative impacts on future individuals and groups, especially in coastal areas of the developing world, as well as impacts on the aggregate distribution of income and wealth.[33] So long as we think that reciprocity-based justice is consistent with there being *negative* duties to those that cannot harm or benefit us, it is consistent with the existence of stringent duties not to worsen the environment we bequeath to our successors even if the latter have no positive claims against us.

How important and far-reaching are negative duties? Is there no connection between reciprocity and the scope of negative duties? Although Gauthier takes the view that the non-contributive do not possess *any* claims against others,[34] other prominent reciprocity-theorists disagree. Jan Narveson, for example, in defending a hybrid of libertarianism and self-interested reciprocity, echoes the influential Nozickian view that *all* persons have some negative rights regardless of how contributive they are to others. He denies, however, that we are bound by any positive duties to aid others or to correct the background system of exchange that brings about inequality.[35]

The separation of certain norms of equality that are not reciprocity-based, and positive duties of distribution which are reciprocity-based, is also defended by White. White defends a hybridisation of fair reciprocity and broad egalitarianism that is informed by 'a picture of the good society as a community of mutual respect between individuals'.[36] Here, 'if one willingly enjoys the fruits of one's fellow citizens' labours, then, as a matter of justice, one ought to provide some appropriate good or service in return'.[37] However, White combines this principle of reciprocity with prior commitments to civil liberties, the dignity and self-respect of members of the community, and to the reversing of underserved economic disadvantages that arise from the workings of the market.[38] If White's version of justice as fair reciprocity is defensible, the non-reciprocity-problem is no serious threat to the application of reciprocity to intergenerational relations.

5.4.2 Non-Reciprocity-Based Theories of Distributive Justice

Most of the distributive theories proposed in recent years seem inconsistent with justice as reciprocity on more fundamental grounds than have been discussed so far. Such theories are not undermined by considerations of non-reciprocity as they deny that positive or negative duties are determined according to social contributiveness. An important set of 'non-reciprocity-based' theories are those that assume that 'basic rights to resources are grounded not in the individual's strategic capacities but rather in other features of the individual herself – her needs or nonstrategic capacity'.[39] These might be called *subject-centred* theories.

Since subject-centred justice severs the link between the scope of justice and contributiveness, intergenerational extensions of it are not obviously undermined by the non-reciprocity problem. This is because a person cannot be excluded from a scheme of justice, on this view, on the grounds of their economic or social *non*-contributiveness – a further argument must always be provided. This might be that, despite everyone enjoying equal opportunities in life, some persons are more successful than others and deserve the greater resource shares they acquire. In such circumstances, to borrow T.M. Scanlon's influential construction, no one could reasonably reject the resulting distributive profile.[40] But it is unlikely that a subject-centred theorist would accept an argument based on 'pure time preference' – the idea that future persons have no, or less weighty, entitlements because they have yet to come into existence.

It is important to note that the disposition to reciprocate might still be regarded as desirable, for subject-centred theorists, in a similar way as the disposition to be honest or trustworthy is desirable on most ethical views. The idea is that reciprocity serves as the 'social glue' that guarantees compliance with the principles of distributive justice. Nevertheless, on most interpretations of subject-centred justice, reciprocity is at most instrumentally valuable.

5.4.3 Counter-Intuitive Features of Reciprocity-Based Justice

Subject-centred theories are attractive because they explain why people who are prevented in some way from engaging in mutually beneficial interaction with others nonetheless have entitlements to social resources. The thought is that these people possess fundamental human interests, and deserve the same level of concern and respect as others. Reciprocity-based theories, as we have seen, struggle with this intuitively plausible thought. In particular, their approach to two key groups of non-contributors is suspect.

Consider, first, the position of the *naturally disempowered*. A number of clear candidates for ethical standing, such as those who are congenitally ill or members of distant future generations, are excluded from the domain of justice as reciprocity because they are unable to benefit others. On the other hand, most of us believe that withholding socially produced benefits (such as education or social housing) from these people would be impermissible. It would be drawing the bounds of justice too narrowly. The key point, here, is that the naturally disempowered are victims of brute *bad* luck and should not therefore be penalised. To recap, 'brute luck' can be defined as 'a matter of how risks fall out that are not in that sense deliberate gambles' and can be contrasted with 'option luck' which is when a person 'gains or loses through accepting an isolated risk he or she should have anticipated and might have declined'.[41] People who are handicapped from birth are victims of brute bad luck since they neither control nor deserve the disadvantages that they suffer as a result of their genetic inheritance. In the same way, no person can choose to come into existence in one generation or another or be held responsible for their life prospects as if they could. To downgrade the ethical status of future generations because of their temporally determined non-contributiveness, then, is equally as suspect as punishing the disabled on the grounds of their genetically determined non-contributiveness.

Consider next, *the able but unwanted*. Suppose a group of existing persons could be enslaved, and subsequently excluded from the terms of voluntary cooperation. These persons could benefit others if they had the opportunity, so their position is different from those (such as the not-yet-born) whose lack of contributiveness seems theoretical not practical. In such circumstances, the slave-owners would appear to owe no obligations of reciprocity to their slaves for justice as reciprocity will only generate entitlements for all if all are included in the relevant scheme of cooperation. This is not a far-fetched example. Such divisions occurred many times in many countries and in many historical periods. The point is that reciprocity-based theories are ill equipped to explain whether the ground-rules of a society's scheme of cooperation are themselves overly narrow, and therefore impermissible. Instead, they provide us with an account of why those who happen to be capable of fruitful cooperation, and who belong to an already existing framework, should recognise each other as having claims of justice. Evaluating whether a certain scheme of cooperation is actually *just* or not, however, is one of the central things we look for in a theory of distributive justice.[42]

5.4.4 Taking Reciprocity Seriously

We have seen that purely reciprocity-based theories are subject to serious problems; that there is an alternative sort of distributive theory which is neither subject to these flaws nor to the non-reciprocity problem; and that if we view reciprocity principles as only ranging over positive (as opposed to negative) duties, this type of theory is consistent with requirements of intergenerational justice. Although it might be questioned at this point whether further investigation into the implications of the non-reciprocity problem is merited, there are at least three considerations in favour of investigating these matters in more detail.

First, the concept of fair reciprocity is deeply rooted in the discussion of equity and climate change, particularly in the exchange between the group of countries led by the USA which is sceptical of the Kyoto Protocol and the group of industrialising countries led by India, China and Brazil that have become significant greenhouse emitters. As well as being highly critical of the Protocol for being a threat to the US economy, the US Administration's position has been that current climate regime is ethically flawed since it exempts the developing world from emissions targets, allowing developing countries to 'free-ride' on the emissions cuts required of the developed world. US involvement in any future climate regime, however, is linked to the 'meaningful participation' of developing countries despite their relative poverty.

This principle, along with several others that are at odds with the present Kyoto architecture, was outlined by George W. Bush at the EU summit in Gothenburg in June 2001 and plays a crucial part in the US Administration's alternative to Kyoto known officially as the Clearer Skies and Global Climate

Change initiative and unofficially as Kyoto Lite. In announcing the approach in 2002, for example, Bush called for action on the part of developing countries stating that 'it is irresponsible to absolve them from shouldering some of the shared obligations'.[43] For their part, administrations in the developing world, such as India, have accused the USA of reneging on its duty of fair play to contribute to the costs of, and solution to, climate change in the light of being a huge beneficiary of the practices that brought it about. They also emphasise the unfairness of setting countries reduction targets when their emissions amount only to a fraction of the developing world's in per capita terms, and when such reductions could not be afforded without great sacrifice.[44]

While there are good reasons for regarding the present US Administration's sceptical approach to Kyoto as motivated purely by national economic interests, there are elements of an ethical approach, appealing to fair reciprocity, in its stance. This is that the USA cannot be expected to make the sacrifices associated with Kyoto unless all other countries that emit significant amounts of greenhouse gases also do this. It is not necessary to take sides on this issue to realise that an equitable, and efficacious, successor to the current climate regime will not emerge until the issue of the distribution of the sacrifices for climate mitigation and adaptation is resolved and this must involve, at some level, norms of fair reciprocity that are acceptable to *all* parties.

Second, justice as reciprocity, in one form or other, remains a popular approach to justice within a generation as well as justice between generations. As Stuart White has observed, there is a 'strong contribution ethic' evident in the broad egalitarian tradition even if reciprocity is rarely adopted as a foundational principle when it comes to determining the scope of justice.[45] Moreover, it seems that at least some of the problems with non-contributors outlined earlier can be solved. It has been argued, for example, that justice as fair reciprocity could quite naturally be extended to recognise the neglected contributions of carers, volunteers and primary care-givers.[46] Moreover, an emphasis on 'cost reciprocity' could extend the realm of actual reciprocators so that disadvantaged persons would need only to match the advantaged in terms of effort, rather than net contribution.[47]

Perhaps the most intriguing recasting of the fair reciprocity theory in this direction is described by Steven Smith. Smith defends an imaginative broadening of how we view the exchange of benefits grounded in the idea of a 'fraternal commitment to others based on mutual recognition and respect'.[48] Crucially, he proposes that fair reciprocity generates both the obligation not to free-ride on the benefits produced by others, but also not to refuse, or neglect, the contributions that others are able to make when they are valuable to us.

Smith further develops the account by introducing a new category of reciprocity grounded not in the exchange of material benefits, but in the dynamics of human relationships themselves. The idea is that there is a sort of 'existential value' that advantaged members of society can derive from living in the same community as the disadvantaged which cannot be reduced to their use-value or the goods they produce. Although this might seem a mysterious use of the reciprocity principle, the central idea is both clear and plausible: that the social presence of those who experience impairment inspires personal and moral development on the part of their compatriots, such as a greater understanding and appreciation of ability, disability, identity and solidarity.[49]

Smith's account is not uncontroversial. He fails to address a number of questions that any fully developed reciprocity-based theory of justice cannot ignore. First, he does not explain fully the relationship between people's entitlements and the difference in the quality of benefits that people contribute to society. How might we balance, for example, the *quality* of reciprocity evident in our dealings between rough equals with the 'existential' reciprocity inherent in our dealings with radically disadvantaged? Let us assume, however, that his view is that any person capable of any type of reciprocity has some entitlements. Second, a full account is not offered of the link between the *quantity* of reciprocity a person is capable of and the share of resources that people are entitled to. Does any amount of contribution guarantee a person a full share of society's resources? Or is the size of a person's share determined in proportion to their contribution? Third, the relationship between fair reciprocity and non-reciprocity principles of justice, such as those that protect negative freedom and equality of opportunity, is not fully explained. How might we resolve clashes between reciprocity and these principles when they occur, for example? Such questions are troubling and need to be addressed. But the overall impact of Smith's account is that justice as reciprocity has more in its favour than is often assumed.

Third, as we shall see in the next chapter, there are serious problems associated with the claim that members of future generations can be *harmed* by actions or policies that predate their existence. As a result, the application of subject-centred justice to the intergenerational domain is more complicated than most assume since it is often presented as protecting the interests and rights of particular people.[50] Problems of non-identity do not obviously plague reciprocity-based theories since the latter utilise an understanding of persons as contributors and recipients, not of persons as unique holders of interests and desires. That is, these theories allocate benefits to people in line with their contribution and not because the withholding of them would be harmful. The upshot is that a more encompassing response to sceptics of intergenerational justice could be constructed if reciprocity-based norms of intergenerational justice were defensible.

5.5 THE CHAIN OF CONCERN MODEL

The chain of concern model of intergenerational reciprocity is grounded in the idea that human beings generally, if not universally, share a sentimental concern for the well-being of their nearest descendants. Since this concern, it is argued, is a central feature of personhood, its object can be treated as a public good, such as national defence or clear air; and, as with other public goods, a principle of general reciprocity requires every member of society to play their part in its upkeep. Here, present persons have duties 'with respect to' rather than 'to' their successors; or, to put it slightly differently, although the duties are grounded in a sentimental concern for future people, they are *owed* to contemporaries.

The chain of concern model generates duties beyond those that safeguard the well-being of proximate generations since it is assumed that one's children care for their children and so forth, extending the chain of concern into the indefinite future. The application of the model to environmental issues is clear. Present acts or policies that worsen the natural environment for many centuries to come, such as those associated with carbon usage, are unjust not merely because they threaten the well-being of our contemporaries, but also because they threaten the well-being of our offspring by compromising their ability to protect and further the well-being of their offspring and so on.

Although various formulations of the model have been defended in the literature[51] we concentrate here on the one advanced by John Rawls in *A Theory of Justice*.[52] The basic elements of Rawls's theory were outlined in an earlier chapter and need not be repeated. Moreover, it was shown above that, as a theory of justice as fair reciprocity, it is an unlikely source of intergenerational duties. This is because environmental conservation will tend to serve the interests of later generations who are (a) already destined to be privileged in terms of well-being relative to their predecessors, and (b) unable to reciprocate the negligence or beneficence of their predecessors. The adoption of conservationist principles would, then, be counter to the Rawlsian principle that primary goods should be distributed for the sake of the worst off, as well as the constraint that principles of justice only apply to those who can interact with each other fairly and cooperatively.[53]

Rawls's response to these difficulties was to make two adjustments to his theory of justice. The first adjustment re-conceptualises the contracting parties to become representatives or heads of 'family lines'.[54] I put this adjustment to one side.[55] The second adjustment changes the motivational base of the contracting parties such that they care deeply about the welfare of their immediate descendants (the 'motivational assumption').[56] Although there has been a great deal of discussion about the factual basis of the motivational assumption, it seems broadly compatible with the other elements of Rawls's theory of justice, such as the understanding of the contracting parties as mutually disinterested members of the same generation (the motivational assumption is a psychological generalisation and it holds between members of different generations not amongst the contracting parties themselves).

The crux of the adjusted theory is that, so long as all in the present generation cares for at least someone in the next, this will be generalised into a constantly regenerating chain of concern that binds members of all generations, and requires a certain amount of environmental, cultural, and economic preservation for the sake of future generations. Rawls writes that: 'Each generation must not only preserve the gains of culture and civilisation, and maintain intact those just institutions that have been established, but it must also put aside in each period of time a suitable amount of real capital accumulation.'[57] Put simply, then, Rawls chooses to represent virtually the interests of future generations in the 'original position'. People seeking agreement on the principles that will be applied to the basic structure, he thinks, will reject all principles that are biased in favour of earlier generations not because we imagine that principles are chosen by all persons at all times, but because the interests of all persons at all times will be considered via the contracting parties' sentimental concern for future family members.[58]

The Rawlsian view can be explained in terms of global climate change. Sustaining present levels of greenhouse emissions will result in a range of adverse effects on human well-being. Because the processes of climate change, such as global warming and sea-level rises, are already under way it is likely that some of the bad effects of climatic change will occur within the lifetime of the immediate descendants of existing persons. According to the chain of concern model, each existing person (who can be thought of as a 'head' of a family line) wishes to secure the conditions necessary for their children and grandchildren to lead flourishing lives – conditions that are vulnerable to adverse changes in the climate system. But in order to preserve these conditions, it is necessary that all members of the present generation (or at least the governments that represent them) agree to implement social policies that protect the climate system. Here the duties of intergenerational justice are in fact owed to other existing people: it would be unfair *to our contemporaries* to avoid contributing to collective efforts to secure a posterity free from the most adverse effects of climate change even if it is not unfair to our descendants.

In the above, Rawls has described a sophisticated implicit contract between proximate generations to safeguard the well-being of later generations. There are, however, two serious drawbacks. The first concerns the position of those who are not motivated to conserve resources for the sake of their immediate descendants. The second concerns the possibility that some human practices might damage the environment of the remote future with little impact on intervening generations.

5.5.1 People Who Are Not Motivated To Save For Their Descendants

The 'chain of concern' model assumes that if A cares for his offspring, B for his, C for his and so on, it will be not only mutually beneficial, but in addition a matter of fairness, for the A–Z population to save for the sake of the next generation. As such, the model assumes that every person is concerned sentimentally for at least one person in the next generation. The problem, though, is that this stipulation is certainly false for at least some people who lack children and have no sentimental attachment to children who are not their own. In such cases, the initial links in the chain break down leaving the model quite vulnerable. Moreover, it does not seem to be a defect of character or irrational to feel this way. Many people do not wish to have children for reasons that others seem unable to reasonably reject, such as an abhorrence of the effects of overpopulation, or a desire to concentrate on projects that clash with child-rearing responsibilities. Although many of these people might have strong sentimental concerns for people who are unrelated, it is clear that this is not always the case. The result is that it seems unfair to require such people to sacrifice their well-being in order to save for the benefit of the children of others in the same way as it seems unjustified to require a person to contribute to other cooperative activities that they derive no benefit from. A similar line of reasoning concerns those biological parents who do not have a strong attachment to their children. To grant uncaring parents and non-procreators an exemption from the duties of intergenerational justice, however, would weaken the robustness of the chain of concern model considerably.[59]

Once we realise that not all people share the sentimental concern proposed by Rawls, there are a number of responses that are available to mitigate the damage to the chain of concern model, although none of these is entirely satisfactory. Perhaps the strongest response is that, since even the childless and loveless derive *present* benefits from additional people in society, such as those related to extra contributions coming into the pension system, it could be argued that the former are also bound by a duty of fair play to treat the well-being of the next generation as a public good. The logic, here, is that all people need society and society needs children, so all people need children, however it is unclear if the obligations of fairness grounded in this logic save the chain of concern model from a severe weakening.[60]

5.5.2 Harming Remote Future Generations

The chain of concern model seems to explain part of the reason why we should preserve the environment for the sake of our descendants. In particular, it works well when the goods being preserved by an earlier generation, G_1, can only be transferred to a much more remote generation, G_n, if it is passed on to, and by, each and every intermediate generation starting with *B*. However, it seems rather more limited in its application for questions of distribution between generations whose members at no stage overlap. The problem is that certain acts or social policies might have adverse impacts on remote future generations without damaging the interests of intervening generations, and the wrong-doing associated with these acts and policies does not seem to be captured by the Rawlsian model. The model, in other words, seems inherently biased towards furthering the well-being of our nearest descendants since it assumes no direct sentimental or ethical connections between existing persons and their distant descendants.

Such a bias is not always problematic. If there is an environmental threat now, and its bad effects are likely to be either equally distributed across generations, or concentrated in the near future, it is a sound policy to frame our response only in terms of the well-being of near generations. After all, the existence of remote generations is, at a deeper level, predicated on the existence of prior generations and their procreative decisions. The problems of rainforest and stratospheric ozone preservation are, I think, good examples of the sort of threat where we cannot but help remote future generations by aiming to help present and near generations. Not all threats are like these, however. Some threats, such as global climate change, are much more complex and alternative policies to combat them will tend to favour either near or remote future generations.

Let me explain. Some of the bad effects of climate change will impact upon members of present persons and their immediate descendants. One example relates to the devastating impact that sea-level rises and extreme weather events will have on the inhabitants of low-lying or arid regions of developing countries.[61] However, it might take several centuries before other climatic changes have any significant negative effects on human populations. One example is the response of the ice caps, oceans and Gulf Stream to global warming. Most climatologists believe that it would take several hundreds of years of pronounced warming before the Greenland or Antarctic ice shelves were submerged. Yet, when they finally occur changes in these and other environmental variables can materialise quite quickly and with huge consequences for human, animal and plant life. Recent analyses of ice cores, for example, suggest that there was a warming of the Arctic of roughly 7°C in just 50 years at the end of the pronounced cold period approximately 11 700 years ago known as the *Younger Dryas*.[62] The chain of concern model cannot explain what would be wrong with human activities that increase the risk of potentially catastrophic climate events like this occurring in the remote future. Moreover, the problem of the remote future seems to undermine all derivations of the chain of concern model. Passmore, for example, who develops a non-contractarian version of the model, admits that the duties derived 'are to *immediate* posterity, we ought to try to improve the world so that we shall be able to hand it over to our immediate successors in a better condition, and that is all'.[63]

It is worth noting that, in *A Theory of Justice*, Rawls briefly sketched a wholly independent argument for intergenerational duties that stretch beyond proximate generations. The idea here is that existing persons have 'a natural duty to uphold and to further just institutions and for this the improvement of civilisation up to a certain level is required'.[64] Human activities that predictably result, at any point in the future, in these institutions being threatened, or in civilisation dropping below a certain threshold, would be unjust according to this supplementary argument because they violate our duty to maintain the 'circumstances of justice' across time. These are the conditions that must obtain for the notion of social justice to make sense, such as that people have sufficient wherewithal to lead 'decent' lives and to be able to form and pursue a 'conception of the good'. Rawls remarks, for example, that the two principles of justice outlined in *A Theory of Justice* 'may be preceded by a lexically prior principle requiring that basic needs be met, at least insofar as their being met is a necessary condition for citizens to understand and to be able fruitfully to exercise the basic rights and liberties'.[65] I would say that this argument, intriguing as it is, is best thought of in subject-centred terms and cannot be used to shore up fair reciprocity as an approach to intergenerational justice.

5.6 THE STEWARDSHIP MODEL

The idea behind the stewardship model of intergenerational reciprocity is that existing persons are duty-bound to protect environmental and human resources for the sake of their successors in return for the benefits inherited from their ancestors. Each generation does not have unlimited rights over the natural and human environment, but is free to make use of the world's resources so long as it does not degrade or destroy the inheritance of later generations. The essence of the view is captured by Edmund Burke, who argued that society is a:

> partnership not only between those who are living, but between those who are living, those who are dead, and those who are to be born. Each contract of each particular state is but a clause in the great primaeval contract of eternal society.[66]

This, of course, does not prevent a generation working to improve the quality of the resource base handed down to their successors by saving or through scientific and cultural achievement, or exempt those generations who have not received a fair inheritance from their predecessors from certain duties of conservation. The model is, in this sense, best seen as a part of a much wider theory of intergenerational justice that generates a duty to preserve environmental and human resources in the absence of reciprocity. Again, a remark from Burke is apposite:

> People will not look forward to posterity, who never look backward to their ancestors. Besides, the people of England well know, that the idea of inheritance furnishes a sure principle of conservation; without at all excluding a principle of improvement. It leaves acquisition free; but it secures what it acquires.[67]

The stewardship model can be usefully contrasted with what might be called the 'communitarian' defence of intergenerational duties. According to this view, community members have a range of duties to safeguard the values necessary for the survival and flourishing of their community.[68] These duties flow, at bottom, from the way in which human identity is bound up with community membership. Since most communities are trans-generational is the sense that they extend much further into the future (and the past) than the lives of their members, a range of duties arise to conserve resources that are necessary for the continued flourishing of the community.

Although communitarianism and stewardship have occasionally been combined in the literature, notably in the writings of Burke, these accounts are in many ways quite difficult to reconcile. One contrast is that communitarianism is usually presented in future-orientated terms in the sense that it recognises no obligation to reciprocate, or continue, the efforts of prior generations. Rather, as de Shalit has put it, 'our obligations to future generations derive from the sense of a community that stretches and extends over generations and into the future'.[69] Here, it is the survival of the community that matters, and this turns in most cases not on the preservation of values that past and present people shared but on what values present and future people could be imagined to share.

Another contrast relates to substantive differences in how the views approach environmental problems. Since the stewardship model specifies the bearers and holders of duties of justice in terms of the language of reciprocal benefit, rather than of communal *identity*, it is more inclusive (I can cooperate with people who are not members of my political community or nation). The result is that notions of stewardship seem better placed to address 'transboundary' problems, such as global climate change, which involve the ethical claims of non-compatriots. If anything, communitarianism implies a rather sceptical view of global climate justice as members of the key polluting states (such as the USA) do not belong to the same communities, or share the same values, as the vast majority of others who are vulnerable to changes in the atmospheric system.

5.6.1 Becker's Model of Intergenerational Stewardship

Elements of the intergenerational stewardship model have been defended by a number of distinguished political theorists and philosophers.[70] However, the most thorough integration of notions of stewardship and reciprocity was set out by Lawrence Becker.[71] Becker's argument runs as follows. A large proportion of the benefits that people receive in their lives is produced by persons with whom they have no face-to-face, or direct, exchanges. In such cases, the identities of the producers of these benefits might be known, yet it might be impossible for the recipients to return these benefits as (1) nothing can be produced which the original producers might value, or (2) nothing could be made which could subsequently be transferred to their possession. This does not mean, however, that there is no obligation to reciprocate for such benefits for an obligation of reciprocity may remain in place even in situations where a mutual exchange of benefits is impossible. To determine whether or not one has an obligation to reciprocate, one must ask whether one has been in receipt of a good 'for which some sort of fitting and proportional return is possible, and it is often perfectly fitting to make our returns to people other than those who have benefited us'.[72]

Becker goes on to argue that the duties of indirect reciprocity – such as those that bind us to help support blood banks – can be owed to persons who belonged to previous generations; and that a subset of such duties can be discharged by producing some benefit for the sake of members of future generations. In fact, there appear to be four steps in his defence of duties of intergenerational stewardship (note that, while Becker focuses on the duties we have to reciprocate for the benefits conferred by past institutions, I assume that his theory can be extended without great difficulty to cover the duties owed to past individuals from whom we have benefited).

1. Many of the assets that present generations benefit from in their lives were produced by past generations who intended them to be passed on to future generations.
2. Although the intended recipients of these benefits are not always specified, these benefits are nonetheless intended for someone.
3. The obligation to pass on these benefits to future persons is analogous to the obligation to reciprocate for benefits received from unknown contemporaries who also had indefinite intentions.
4. It is 'fitting and proportionate' that we pass on these benefits by producing goods for the future, and in this sense acting in this way will 'in principle satisfy the moral requirements of reciprocity'.[73]

So the 'fitting and proportionate return' in Becker's argument is owed to *past* persons, the obligation binds *present* persons, and the performance associated with this obligation is directed towards *future* persons.

The stewardship model, as presented by Becker, offers some important insights about relations between generations. Because it fuses elements of benefit, cost and indirect reciprocity, the model does not require later generations to pass on goods they have inherited if they could only satisfy their basic needs by consuming them. The cost of providing an equivalent benefit in such cases would be too high and would violate the ideal of 'balanced exchange' according to which equivalent exchange of benefits amongst reciprocators is desirable but must also be weighed against other considerations. Becker stops short of endorsing 'cost reciprocity', however, since the effort required to produce a given benefit is allotted no independent value of its own. The upshot is that the benefits to be secured for future generations are determined primarily by the actual bundle of goods inherited, rather than the capacity of each generation to preserve.

The main limitations of Becker's model are revealed by an analysis of steps (1) and (4) of the argument. Suppose we grant that certain duties can be discharged only if we perform actions that benefit someone other than the party who is owed these duties, and that these duties can, at least in principle, be owed to past persons and discharged by benefiting future persons. Step (1) is vulnerable since the vast majority of benefits passed down through the generations were not explicitly bequeathed on the understanding that they be preserved for the sake of remote future generations. Step (4), by contrast, assumes precisely that it is fitting and proportionate that such goods be saved rather than consumed by present persons and this might seem hard to believe when the persons concerned are impoverished members of developing countries. I discuss each of these problems below.

The claim that benefits arising as unintended side-effects of actions give rise to duties on the part of recipients to reciprocate for them is highly controversial. Suppose, for example, that a government adopts an initiative to reduce CO_2 emissions solely for the benefits this will have for the well-being of existing members of that society. A century later it is demonstrated that this prior initiative also led to a reduction, for reasons that are poorly understood, in the incidence of certain varieties of cancer. We would not usually suppose that those belonging to later generations owe any debt of gratitude to their predecessors for this unintentionally produced benefit. It just seems a matter of good fortune.

Becker, however, argues that the receipt of unintentionally produced goods gives rise to a range of duties of reciprocity on the part of those that receive them, in particular to sustain and preserve the institutions or practices which enabled their production. 'We owe to the future' he argues 'only as much as we were given, and we must make our "returns" in the very way we were benefited (e.g. intentionally or unintentionally), and to the very institutions that benefited us'.[74] But this seems to be as much a worrying, as it is a liberating, conclusion for defenders of intergenerational justice. For if we accepted that unintentionally produced benefits gave rise to the same duties as intentionally produced benefits we would be overloaded by duties of reciprocation. Are the present inhabitants of the UK indebted to the Romans, for example, for their unwitting contribution to the current road transport network? Aside from the difficult issue of which goods it is appropriate to pass on, there is the problem of how one makes a fitting and proportionate return for an indirectly produced good.

I say no more about the problem of unintentionally produced benefits because it seems clear that at least some of the benefits created for present persons were intentionally produced. Turning to the issue of *involuntary receipt*, the problems raised here seem less soluble. This is because most of the benefits which our predecessors have passed down to us were forced upon us in the sense that we could not have refused them; and there is a large literature which calls into question whether benefits that are not received voluntarily confer any obligations of reciprocity on their beneficiaries.

Consider, for example, the question of whether, as someone who is benefiting from a certain social practice, a person has a duty of fairness to pay his fair share of the costs of this practice. In *A Theory of Justice*, Rawls claims that there are two conditions on an affirmative answer. First, that the benefit providing institution is just and, second, that the benefits concerned are voluntarily accepted.[75] Let us put the first condition to one side on the grounds that it brings unnecessary complications into the discussion. If, as in Rawls's view, fairness is about making a fitting and proportionate contribution to benefits one receives from *voluntary* social cooperation, the fact that one did not willingly cooperate in the production or receipt of certain goods would mean (1) one has no duty to contribute to the production costs of such benefits, and (2) one has no right to such benefits in the first place.

A version of the 'voluntary acceptance' condition is also canvassed by Nozick. In *Anarchy, State, and Utopia*, Nozick argues that benefits that have not been voluntarily accepted generate no duties of distributive justice against the receiver to reciprocate for these benefits.[76] Nozick cites the case of the nuisance who hurls books onto the front porches of several homes, without prior solicitation, and later demands payment. He goes on to conclude that in both this case, and in any relevantly similar case of involuntarily received benefit, there are no grounds for thinking the decision *not* to reciprocate for such benefits is unjust: 'One cannot, whatever one's purposes just act so as to give people benefits and then demand (or seize) payment'.[77]

The Rawls–Nozick view, however, is not endorsed by all contributors to this debate. A number of writers, such as Richard Arneson, have argued that the voluntary acceptance condition should be relaxed in certain situations.[78] The idea is that there are cases in which involuntarily received benefits can give rise to obligations of fairness, but that these cases are limited to public goods which are non-excludable in the sense that they cannot be provided for some without being provided for others.

Unfortunately, I do not have the space to discuss this interesting argument except to say that it is a promising response to those who claim that duties of reciprocity only bind those who accept benefits voluntarily. In particular, note that the inherited benefits with which we are concerned are non-excludable goods, such as clean air and a hospitable climate system which cannot be enjoyed by some without being enjoyed by all, and which can be seen as necessary features of a life of acceptable quality.

5.7 POSTHUMOUS HARMS AND INTERGENERATIONAL JUSTICE

There is a further way in which reciprocity theorists might save their commitment to intergenerational justice. This is to claim that members of later generations can affect their ancestors for better or worse, even though they cannot do this by affecting the bodies or minds of their ancestors directly. This might seem very obscure indeed. Philosophers through the ages, however, have defended this very idea when they have argued for the idea of posthumous harm.[79] As we shall see, this idea is much less bizarre than it might seem at first glance, and, if defensible, has an obvious application to the notion of intergenerational reciprocity.[80]

First, we must deal with an obvious, but I believe mistaken objection. Many of those sceptical of the notion of posthumous harm have argued that it presupposes that events that occur at earlier moments in time can be caused by events (or actions) that take place (or are performed) at later moments in time. That is, they think that the notion of posthumous harm presupposes the presence of *backwards causation*. According to the most intuitive account of posthumous harm, however, the presence of backwards causation is unnecessary for posthumous harm to occur because it is unnecessary for an act or social policy to affect a person's well-being that this act or social policy bring about any change in this person's bodily or mental states. This is important for, as Aristotle observed, even God cannot change the past.[81]

Consider the case of Smith, who is ridiculed by his friends and acquaintances without knowing about it. According to most views of well-being, Smith is worse off than he would have been without this treachery. This is because they hold that people should want not only to experience things in life, but also that they experience the world as it is. And they want to avoid being slandered, or lied to, even if the offending behaviour does not bring about any noticeable unpleasantness, such as being humiliated in public, or being the victim of threats or abuse. How might we explain this? The most obvious answer is that a person's well-being can be affected by an action or event even if it does not alter any of their intrinsic properties (states of their mind and body). The act or event might, instead, bring about a change in a person's *relational* (or *extrinsic*) properties (those that concern their relations to other people and objects).

Consider, next, the case of Jones who is ridiculed by his friends and acquaintances after his death. The idea is that he is harmed by these 'non-experienced' posthumous events just as Smith was harmed by events while he was still alive despite the fact that the physical or mental properties of neither were altered. So just as we should not be misled into thinking that the harm in the first case required some sort of 'instantaneous causation at a distance', we should not be misled into thinking that the harming of Jones in the second case involved 'backwards causation'.[82]

The intergenerational reciprocity created by the notion of posthumous harms would not, of course, mirror in every respect the paradigmatic dealings of mutual benefit between members of the same generation. The existence of posthumous harm does not mean that members of remote generations, despite being non-contemporaries, can enter into face-to face dealings with each other. Nor can posthumous interventions change a whole range of well-being components tied to the state of intrinsic properties of the person (such as pain or pleasure) or the achievement of self-regarding ambitions (such as physical strength or self-improvement). Nevertheless, a certain sort of reciprocity would be generated which would appear to solve the non-reciprocity problem by permitting us to revise belief (3) to become:

3C. Reciprocity exists only between those persons who can interact with each other either through some direct or indirect causal pathway, or through some *relational* or *intrinsic* pathway.

The posthumous harms idea suggests that there is a certain amount of reciprocity between members of remote generations that provides earlier generations with both fairness and self-interested reasons to bequeath their successors a flourishing natural, cultural or socio-economic environment. If members of present generations act responsibly with regard to the preservation of the climate system, for example, our successors will be in a position to judge present persons favourably as far as their posthumous reputations are concerned, as well as being generally disposed to continue and fulfil our posthumously surviving projects and goals.

In order to evaluate this new and controversial conception of reciprocity, it is useful to find out whether posthumous harms can be accommodated into a cogent theory of human well-being. This will involve us revisiting some of the theories of what it is for a life to go well that were discussed in relation to the 'equality of what?' question in Chapter 3.

Conscious-state (or *mental-state*) theories, hold that well-being consists in the possession of certain states of the mind.[83] A useful example is *hedonism*, which holds that well-being consists in 'happiness' – the presence of pleasurable, and the absence of painful, mental-states.[84] For hedonists, as for other conscious-state theorists, an event cannot be bad for a person if it does not affect their conscious experience, so, on this view, there can be no unexperienced or posthumous harms.

Despite great progress in recent years in the measurement, and interpersonal comparison of, positive and negative affect[85] hedonism remains an implausible account of well-being. It cannot explain the widely held conviction that some events improve a person's well-being even if they are not experienced as enjoyable. Nor can it explain how there might be things in life that reduce a person's well-being even if they are experienced as enjoyable. So, whereas hedonism seems to capture something important about this debate – that a person whose life is lacking in enjoyment is unlikely to be leading a life high in well-being – it is clearly too simplistic.

Once mental-statism is abandoned, it becomes much less obvious why people cannot, at least in theory, be harmed after their death. According to the *desire theory*, a person's well-being consists in having their desires fulfilled. Perhaps the most compelling way to interpret desire theory is to claim that what is best for a person is that which would best fulfil those, and only those, desires which they have about their own lives. This has been called 'success theory'.[86] The main contrast between the success theory and mental-statism is that the former is consistent with the thought that certain things, such as slander and unpopularity, can affect a person's well-being without entering their conscious experience.

The success theory seems reconcilable with the existence of posthumous harms. Suppose Brown, who is totally dedicated to his family's success, dies before it becomes clear that his family, due to his incompetence as a parent, lead less successful lives than he had hoped for. According to many variants of success theory, Brown's life could be judged to have gone worse than if the family decline had not happened. This is because it regards some desires as being fulfilled by states of the world rather than by subjectively discernible states. Note that, in this case, Brown's desire is partly *vicarious*. That is, it picks out a desired state of the world that does not concern Brown's own life. Suppose that such desires are legitimately included in judgements of people's well-being while they are still alive. Is it critical that the fulfilment of these vicarious desires occurred before a person dies? It seems not. All that death seems to do is to ensure that people will never know or experience that their desires have been frustrated.

To sum up the discussion so far: mental-statism denies that posthumous events can benefit or harm a person, but is a flawed account of well-being, whereas plausible versions of the desire theory seem compatible with the idea. A third theory of well-being, *objectivism*, holds that a person's well-being consists in the possession of an assortment of objectively valuable goods (wisdom, knowledge, courage) while avoiding objective bads (being deceived, slandered or betrayed).[87]

The exact list of these objective goods is the subject of great dispute. When this list focuses on excellences of the human species, objectivism coincides with *perfectionism*. Perfectionism is a popular version of objectivism, and can be thought of as the doctrine 'that the good or intrinsically desirable human life is one that develops to the maximal possible extent the properties that constitute human nature'.[88] However, there are a number of additional possibilities. The unifying factor for all of these is that the 'well-being value' of goods is set independently of people desiring or finding pleasure in them, although this is not to say that coming to identify with these goods is not part of well-being.[89]

Objectivist theories appear to provide a more convincing approach than their subjectivist rivals in a number of problem cases. Consider Nagel's example of a person whose most intense desire is to pass his days attempting to communicate with asparagus plants.[90] This person possesses a desire that seems so bizarre that its fulfilment seems unrelated to their well-being. Suppose that this desire is nevertheless *informed* in the sense that it is held in the light of a full consideration of the alternatives and is central to its owner's life plans. Neither mental-statism nor success theory can easily avoid the thought that this person is high in well-being. According to the success theory, for example, they would be fulfilling their strongest, informed, and global desires. According to mental-statism, on the other hand, fulfilling their desires enables their owners to obtain great enjoyment. Can this be right? Can a person spending much of his time talking to asparagus plants make his life go well? Objectivist theories, because they can view the fulfilment of a preference or desire as being well-being enhancing, diminishing or neutral can explain what is going wrong in cases like this. This is that he is mistaken about the types of preference that are worth fulfilling.

Objectivism can also explain what is going on in cases where people, such as Smith, are victims of unexperienced harm. To be betrayed, on this view, is not bad for people because it is the source of some conscious pain as the mental-statist argues, nor that it frustrates his desires as proponents of success theory argues. Rather, it is bad for him because possessing a good reputation, if it is merited by his conduct, is one of the goods whose possession comprises human well-being. When we switch to the case of the dead, there is indeed a difference to be accounted for. The difference is that the dead person's intrinsic properties are logically immune from change, since they no longer exist whereas, before death, their intrinsic properties were only contingently immune from change. Does this make a difference? It seems not. There is no decisive reason for an objectivist to think that posthumous events cannot affect a person's well-being except that the idea seems implausible on commonsense grounds.

I have space here to mention just two considerations that suggest that the appeal to posthumous harms would only lead to a partial solution to the non-reciprocity problem. The first concerns the *quantity* of the reciprocity at issue. Not all people have deeply held desires that will be liable to fulfilment, or frustration, by states of the world subsequent to their death. So, even if the success theory can be defended, the number of people whose well-being will be vulnerable to posthumous harm may turn out to be far less than the number of future people whose well-being will be shaped by events which take place before they are born. On the other hand, even if the objectivist view can be defended, it will be the case that the status of many well-being enhancing goods cannot be altered posthumously because they are tied to changes in a person's mental and physical states. In each case, much of what determines a person's well-being seems immune to posthumous events.

Second, the *quality* of the reciprocity generated by the existence of posthumous harms is in doubt. Usually we think of reciprocity as arising from relations that involve fitting and proportional exchanges of goods. However, the goods being traded in the case of posthumous reciprocity appear qualitatively different. Perhaps they are even incommensurable too, for how can we compare the good of a posthumous reputation, or of having one's unfinished plans and projects continued posthumously, with the good of a habitable biosphere?

5.8   SUMMARY

In this chapter, I have dealt with some of problems with applying reciprocity-based theories of distributive justice to the intergenerational domain. I began by outlining what I called the non-reciprocity problem. I then explored three ways in which theories of justice as fair reciprocity might respond. As I explained, all three responses are subject to formidable objections, particularly if conceived as complete solutions to the problem of intergenerational distribution. But all seemed to generate at least some duties.

While the environmental duties that can be grounded in intergenerational reciprocity are limited, and in need of much further exploration, it is the view of the author that they provide a useful addition to the growing ethical consensus in favour of stringent policies to protect the atmospheric commons for the sake of future generations. Intergenerational and environmental justice sceptics typically hold that such policies should not be adopted because they obscure more pressing problems of intragenerational justice, such as global poverty, famine and overpopulation.[91] The normative idea behind this approach appears to be that future persons do not yet count from the point of view of justice in the strictest sense, an idea underpinned by an empirical premise that members of later generations are destined to be far richer than their predecessors because of inescapable features of economic development. Climate policy enthusiasts, on the other hand, such as the EU and many NGOs, have generally avoided the language of mutual benefit and reciprocity in their defence of the Kyoto Protocol and associated policy instruments. This is because other arguments, mostly concerned with the *harms* we inflict on our descendants through our negligent use of carbon resources, have seemed less equivocatory.[92]

The message of the above discussion, however, is that the approach of both sceptics and enthusiasts needs revising. A small, but significant, measure of intergenerational reciprocity is a direct challenge to sceptical views that downgrade the ethical status of future persons because they are viewed as being unable to reciprocate ongoing attempts to mitigate global climate change. But it also suggests that the current focus of enthusiasts on subject-centred principles of justice should be widened to make space for other, less fashionable, principles, such as those of fair reciprocity.

NOTES

1. Addison, 1714.
2. Arendt, 1961, p. 6.
3. Gauthier, 1986, p. 4. His theory of self-interested reciprocity is refined in Gauthier, 1990a, pp. 129–206.
4. Hobbes, 1968, p. 185.
5. Hobbes, 1968, p. 186.
6. See Kavka, 1986; and Gauthier, 1990b.
7. See, for example, Narveson, 1991.
8. See, for example, Binmore, 1998, pp. 78ff. See also the contributions to Morris and Epstein, 2001.
9. Layard, 2005, p. 102.
10. These findings are discussed in Layard, 2005, pp. 100ff.
11. Gintis, 2000; and Bowles et al., 2005.
12. Rawls, 1971, p. 112. Rawls's discussion of the duty of fair play draws upon an earlier treatment of this idea by H.L.A. Hart (Hart, 1955, pp. 185ff).
13. See Arneson, 1997, pp. 339ff; and Steven R. Smith, 2001, pp. 32ff.
14. See, for example, White, 2003b, pp. 66ff.

15. Arneson, 1997, p. 340.
16. Singer, 2002, pp. 22ff; Athanasiou and Baer, 2002, pp. 98ff.
17. See, for example, DeSombre, 2004.
18. See, for example, Gardiner, 2004a.
19. Lomborg, 2001, pp. 302ff.
20. Wigley, 1998. See also Wigley, 2005; and Reilly et al., 1999.
21. Versions of this problem have been discussed in Barry, 1989a, pp. 483ff; Barry, 1977, p. 270; Goodin, 1985, p. 177; Rawls,1971, pp. 291ff; de Shalit, 1995, pp. 17ff; and Kymlicka, 1990b, pp. 105ff.
22. Barry, 1989c, p. 189; see also Gardiner, 2004a, pp. 29ff.
23. Gauthier, 1986, p. 298.
24. See de Shalit, 1990, p. 229.
25. Gauthier, 1986, p. 299.
26. Gauthier, 1986, p. 299.
27. Sauvé, 1995, p. 166.
28. See de Shalit, 1990, pp. 227–8; and Gardiner, 2004a, pp. 31–3.
29. Rawls, 1971, p. 290.
30. Rawls, 1971, p. 290.
31. White, 1997, p. 318.
32. An intrinsic pathway is a means by which one agent might affect another agent's intrinsic properties, which are those that involve their body and/or mind.
33. McMichael and Githeko, 2001, pp. 451ff; Tol, 2002, pp. 47ff.
34. See Gauthier, 1986, pp. 283–7.
35. See Narveson, 2002.
36. White, 2003b, p. 67.
37. White, 2003b, p. 49.
38. White, 2003b, pp. 25ff.
39. See Buchanan, 1990, pp. 231ff.
40. The idea of 'reasonable rejection' as an approach to ethical motivation and justification was pioneered by Thomas Scanlon. See Scanlon, 1981, and 1999. See also Barry, 1995, pp. 10ff.
41. Dworkin, 1981b, p. 293.
42. See Buchanan, 1990, p. 236; and Barry, 1995, pp. 33ff.
43. Speech to the National Oceanic and Atmospheric Administration, Silver Spring, Maryland, 14 February 2002 (available at: http://www.whitehouse.gov/news/releases/2002/02/20020214-5.html).
44. The Indian Prime Minister Atal Behari Vajpayee, for example, has consistently argued this case. See BBC Online, 'India rejects climate change pressure', Wednesday 30 October 2002 (http://news.bbc.co.uk/1/hi/world/south_asia/2374551.stm).
45. White, 2003b, pp. 50ff.
46. Steven R. Smith, 2003, p. 245. Elements of Smith's account are also shared by Stuart White: see White, 2003a, and 2003b, pp. 49ff.
47. White, 2003b, pp. 66ff.
48. Steven R. Smith, 2003, p. 260.
49. Steven R. Smith, 2003, pp. 249–50.
50. Feinberg, 1988, pp. 25ff; Partridge, 1990, pp. 40ff; Heyd, 1992, pp. 80ff.
51. Versions of the model are defended in Passmore, 1974, pp. 90ff; Howarth, 1992, pp. 133–40; and Rawls, 1971, pp. 284–98.
52. The Rawlsian chain of concern model has generated a considerable secondary literature. See, for example, English, 1977; Hubin, 1976; and Paden, 1996.
53. Rawls, 1971, p. 292.
54. Rawls, 1971, p. 292.
55. See English, 1977, pp. 91–6; and Okin, 1989, pp. 235ff.
56. Rawls, 1971, p. 292.
57. Rawls, 1971, p. 285.
58. Although Rawls at no stage repudiates the account discussed in the text, in later work he argued that principles of conservation will be agreed to by the contracting parties on the

assumption that all previous generations have also conserved an appropriate amount. Given an 'ideal theoretic' approach that assumes full compliance with principles of justice, and given the veil of ignorance prevents the parties from knowing which generation they belong to, the problem of a generation free-riding seems to be removed. See Rawls, 1993, p. 274; and Paden, 1996, pp. 251ff.

59. See Partridge, 2001, pp. 383–4.
60. This argument is discussed in Casal and Williams, 2004, pp. 156–60; and Casal, 1999.
61. See 'Coastal zones and marine ecosystems' (pp. 343–80), 'Africa', (pp. 487–532) and 'Small island states' (pp. 843–76) in McCarthay et al., 2001.
62. See John Houghton, 2004, pp. 73–5.
63. Passmore, 1974, p. 91; de Shalit, 1995, pp. 32–3.
64. Rawls, 1971, p. 293.
65. Rawls, 2001, p. 44n. See Bell, 2002, pp. 707ff; and Preston, 2004.
66. Burke, 1968, pp. 194–5.
67. Burke, 1968, pp. 120–21.
68. See, for example, de Shalit, 1992; and 1995, pp. 13–65; and Marshall, 1993.
69. de Shalit, 1995, p. 14.
70. Burke, 1968, pp. 120ff; Baier, 1981, pp. 171ff; Laslett, 1992, pp. 24ff.
71. Becker, 1986, pp. 229–51.
72. Becker, 1986, pp. 230–31.
73. Becker, 1986, p. 231.
74. Becker, 1986, pp. 238–9.
75. Rawls, 1971, pp. 111–12. See also Cullity, 1995, pp. 9ff.
76. Nozick, 1974, pp. 95ff.
77. Nozick, 1974, p. 95.
78. Arneson, 1982, pp. 623ff.
79. See, for example, Aristotle, 1953 translation, Book I, Chapter X, 1101a–b; Partridge, 1981; Feinberg, 1988, pp. 79–93; Pitcher, 1984; Grover, 1987, pp. 350ff; Callahan, 1987; Levenbrook, 1984.
80. The link between posthumous harm and intergenerational justice is explored by John O'Neill, 1995a, pp. 35ff; and 1995b; and Page, 2000.
81. See Aristotle, (1953 translation), 1139b, 6–10.
82. Pitcher, 1984, p. 186; Grover, 1987, pp. 335ff.
83. See Parfit, 1984, pp. 493–502; and Griffin, 1986, pp. 13ff.
84. A useful discussion of hedonism is provided by Sumner, 1996, pp. 81ff.
85. This research is reported by Layard, 2005, pp. 17ff.
86. Parfit, 1984, pp. 494ff; Griffin, 1986, p. 21.
87. Parfit, 1984, pp. 493–502; Griffin, 1986, pp. 40ff.
88. Arneson, 1999, pp. 119–20; and Hurka, 1993, pp. 17ff.
89. See Kraut, 1979; Parfit, 1984, pp. 501–2; and Raz, 1986, pp. 288ff.
90. Nagel, 1979, p. 5.
91. Lomborg, 2001, pp. 258ff.
92. Jamieson, 2003, pp. 290ff; Shue, 2001, pp. 449ff.

6. The non-identity problem

By burning fossil fuels prodigally we accelerate the green-house effect and may dramatically harm successors, who can do nothing to us.[1]
Onora O'Neill

It may help to think about this question: how many of us could truly claim, 'Even if railways and motor cars had never been invented, I would still have been born?'[2]
Derek Parfit

6.1 INTRODUCTION

In the previous chapter, it was argued that theories of justice as reciprocity are compatible with at least some norms of intergenerational justice. In this chapter, a second argument is explored that calls into question the widely held view, expressed by O'Neill above, that imprudent environmental policies are unjust because they *harm* members of future generations. The argument flows from an analysis of a unique philosophical puzzle confronting those who wish to explain our duties to future generations in terms of the language of harms. Put simply, the puzzle is that actions or social policies that will lower future quality of life will harm few, if any, members of future generations because they are also necessary conditions of these people coming into existence. This has been called the *non-identity (or contingency) problem*.[3] The problem, as we shall see, presents a serious challenge for any theory of intergenerational justice that assumes that actions or policies can be wrong only if they harm particular humans or non-human animals (these can be called *identity-dependent* accounts).

In what follows, I first provide a critical discussion of the non-identity problem and explain its relevance for ethical evaluations of climate policies. I then go on to consider the way in which theories of individual and group rights might be adapted to respond to the problem.

6.2 THE NON-IDENTITY PROBLEM

Decisions concerning alternative environmental, and other, policies will influence not just the quality of life of future generations, but also their size and composition. As a result, they are not easily evaluated in terms of ethical concepts, such as harm and benefit, which assume that the same people will live, and be harmed or benefited, however we act. Consider the following.

The Battle for Kyoto II

An intergovernmental conference is organised to discuss what should follow the Kyoto Protocol when it expires in 2012. The large range of options is cut down to two, both of which possess a wide following.[4] The first option, *Kyoto Lite*, would set targets based on the ratio of national carbon emissions to economic output. The idea is that countries would reduce the 'carbon intensity' of their economies helped by incentives for moving to cleaner technologies. Because there would be no direct emissions targets, however, it is predicted that a future climate regime based on this option will fail to prevent total carbon emissions from growing. The result would be disastrous for future generations of all countries, but rather beneficial outcomes, on balance, for existing and proximate generations in developed countries who will gain from modest reductions in climate risks and relatively uncompromised economic growth.

The second option, *Contraction and Convergence*, is driven by three ideas. First, each person on the planet is granted an equal right to emit carbon. Second, a 'global ceiling' for greenhouse emissions is calculated based on the amount the global environment can withstand without dangerous impacts. Third, each country is allocated a yearly 'carbon emissions budget' consistent with the global ceiling not being exceeded, and calculated according to their population size relative to the base year of 2005.[5] If a country wishes to emit more than its fair share in a certain year they must buy emissions 'credits' from a country that intends to emit less. The suggested figure of roughly one tonne of carbon per person per year would mean that many developing countries (such as China and India) could raise their per capita emissions a little whereas all developed countries would have to reduce their per capita emission substantially.

Because the contraction and convergence option will be associated with much greater use of renewable energy sources, as well as tight restrictions on greenhouse emissions, it is predicted that it will reduce the extent of climate change substantially. In fact, it is predicted that, after one or two centuries, many more of the people who would later live if Kyoto Lite is chosen will enjoy a much lower quality of life than those who would live if Contraction and Convergence is chosen.

Consider the following line of argument, which undermines the reasoning behind many people's intuition that Contraction and Convergence would be the most just, if not the most realistic, option. As a consequence of the profound impact it will have on even the smallest details of all people's lives, whatever decision is made in regard to the two options will predictably, if indirectly, affect who mates with whom and when, and thus which individuals will be born in the future. This is because all persons owe their existence to the coming together of a particular egg and a particular sperm – and this 'coming together' is highly sensitive to antecedent events. In fact, after a few generations, and depending on which option we choose, completely different sets of people will come into existence and these sets of people will in a sense owe their existence to this prior choice of option (they would not have been born if that particular option had not been chosen).

If it is assumed that the adoption of neither regime will result in any of our distant successors leading lives that are not worth living, it appears that choosing Kyoto Lite over Contraction and Convergence will not result in any particular future person being harmed so long as we hold that being harmed means being made worse off than one would have been had the harming action(s) not been performed. On the other hand, choosing Kyoto Lite would predictably benefit more members of present and proximate future generations since even the extensive sacrifices that Contraction and Convergence will require of developed countries will reduce the well-being of many persons in these countries, even if not by a significant amount. If we believe that ethics and justice are identity-dependent in structure – that is, we are concerned with how our actions affect the well-being of particular ethical beings for better or worse – then it seems paradoxically that it would be wrong not to adopt Kyoto Lite.

This line of reasoning, which has been called the *non-identity problem*,[6] calls into question many, though by no means *all*, of our duties to future generations. It leaves intact, for example, duties to those descendants whose identities are beyond our influence, as well as those whose lives will not be worth living as a result of our behaviour (they are, as it were, worse off than if they had never been born). It also leaves intact objections to Kyoto Lite grounded in identity-independent goals such as utility maximisation or the perfection of the human species. Finally, it leaves intact 'deontological' objections that explain the wrong-doing in such cases to the intentions and state of mind of the policy-choosers, not to the outcomes of the various policy choices. Nevertheless, since harm-based, or identity-dependent, reasoning is deeply ingrained in the ethics, law and commonsense morality of most countries, the non-identity problem suggests that our duties to posterity may be weaker, and less extensive, than is often supposed.

6.2.1   Resourcism, Contractualism, and the Non-Identity Problem

As a starting point for our evaluation of the non-identity problem, consider its implication for Brian Barry's theory of justice as resource equality, which was outlined in Chapter 3. The non-identity problem appears to pose a serious challenge to the scope of Barry's theory as, in addition to holding that each generation is entitled to at least as habitable environment as their predecessors, it appeals at a deeper level to the avoidance of harm. While Barry does not discuss the implications of the non-identity problem for resource equality, and he generally avoids describing environmental injustice in terms of harms to specific individuals, his general approach to political philosophy, which he calls 'justice as impartiality', attributes great weight to the notion of harm and its avoidance. A representative comment is the following:

> I acknowledge that harm may be conceived more or less expansively, shading over into inconvenience, annoyance, or offence. Since I am saying that a society is unjust if it does not prohibit harm, a narrow construal of harm fits the theory best . . . The positive harm principle says that a just society will prohibit people from inflicting harm on other people.[7]

The upshot is that an important aspect of the injustice associated with depleting natural resources, or exacerbating climate change, is that such behaviour will harm future individuals (Barry, like most liberal egalitarians, embraces a theory of value that restricts basic ethical entitlements to individual human beings). The non-identity problem, however, shows us that very few future persons will be harmed by the adoption of Kyoto Lite since, if a different approach to climate change had been taken, a different set of persons would have come into existence. So long as these future persons lead lives worth living, they would have no way of comparing their actual state of being with an alternative, preferable, state.

Other theories of intergenerational justice that endorse identity-dependent principles of harm are also vulnerable to the non-identity problem. An interesting case is that of the 'contractualist' family of theories, of which Barry's is a member. According to contractualism, the source of ethical motivation is 'the desire to be able to justify one's actions to others on grounds they could not reasonably reject',[8] and an act is wrong only if its performance 'would be disallowed by any system of rules for the general regulation of behaviour which no one could reasonably reject as a basis for informed, unforced general agreement'.[9] Although contractualism can be interpreted as an impersonal, or identity-independent theory, a more natural interpretation of 'reasonable rejection' takes it to mean that, for a person to raise a decisive objection to an act or social policy, they must (1) be disadvantaged by it in some sense and (2) have a complaint grounded in this disadvantage that is unanswerable, where (1) and (2) are explained in person-affecting terms.[10]

Contractualism is quite clearly a non-reciprocity-based theory, so it is not prone to the non-reciprocity problem.[11] The core of this theory is that judgements about the wrongness of actions or social policies are made in relation to non-strategic features of persons, principally their interests and how these can be furthered and harmed. It is, therefore, open to the thought that future persons, as well as other entities that cannot contribute to social well-being at present, possess full ethical status. Scanlon, for example, remarks that, 'it should be clear that this version of contractualism can account for the moral standing of future persons who will be better or worse off as a result of what we do now'.[12] Nevertheless, contractualism cannot easily be applied in order to explain our duties to very many future persons, as the Kyoto II case shows. This is because there appear to be no particular people belonging to future generations whom our acts will affect for the worse, and will possess a decisive complaint against us, if we choose Kyoto Lite.

For further clarification, let us call all those future persons who will only come into existence if Kyoto Lite is adopted, the *Kyoto Lite people*, and all those who will only come into existence if Contraction and Convergence is chosen, the *Contraction and Convergence people*. Can sense be made of the idea that the Kyoto Lite people have reason to reject the line of reasoning of those who decided to adopt this policy? The Contraction and Convergence and Kyoto Lite people, though contingent on our choice of climate regime, will possess interests that can be harmed once they have been brought into existence. No one seriously doubts, I suspect, that people in the future will have the capacity to be lower or higher in well-being, however this is defined, or that their well-being will be influenced by the state of the natural, cultural and socio-economic environments which these people inherit from their predecessors.

The problem lies rather in the idea that the ethical basis of certain acts or social policies could be reasonably rejected on the grounds of the interests of persons that would not have been served better on balance, or *all things considered*, had Kyoto Lite not been adopted. The only alternative for the Kyoto Lite people to being born into the polluted future world, however, would have been non-existence; and the claim that a person's not being brought into existence might be in some respect *better* for that person than leading a life which is worth living (if limited in certain ways) does not seem plausible. As a result, it appears that those who are responsible for choosing a successor to the Kyoto Protocol appear neither to be harming nor wronging the vast majority of future persons if they adopt Kyoto Lite.

Suppose, for the sake of argument, that the same people will exist whatever policy was adopted – that is we simply ignore for a moment the sensitivity of human identity to pre-conception events. On this scenario, a contractualist explanation could be provided for the wrongness of adopting Kyoto Lite. This would be that many future persons will be worse off when they come into existence than they might otherwise have been – for, in this case, the Kyoto Lite and Contraction and Convergence people will be one and the same. That is, in the one possible future people will inherit a world in which vector-borne diseases, rising sea levels, and extreme weather events customarily injure and kill many more than in the alternative possible future.

When we re-introduce ourselves to the reality of the non-identity problem, however, this objection – and the complaints that sustain it – disappears. So the problem is that it is unclear how contractualism can cope with the problem raised by future people who owe their existence to actions that worsen the conditions in which they live. Intriguingly, perhaps, contractualists are in this way forced into following their rivals, reciprocity theorists, into accepting a much narrower account of the scope of justice than is intuitively plausible. In fact, if considerations of posthumous harm and non-identity are combined in a single theory, the contractualist account looks yet narrower than its rival since future persons could on this view harm their ancestors (posthumously) with no possibility of requital (non-identity)!

Yet the problems for contractualism and related theories do not end here. The non-identity problem also undercuts the application of these theories to a vast range of past injustices. The problem is that, just as future persons will owe their identities to innumerable combinations of events, acts and policies that pre-date their existence so present persons owe their existence to events in the past. This is the basis for Parfit's suggestion that the reader ask himself whether he would have been born if rail travel had not been introduced, and decisively repopulated the future, in the 19th century. As a result, it seems incoherent to argue that existing persons have been made worse off by large historical events that occurred even a few months before they were born. These people might regret that these events took place, but, as they would not have existed otherwise, they cannot plausibly argue that they have been harmed by them.

One aspect of this backwards-looking version of the identity problem is its application to the problem of apologising for historical injustices. There have been a range of governmental apologies to the descendants of victims of historical crimes in recent years. The Irish Potato Famine and American slave trade[13] are just two examples of past events that have received attention. However, the fact that both the descendants of slavers and slave-owners, British and Irish, would not have existed but for the original crimes undercuts the conceptual basis of an apology, as well as the resentment and shame that such events generate in their victims and perpetrators. There may be some symbolic meaning in an apology to the *un*harmed descendants of a long-deceased group, but it does not seem to have any basis in terms of justice or entitlement.[14]

This point can be framed in terms of global climate change. For, if it is nonsensical to compensate present persons for ancient wrongs committed to their ancestors, it is likewise nonsensical to insist that countries that contributed the vast majority of greenhouse emissions prior to 1990, have more than a modest harm-based duty to pay for the costly measures needed to reduce emissions. This is because the greenhouse emissions that contributed to the climate problem originated in acts and policies that also modified the size and composition of subsequent generations of all countries. If we find this implausible, it is worth asking whether a world without carbon industries would have supported a rise in world population from 2.5 billion in 1950 to over 6.4 billion people in 2005.[15]

6.2.2   Four Beliefs

Recall that *identity-dependent* theories of justice direct us to make particular ethical subjects healthier or happier or rescue them from harm or disadvantage. The most popular subset of such theories are *person-affecting* theories, which hold that only particular human beings can be full ethical subjects. Identity-dependent theories can be contrasted with *identity-independent* theories of justice, according to which it can be wrong to perform acts or adopt policies, even if they do not harm any particular ethical beings. The most popular subset of such theories are *impersonal* theories, which direct us to improve human well-being, but from a standpoint that is neutral to the way in which this affects particular persons.

One way of illustrating the problem that non-identity considerations pose for identity-dependent theories is to note that it tempts their proponents into holding four, mutually inconsistent, beliefs.

1. To adopt Kyoto Lite would be wrong.
2. An act or social policy can be wrong only if it harms or disadvantages a particular person.
3. An act or social policy harms or disadvantages a particular person only if it makes them worse off than they would have been had it not been undertaken.
4. The adoption of Kyoto Lite is a remote, but necessary, condition of the Kyoto Lite people coming into existence and leading lives that are worth living.

If we are inclined towards an identity-dependent view, it seems that we are faced with serious difficulties in constructing a consistent approach to questions of intergenerational distribution. For example, if we are to construct an account that explains why choosing Kyoto Lite violates some requirement of distributive justice, it would seem that one or both of (2) or (3) must be revised. However, both of these beliefs appear to command a strong measure of support in the literature.

David Heyd, for example, has defended the view that the price of abandoning either (2) or (3) and with them the identity-dependent view, is simply too high.[16] Endorsing a view that he calls *generocentrism*, Heyd claims that ethical obligations can be owed only to persons whose identities lie beyond the reach of the non-identity problem. But because persons whose identities do not depend on present decisions will almost invariably belong to the present generation, Heyd claims that we have no ethical obligations to the vast majority of future individuals. A similar view is held by Thomas Schwartz who claims that, 'whatever we may owe ourselves or our near posterity, we've no obligation extending indefinitely or even terribly far into the future to provide any widespread, continuing benefit to our descendants'.[17] If this *rigidly* identity-dependent view could be defended, it would appear that the non-identity problem has large implications for the nature and scope of intergenerational and environmental ethics. It would imply, for example, that acts or social policies that result in the emission of huge amounts of greenhouse gases into the atmosphere, and a significant lowering of the quality of life of future generations, do not violate any requirements of distributive justice.

Putting Heyd's approach to one side, there appear to be at least two ways in which we might retain belief (1) in the context of social policy non-identity cases such as Kyoto II, while also retaining an identity-dependent view of ethics. First, we might revise belief (2) in order to retain beliefs (1), (3) and (4). This suggestion has been developed in quite different ways, but the most interesting of these proposes that, although no particular future members of the Kyoto Lite people population will be harmed by Kyoto Lite's adoption, certain collectivities will be harmed by it. Second, we might revise belief (3). The idea here is that the concept of harm should be broadened in some way, for example by abandoning the constraint that a person must be made worse off, on balance, for them to be harmed by an act or policy.

6.2.3 The Limits of the Non-Identity Problem

Even if we suppose that considerations of non-identity are relevant to theories of identity-dependent justice, they do not appear to be problematic for many other theories. One way of explaining why this is the case is to see how the problem relates to four groups of theories of environmental ethics or justice: anthropocentrism, zoocentrism, biocentism and ecocentrism.

Anthropocentric theories are those that attribute value only to states of human beings. One prominent example is the 'green theory of value' proposed by Robert Goodin. According to this theory, the value of the natural world can be traced only 'to its value to human beings and the place it occupies in their lives'.[18] A similarly anthropocentric stance on the value of the natural environment is endorsed by the World Commission on Environment and Development (WCED)'s influential report *Our Common Future*. In the foreword to this report, it is claimed that human well-being 'is the ultimate goal of all environment and development policies', a view that is very widely held.[19]

The anthropocentric accounts defended by Goodin and the WCED, as well as most of the theories discussed in the book, are 'consequentialist' in the sense that they evaluate acts and policies in terms of their consequences. They are also impersonal, in the sense that they are not concerned with how these acts and policies harm and benefits particular persons. Other anthropocentric theories, however, are neither consequentionalist nor impersonal. They focus instead on the intentions of the actor or on the extent to which a course of action was adopted by a person with a high capacity for practical wisdom and other virtues such as a disposition to care about wild nature. The key point, for our purposes, is that anthropocentrism can be person-affecting or impersonal, consequentialist or non-consequentialist.

According to *zoocentrism*, value and ethical status should be attributed to all sentient creatures, and not only individual human beings. The idea is that the traditional reduction of environmental value to the states or well-being of human beings represents a sort of 'human chauvinism'[20] that ignores the fact that species membership is essentially 'a morally irrelevant difference between individuals'.[21] According to Peter Singer, for example, if we are committed to the fundamental principle that each human being's interests must be treated with equal concern, we are also committed to accepting a principle of equality 'as a sound moral basis for relations with those outside our own species [such as] non-human animals'.[22] While Singer's zoocentrism is developed in terms of utility maximisation, other influential versions have been couched in the language of rights. Tom Regan, for example, has argued that many animals possess rights in virtue of being 'subjects of a life' in the sense that they possess fundamental interests that should not be sacrificed even if they conflict with the interests of humans.[23] Zoocentric theories may or may not focus on consequences for animal welfare, or be identity-dependent or identity-independent.

According to the third outlook, *biocentrism*, all, or at least many, living entities can be viewed to some extent as ethical subjects. The idea is that individual living things (such as plants and trees) can be valuable independently of their contribution of the flourishing of humans or other animals despite not being conscious. Holmes Rolston III, for example, invokes this mode of thought when he argues that ethical status be attributed to all creatures that can be said to be alive. On this view, something possesses a life not only if it is conscious but also if it can be said that it has a goal or purpose.[24] A related theory, proposed by Paul Taylor, holds that all organisms that can be benefited or harmed are ethical subjects. According to Taylor's 'life centred theory', animals and even some wild plants possess non-instrumental value by virtue of possessing a 'good'.[25] Biocentric theories, which are generally consequentialist, can be either identity-dependent or identity-independent.

According to *ecocentrism*, our ethical concern should extend beyond living things in order to protect 'environmental objects', or the biological and physical systems that provide the background conditions for life. Robert Elliot takes the former, atomistic route when he argues that every separate component of the biosphere (flowers, trees, rocks) deserves our respect, potentially to the same degree.[26] A proponent of the holistic route is Aldo Leopold. In his influential book *A Sand County Almanac*, Leopold argued that the ecosystem as a whole must be protected, and if necessary it should be given priority over its individual components. 'A thing is right', he observed, 'when it tends to preserve the integrity, stability, and beauty of the biotic community. It is wrong when it tends otherwise'.[27] Ecocentrism is a peculiarly broad tradition, but it is united by a fundamental mistrust of ethical theories that deny the natural environment has value independently of its use-value for individual humans, animals or other living creatures. Ecocentric writers are generally consequentialist, although they can be identity-independent or identity-dependent.

It is not necessary to choose between these contrasting four models of theorising about the environment to recognise that the non-identity problem only undermines the intergenerational application of a rather limited range of anthropocentric, zoocentric and biocentric thinking, namely, those that emphasise how things are for particular individual humans, animals or other living creatures. The problem affects intergenerational duties derived from zoocentric theories of rights, for example, because of the similarities in reproductive systems between human and many animal species. Considerations of non-identity, however, do not undermine the intergenerational extension of identity-independent versions of the above theories since these do not hold that damaging the environment is wrong because it harms particular persons, animals, or things.

It transpires that, most of the theories, principles and norms habitually applied to the climate issue have taken an identity independent, specifically *impersonal*, form. For example, the key principles of equity mentioned in climate negotiations and documents are impersonal in form.[28] Moreover, the general principle of sustainable development although it is open to a number of interpretations, balances the needs of future and present generations without reducing this to how particular persons fare on different paths of development. Proponents of such principles will not be overly concerned about issues of non-identity if they cannot be persuaded that a full theory of environmental justice must also appeal to identity-dependent principles.

6.2.4 Taking Non-Identity Seriously

Despite its restricted scope, and esoteric origins, there are at least two reasons why theorists concerned with intergenerational and climate justice should pay closer inspection to the non-identity problem. First, environmental theories which make no reference to how things are for particular individual entities, such as impersonal utilitarianism or holistic ecocentrism, are contentious to say the least. One problem raised by Parfit is that impersonal utilitarianism could require us to adopt environmental policies that lead to a huge number of people existing in the future who lead lives of poor overall quality instead of policies which lead to a much smaller number of people existing in the future who lead lives of a much higher quality, if the former future contained more utility. He calls this the repugnant conclusion.[29] By ignoring the effects of acts and policies on particular people, similar conclusions will plague identity-independent versions of zoocentrism, biocentrism or ecocentrism.

Second, even if we reject the view that justice is mainly, or exclusively, identity-dependent, the principle that it is wrong, and unjust, to harm other human and animals if it is avoidable to do so is very widely held and a number of writers have argued that it must form a part of a plausible theory of justice.[30] The principle that harm should be avoided, or compensated for, is found at the heart of the legal systems of most countries, notably in criminal and tort law, as well as in medical practice, where practitioners traditionally take, or at least abide by, the hippocratic oath never to inflict avoidable harm. Indeed, some authors have argued for the adoption of an 'environmental hippocratic oath' that would outlaw environmental practices that exacerbate the risks of dangerous climate change.[31]

The appeal of harm-based analyses of environmental problems comes out well in the work of Henry Shue and Dale Jamieson, who specifically address the injustice of climate change in terms of the language of harm. Jamieson, for example, despite acknowledging that evaluations of climate impacts are complicated by the fact the causes and harms of climate change are temporally and spatially diffuse, argues that 'serious, clearly identifiable harms will have occurred because of human agency.'[32] Jamieson, then, does not seriously call into question whether we can harm future persons by our profligate environmental behaviour but argues instead that we need to modify conventional understandings of culpability to tie these harms to their present perpetrators.

Shue, on the other hand, has claimed that we should conceive of the harmful effects of climate change as analogous to those of passive smoking, the idea being that both the activity of smokers, and of profligate emitters of greenhouse gases, render other non-smokers and non-emitters *worse off* through no fault of their own.[33] Shue, however, fails to acknowledge that the fact that future persons owe their existence to the profligate actions of previous generations in these cases means that they cannot complain that they have been harmed, or rendered worse off, by them. In this respect, the analogy between the effects of passive smoking and the effects of depletionist policies on future generations needs further clarification.

6.3   INDIVIDUAL RIGHTS AND THE NON-IDENTITY PROBLEM

Recall that the problem with applying identity-dependent theories, such as contractualism, to the Kyoto II case is that no person who owes their existence in part to the adoption of Kyoto Lite would have a complaint against its adoption even if it would lead to a lower quality of life in the future. This is because this regime, although it appears objectionable, does not render any particular future people worse off than they otherwise would have been.[34] It appears that what proponents of identity-dependent principles need to do if they are to explain what is wrong with adopting Kyoto Lite is to show how it can be harmful, and therefore impermissible, even though it will not render future individuals worse off than they otherwise would have been. This is the challenge that I take up in the remainder of this chapter.

6.3.1 Interests, Choices, and the Rights of Future Persons

There are several objections to the claim that future persons, such as the Kyoto Lite people, possess rights against their predecessors. According to the first, and perhaps the most sweeping, it is objected that the formal nature of rights discourse rules out non-existing entities from being the bearers of rights. The objection is raised quite explicitly in the work of Hillel Steiner,[35] but will be endorsed by all proponents of what has become known as the *choice theory of rights*. According to this theory, rights are associated analytically with their bearers in a particular sort of way. In short, the right-bearer possesses a right, not in virtue of any benefit he will derive from another being constrained not to violate it, but rather because 'he is ethically in a position to claim the performance of a duty from another, or to waive it, and therefore to determine by his choice how the other ought to act'.[36]

This aspect of the choice theory – that right-bearers are viewed as active, choosing agents – means that ascribing rights to entities which are incapable of making the sorts of choices that rights-possession requires is a conceptual mistake. As Steiner puts it, 'it is precisely because future persons are necessarily incapable of choice, that they cannot [according to the choice theory] be said to have rights against present persons'.[37] This does not necessarily mean that existing persons have no duties to protect the environment which future generations will inherit from us. Such duties may exist, but are not explicable in terms of an appeal to rights.

I take the liberty, here, of not reviewing the strengths and weaknesses of the choice theory of rights. I think that Steiner is correct that such a theory is not consistent with the possibility of a right-based objection to the sorts of actions (and policy decisions) with which we are concerned. Moreover, this incompatibility has nothing essentially to do with the non-identity problem, for Steiner's view also rules out future persons whose identities have already been fixed, such as unborn children, from possessing rights. I do not think that those sympathetic to rights-based principles in general ought to be overly concerned about this, however. This is because there is another theory of rights that seems much more in tune with our considered convictions about the nature and scope of rights discourse. As such, I think that we have reason to put the choice theory to one side in order to see the implications of holding the alternative *interest theory* of rights in contexts where non-identity considerations obtain.

According to the interest theory, to say that an agent, X, has a right implies that 'other things being equal, an aspect of X's well-being (his interest) is a sufficient reason for holding some other person(s) to be under a duty',[38] and in contrast to the choice theory, there is little in the formal nature of this account which, considerations of non-identity aside, excludes the not-yet-born from possessing rights. It can be assumed that there will be people who exist in the future, that these people will possess interests that will be vulnerable to harm, and that the actions of existing persons – particularly those affecting the integrity of the natural environment – will have profound effects on these interests.[39] As Feinberg puts it: 'the identity of these interests is now necessarily obscure, but the fact of their interest-ownership is crystal clear, and that is all that is necessary to certify the coherence of present talk about their rights'.[40]

However, there are some serious *substantive* objections to the idea that future persons may possess rights even on the interest theory, and the most problematic of these flow from considerations of non-identity. Consider, for example, the following line of argument. Persons whose rights are in danger of being violated in cases of non-identity can *only* exist in the state in which their rights are violated. It follows that the only way in which these persons' rights could have been fulfilled would have been for their owners not to have been born. To ascribe rights to such persons would be to ascribe rights that could not possibly be enforced to persons who owe their existence to these rights being violated. But if one cannot, even in principle, honour or respect any of the rights a person allegedly possesses, that person cannot actually possess any such rights.[41]

One response to this line of argument is that, in certain situations, respecting a right might require that we act so as to ensure that no one comes to possess that right. Take the Kyoto II example. The idea here is that Contraction and Convergence should be adopted because not doing so would predictably result in many more people coming into existence bearing rights that could not possibly be fulfilled.[42] One example of such a right would be the right not to be brought into existence when one would thereby not be able to enjoy access to life-preserving natural resources that are highly sensitive to climate change, such as clean air and water.

If defensible, the presence of 'unavoidably violated rights' would seem to defeat the argument against future persons possessing rights mentioned above. It enables us to grant the claim that it is a necessary condition of a right being violated that a recipient of that right actually exists (obligations cannot be owed to possible people on this view – no one has a right to be born, for example). On closer inspection, however, this approach is subject to at least one serious objection. Since we have assumed that the Kyoto Lite people will not have existed if their ancestors had chosen Contraction and Convergence, and since we have supposed that they will lead lives that are worth living, it might be assumed that, once they came into existence, they could be expected to *waive* their rights not to be brought into existence in a state where their rights would necessarily be violated.[43] The idea is that, although the Kyoto Lite people may think that it would have been wonderful to have been born into better environmental circumstances, they would come to feel glad to be alive, and view their ancestors' decision not to conserve as one which actually furthered, rather than set back, their interests taken as a whole! Of course, if it could be predicted that future persons would not lead lives that were worth living, then the right-waiving response would seem to be far less plausible. In such cases, one might think that it would be much worse for someone to exist than for them not to exist at all and, as a result, it would not be reasonable to expect these people to *waive* their rights not to be brought into existence suffering great misery.[44] However, to the extent that many persons belonging to future generations will lead lives that are well worth living, it could be predicted that many of these persons would wish to waive their rights not to be born with rights and interests that could not be fulfilled.

The application of notions of right-waiving to the climate change issue is clear: the adoption of Kyoto Lite is not objectionable because it violates the Kyoto Lite people's rights for, if these people were in possession of the facts, they would not regret, and could be expected to waive their rights against, the adoption of the Kyoto Lite regime.[45] Again, we have not shown that the policymakers do no wrong if they choose Kyoto Lite. Rather, we have shown that the explanation of the wrong-doing is not easily framed in identity-dependent terms.

6.3.2   Specific Interests, Specific Rights, and the Non-Identity Problem

One way of constructing a rights-based objection to the adoption of Kyoto Lite is to modify the standard 'all things considered' understanding of harm, according to which a person is harmed only if they are rendered worse off than they otherwise would have been *on balance*. Perhaps the most plausible way in which this modification might be accomplished is by exploiting the distinction between rights that are grounded in considerations of overall well-being (general rights) and rights that are grounded in more specific interests (specific rights).[46] According to James Woodward, for example, people have relatively specific interests (e.g., in having promises kept, in avoiding bodily injury, in getting their fair share) that are not simply reducible to some general interest in maintaining a high overall level of well-being and that many moral requirements function so as to protect against violations of such specific interests. That an action will cause an increase in someone's overall level of well-being is not always an adequate response to the claim that such a specific interest has been violated.[47]

The 'retroactive right-waiving' response appears to deal a mortal blow to the idea that the general rights of the Kyoto Lite people can provide the basis for an objection to Kyoto Lite. But it is less clear what its implication is for the notion of specific rights, such as the right not to be born into a life lacking in dignity or autonomy. There are two reasons for thinking that the specific rights of future persons might not fall victim to the retroactive right-waiving objection. First, at least some specific rights might be viewed as inalienable in the sense that they cannot be waived when their possession is not conducive to the maximisation of their possessor's well-being. Second, there are considerations which suggest that future persons, while they might wish to waive their specific rights, have some reason *not* to do so.

Let us put the idea that specific rights are inalienable to one side for the moment in order to focus on the issue of retroactive right-waiving.[48] I start with the thought that there are certain advantages in maintaining the distinction between *specific* and *general* rights in dealings between contemporaries. Recall that, according to the interest theory of rights, a person has a right only if an aspect of their well-being is a sufficient reason for holding some other person to be under a duty to him (as Raz puts it, 'rights are always to what is in the interest of the right-holder').[49] The merit of making space in such a theory for specific rights and interests is that this solves the otherwise puzzling phenomenon that the possession of certain rights appears to be in one's interests in some respects but not in others.

A revealing example is discussed by Raz. In certain contexts, a person might enjoy a right against others correlative to the important interest tied to some piece of property that they have acquired. On the other hand, the person's exclusive right over the disposal of this property might render them the target of theft, fraud, or of temptation. In fact, if certain conditions hold (say, that the temptation and malice of some band of criminals passes a certain threshold) it could be the case that the right-holder's interests taken as a whole may cease to be served by his possessing their property rights (it may put the right-holder in danger of being robbed, for example). If rights merely served to protect their holders' all-things-considered interests, then this would imply that being the subject of malicious criminals could lead to one's ceasing to possess the right to dispose of one's property as one sees fit. But this seems absurd. A more plausible view is that, to the extent to which possessing the property is at least in its owner's interest in at least one respect, then this is sufficient, all things being equal, to justify that person possessing a right to it.[50]

Raz's intragenerational example suggests that we ought to abandon the view that all rights function so as to protect a single, all-things-considered interest in their holders' well-being. As such, it also seems to provide some reason to embrace the view that actions can harm (and therefore wrong) a person even if they do not render that person worse off than they would otherwise have been. This is because such actions might violate a person's specific interests and rights without endangering that person's overall well-being.

It is important to note that embracing the notion of specific rights and interests need not mean abandoning the identity-dependent framework altogether because the exact nature of this framework is open to interpretation. It might, for example, hold that 'an act cannot be wrong *in any respect* if it is not worse for people than any alternative *in any respect*' or that 'an act cannot be wrong *in any respect* if it is not worse for people than any alternative *all things considered*'.[51] Although many contributors to the literature have assumed that the second of these formulations is self-evidently the correct one, much work still needs to be done to clarify the scope and content of the harm principle.[52]

Moving to the intertemporal application of this line of thought, consider the case of *Green*, who is a member of a distant future generation in the possible future world where Kyoto Lite has been adopted, and who has difficulty in breathing clean air due to pollution caused by climate change. According to the appeal to specific rights and interests, Green's specific right of access to an important life-sustaining resource (i.e. clean air) appears to have been violated as a result of the greenhouse emissions of previous generations.

Suppose, next, that had Green's ancestors adopted more stringent policies on greenhouse emissions, Green's difficulties would have been avoided. Applied to this case, the appeal to specific rights suggests that Green's right to breathe clean air has been violated by the negligent actions of his ancestors, despite the fact that the actions that led to this right being violated rendered Green, on balance, no worse off. If stringent policies had been adopted, Green and his contemporaries would not have been born with specific rights to resources which could never have been fulfilled and, in this specific sense, Green and his contemporaries would have been better off *not being born*. That is, if they had never been born, they would not have been put in the position where their specific interest in breathing clean air had necessarily been violated.[53]

Unfortunately, even if we follow Woodward and Raz in holding that people possess fairly specific interests which ought to be respected by others, this does not seem to provide a full response to the retroactive right waiving idea. Suppose we adopt the perspective of the potential recipient of some specific right. The main defect in a rights-based objection to Kyoto Lite would be that we could expect the Kyoto Lite people to be grateful that they had been born and that as a result they would waive any rights that would be violated by this policy. But why, it might be asked, should this objection not also be directed towards the notion of specific rights? So long as the Kyoto Lite people lead lives which are worth living, and they do not regret their existence, we might assume that they would waive *any* rights or entitlements that require us not to choose Kyoto Lite on their behalf. This suggests that rather more of the specific rights approach than seemed at the outset turns on the controversial idea that some rights and entitlements are inalienable, and cannot therefore be waived.

6.3.3 Responses to the Retroactive Right-Waiving Objection

Are there any considerations that cast some doubt on whether the Kyoto Lite people would, in actuality, wish to waive either their specific or general rights not to have been born with interests which could not possibly be fulfilled? I think there are, and I consider some of these below.

The retroactive right-waiving idea rests on an analogy between the way in which agents typically waive certain rights that they do not regret being violated in *intra*generational contexts and the way in which future persons could be expected to waive certain rights that they do not regret being violated by their ancestors. Parfit's example of the former sort of case is that of the person who wishes to marry and who does not regret his future wife violating his rights of privacy.[54] It might be argued, however, that there is a crucial difference between intragenerational and intergenerational right-waiving. This is that the person who gets married explicitly consents to their subsequent loss of privacy in advance of the marriage ceremony, whereas there is no such consent from the Kyoto Lite people available at the time of its adoption.

One aspect of this disanalogy is that we cannot be certain that the Kyoto Lite people would waive these rights in actuality. However, the disanalogy also renders problematic the whole notion of retroactive right-waiving when the right-waiver does not yet exist. There are, for example, formidable problems with the idea of retroactive right-waiving in cases where future persons lead lives of very poor quality, but where it is uncertain whether they lead lives which are on the whole worth living or not. The examples offered by Parfit are perhaps overly simplified in this regard – he stipulates that the characters in his examples are not so miserable that they would ever consider their lives not to be worth living. However, in reality there seem to be many cases in which people are born with medical conditions that make their lives doubtfully worth living and it is very likely that climate change will bring about, if it has not done so already, a large increase in such cases. How, though, might we establish whether the people who will belong to future generations blighted by climate change would *in fact* wish to waive either their specific or general rights?

Consider once more the Kyoto II example. Suppose it was suggested that it does not matter that we cannot predict if the Kyoto Lite people would waive their rights in actuality, but rather what matters is whether we can say that it would be *reasonable* for them to refuse to waive their rights. The Kyoto Lite people have at least three good reasons to regret the choice of Kyoto Lite that might lead to such a refusal.

First, a person might argue that it would have been better if they had never existed in cases where they fall short of some standard of perfection and believe strongly that it is a terrible thing to live and fall short of this standard.[55] It might be the case, for example, that many of the Kyoto Lite people come to resent the fact that their reduced physical capabilities prevent them from perfecting their pursuit of some physical activity (such as running or walking) even though they accept that their lives are on balance well worth living.

Second, the right-waiving approach assumes that if it is known with some degree of certainty that a person will not regret an act's performance then this act does not violate any of this person's rights. However, this claim seems questionable to say the least. Many people would think it wrong to enslave or to torture another person even if this person gave their consent and subsequently argued that they did not regret giving it. In a similar way, it could be argued that any lack of regret that the Kyoto Lite people express towards the adoption of Kyoto Lite does make it less objectionable.

Third, the Kyoto Lite people might resent the adoption of Kyoto Lite because it harmed them in a way that did not reduce their well-being. The idea here is that there might be victim-involving acts that do not in fact diminish well-being, but are nevertheless *interest-violating*. Perhaps the Kyoto Lite people can be viewed to be harmed in virtue of being frustrated, and bitter, that their ancestors made no attempt to solve the climate change problem, effectively robbing them of their dignity by giving them the gift of blighted life rather than giving another set of people the gift of a much better life. The complaint against the original policy negotiators would be that, by adopting Kyoto Lite, the 'standards of due care' owed to successor generations were violated.[56] Such a complaint, although it would not be easily framed in identity-dependent terms, would provide one reason why the Kyoto Lite people might not want to waive their intergenerational rights.

The above discussion shows that the appeal to specific interests is an ingenious response to the non-identity problem. But it cannot possibly provide a full solution to it. It could never be established how many future persons would refuse to waive their specific rights not to be born into a world blighted by climate change. Moreover, the specific interests of future persons do not seem weighty enough to override the specific, and general, interests of present persons when they conflict as they seem to do in the context of climate change. Finally, the appeal to specific rights/interests is not easily located within the identity-dependent tradition of thought which it is designed to rescue. The idea that we can harm someone even if we do not make them worse off on balance is, for example, counter to the vast majority of identity-dependent analyses of what it means to harm a person, which do not distinguish between specific and general interests when they evaluate whether or not a person has been harmed by an act or policy.[57] We have reason, then, to seek out other solutions to the non-identity problem that do not involve such drastic modifications in identity-dependent reasoning. In what remains of the chapter, I argue that a promising solution to the non-identity problem can be found in the general rights of future groups and collectivities.

6.4   GROUP RIGHTS AND THE NON-IDENTITY PROBLEM

In order to establish whether an appeal to the ethical status of certain groups or collectivities (I use the terms interchangeably) can solve the non-identity problem, it is necessary to survey briefly the two alternative forms the appeal might take. The first of these takes the rights of groups to be merely the aggregation of the rights of their members. Here, the group itself has no ethical status above and beyond that possessed by its members. I call this the *reductionist* view of group rights, the most distinguished exponents of which are Joseph Raz and Will Kymlicka. The second articulation of group rights regards the *ethical* rights of groups in a similar way as the *legal* rights of certain corporations. These rights are not reducible to the rights shared by its members. The group is, rather, viewed as bearing ethical status independently of its individual members. I call this the *holistic* view of group rights, one proponent of which is Vernon Van Dyke. The distinction between the two positions they represent is important, I will argue, because while the holistic view appears more likely to be of useful application in cases of non-identity, the reductionist view is much less controversial and appears more readily reconcilable with broad egalitarianism.

Recall that, for Raz, a person, X, 'has a right if and only if X can have rights, and, other things being equal, an aspect of X's well-being (his interest) is a sufficient reason for holding some other person(s) to be under a duty'.[58] The key idea here is the extent to which a *group* might be thought of as possessing some interest that is important – or significant – enough to create a duty on the part of another group or person. Raz requires three conditions to be met in order for this to happen. That is, a group will possess a right whenever some joint interest of its members satisfies the following conditions. First, it must be important enough to justify the creation of duties upon others. Second, the interest must concern the members' interests in securing access to an 'inherent public good'.[59] Third, the interest of each of the group's members in this public good is insufficiently strong for it to justify the creation of duties on the part of others.[60]

In Raz's view, it is not the way in which a group possesses the quality of being an independent, and ethically important, entity in its own right which gives rise to it being the recipient of rights, but rather the feature that the individuals which comprise it possess interests which combine in order to be sufficiently weighty to ground duties on the part of others. For Raz, a group as thinly defined as a set of individuals with one common interest on a shared matter can possess group rights if their combined interests are weighty enough. Raz is clearly defending a reductionist theory of group rights in this sense. He argues that 'collective or group-rights represent the cumulative interests of many individuals who are members of the relevant groups. It follows that there is nothing essentially non-aggregative about rights'.[61]

The core of Kymlicka's defence of group rights has several steps.[62] First, individuals must have access to some structure in order for them to be provided with the conditions necessary for autonomous choice among an adequate range of options. Second, only membership of a flourishing and secure cultural group provides such a structure. Third, many cultural groups are vulnerable, and can only flourish if they are allocated certain group rights which are not relevant in respect of other, more robust, groups; possessing these rights may in certain cases be a necessary condition of a group, or culture, preserving the distinctive culture and way of life that its members identify with. Fourth, a defensible theory of justice must accommodate certain group rights, at least with respect to those groups that have been especially vulnerable to historical injustices, in order to protect the context for autonomous choice.

If reductionist group rights are grounded in the claim that the objects of group rights – e.g. national self-determination – are essential to the continued well-being of that group's members, holistic group rights are grounded in the notion of respect for groups as entities 'with a distinct identity and life of its own which others must recognise and respect'.[63] Consider the paradigm of a group that bears rights in international law, the *nation state*. Nation states are often recognised as being singular ethical, as well as legal, entities – possessing a separate identity and the right of self-determination. It is this identity that gives rise to the demands of many nations to be seen as ethical subjects in their own right, and not the idea that the members of these communities have interests which add up with sufficient weight to create a right of self-determination. The idea behind the holistic view is that this sort of reasoning can be extended to the case of sub-national groups.

There are obviously several problems with this last claim. One is the problem of vagueness of identity. The identities of groups do not appear to be as easily defined as those of their individual members. This makes it difficult to establish the point of origin, as well as extinction, of any given group. It also suggests that one of the formal requirements of rights-allocation – that the bearer is identifiable or specifiable in some reasonably clear way – will not be met by the sorts of groups which the holist wishes to enfranchise. A different problem associated with group identity is the intuitive condition that the identity of potential right-bearers should be robust to the point where they are not better viewed as the parts of a wider entity or merely an amalgam of smaller entities. The idea of 'species rights', for example, seems implausible in a way that could not be said of individual human rights since parts of the body do not possess ultimate ethical value in the same way as particular members of species.[64] A third problem concerns the *directionality* of the rights that the holistic view defines. This conception of group rights is prone to the objection that the rights it defines will in some cases conflict with the rights of its individual members. Such group–individual conflicts are not possible under the reductionist view as with this view a person simply ceases to be a member of a group if his interests conflict with it.

To address these issues, proponents of holist group rights such as Vernon Van Dyke propose stringent standards for differentiating entities that can be regarded as the genuine possessors of rights from those which cannot.[65] Here the strength of any given group's rights-claims will vary in proportion to:

1. the desire it has to preserve itself;
2. the reasonableness of its chance to preserve itself;
3. the extent to which it possesses clear criteria of membership;
4. the significance it has to its members;
5. the importance of the rights it would be afforded;
6. its ability to act and assume responsibilities;
7. the extent to which it is already treated as a group;
8. the extent to which the rights the group wields are compatible with a commitment to an abstract understanding of equality for those affected.

The above standards, Van Dyke argues, are not to be seen as being a list of necessary, or jointly sufficient, conditions for a group to possess rights, but rather 'permit varying degrees of decisiveness in judging whether a group is entitled to status and rights'.[66] He notes that taken together they will 'not suggest any great proliferation of the kinds of groups to be recognised', and more importantly that interest groups and social classes are particularly unlikely to qualify. The extent to which other groupings, such as generations, might meet these conditions is a further source of debate.

It is obviously much easier to sketch a theory of holistic group rights than it is to defend the theory of value that lies behind it, namely, that groups possess interests – and therefore ethical status – in the same way as individual humans. There are several considerations, however, that at least point in the direction of holistic rights. Some of the most interesting of these reflect the behaviour and attitudes of individual persons. Many people believe, for example, that the destruction of entire communities or cultures is bad over and above the fact that this is often accompanied by the deaths, or reductions in well-being, of their individual members. On the other hand, people are disposed to view a natural, or human originating, disaster as being more regrettable if it involves the destruction of a whole community than if it involves an identical amount of human misery though dispersed amongst strangers in different communities.

The idea is that, if we adopt a 'practical' approach to ethical standing, we should not be deterred by the lack of a clearly definable list of conditions that will rule certain entities in, and other entities out, of the bounds of justice. Rather, we should ask which entities we already make assumptions about and build 'into our actions, habits, practices and institutions'.[67] Here, a number of groups and cultures can be attributed ethical status in a roughly analogous way as individuals because this is how they are already treated in practice. This might seem a rather ad hoc approach to the grounding of group value and group rights, but it is worth remembering that the attribution of ultimate value to any entity, including individual humans, is problematic for there can be no clear answer to the sceptic who asks 'why should individual humans be treated with dignity and respect? Why are people morally equal?'

6.4.1 Climate Change and the Rights of Future Groups

To explain the relevance of holistic group rights for the non-identity problem it is useful to revise the Kyoto II example. As we have seen, climate change is expected to have a range of effects, both positive and negative, on the socio-economic fabric of many nations. There is possibly no better example of this than the way in which climate change is expected to cause significant sea-level rises in the coming decades and centuries. Moreover, as we have also seen, the IPCC also predicts that this will have serious consequences for many nations in the future, but in particular for developing countries.

Sea-level rises are expected to damage coastal cropland, and displace millions of persons from low-lying and coastal communities. Just some of the low-lying nations that the IPCC thinks are in most danger are the north-east coastal nations of Latin America, Bangladesh, Egypt and Holland.[68] Perhaps the most disconcerting examples of nations vulnerable to sea-level rises, however, are the small island states of the South Pacific. The IPCC singles out these nations for special attention because of the especially adverse effects of sea-level rises on these states, including, in the worst case scenario, complete destruction.[69]

Suppose next that the IPCC's mid-range estimate for global sea-level rise of half a metre by the year 2100 is proved accurate. Consider the following:

The Case of the Displaced Islanders

At the end of the 21st century, the remaining inhabitants of a Pacific Island state have assembled to assess the damage that climate change has caused their small community. In line with earlier analyses of the climate regime that was adopted by previous generations – *Kyoto Lite* – their island has already been partially submerged by the Pacific Ocean and their agricultural industry all but destroyed by a combination of soil erosion and soil infertility. Because of the lack of employment prospects and general social upheaval, the indigenous population has been cut to a small percentage of its 20th-century level, although the existence of alternative sources of employment and sustenance outside the Island have meant that no particular Islander has failed to lead a life which was at least worth living. Finally, because of the combined impact of population displacement and other impacts, many cultural practices – practices which had been handed down through the generations – have been abandoned. The community, all agreed, was on the verge of physical and cultural ruin.

Let us put aside the economic, social and health impacts of climate change on existing and proximate generations of islanders, and in particular the important issues of global justice which this case raises. Granted that such issues will be dealt with by other aspects of our theory of justice, the question I want to ask is this: has the island community itself been harmed by, and has it a complaint against, the failure of previous generations to adopt climate policies which may have prevented dangerous climate change? Can this complaint be transposed to the choice of climate regime at the time it is made?

According to the holistic view, there is at least some cause to think it can. Despite the fact that no particular individual will exist in the future where Kyoto Lite is adopted who would have existed had it not been, various groups and associations will, and are thus at least candidates for complaint-bearing status. Moreover, even if the island community ceased to exist following a catastrophic increase in sea levels, this would not mean that we could simply assume that it had never existed. Rather, we would conclude that the nation had been destroyed primarily as a result of the impact of climate change. The idea, then, is that the interests of the groups that constitute the island community were violated as a consequence of adopting Kyoto Lite. These violations would not be connected to the interests of the island as such – we should reject the ecocentric view that the destruction of physical or biological systems can be wrong wholly independent of human well-being. Rather they concern the human cultures and groups that cannot survive if the island is destroyed.

It is worth locating the above claims within the context of some of the theories of group rights discussed above. Recall that, for Kymlicka, the adoption of certain acts or social policies can be wrong because they undermine the needs that particular individuals have to access a flourishing cultural or communal context. In his treatment of the issue of the claims of minority communities, Kymlicka claims that 'membership in a cultural structure is what enables individual freedom, what enables meaningful choices about how to lead one's life',[70] and he goes on to suggest that the ethical importance of individual freedom is such that persons belonging to disadvantaged minority cultures should be afforded additional rights and resources to compensate for the special disadvantages they face. But, as we have seen, while these rights are collective in the sense that they are exercised collectively rather than individually, they are nonetheless individual rights in the sense that they are grounded in the interests of particular persons.[71] According to the holistic view, by contrast, the communities which future people will belong to deserve concern and respect in their own right; present actions that predictably result in these communities being impaired, or being destroyed altogether, are unjust. Such injustice cannot be explained in terms of Kymlicka's theory of group rights, however, since he rejects the idea that communities can have ultimate ethical importance.

The holistic view of group rights has seldom been discussed in the context of intergenerational justice. It seems reasonable to assume that this is because the notions of group value and holistic rights are so controversial. One author that has proposed a similar approach, with rather different terminology, is Edith Brown Weiss. According to Brown Weiss, a basic requirement of intergenerational distributive justice is that each generation respect the rights of successor generations to inherit an equal share of natural resources; and that these 'planetary' rights:

> may be regarded as group-rights, as distinct from individual rights, in the sense that generations hold these rights as groups in relation to other generations – past, present and future. They exist regardless of the number and identity of individuals making up each generation.[72]

Brown Weiss goes on to claim that the notion of planetary rights escapes considerations of non-identity, which only call into question 'the traditional conceptual framework of rights as rights of individuals'.[73] Planetary rights, on the contrary, 'are not rights possessed by individuals' but are rather possessed 'by generations themselves against other generations'.[74]

I am sceptical, however, of the idea that generations can possess rights; a generation as a whole, as opposed to a future cultural group or nation, seems a rather abstract entity on which to ground a theory of intergenerational justice. It is extremely difficult, for example, to define a generation in a way that caters for the overlap between it and another generation. Moreover, and unlike the cultural groups they belong to, people do not generally act as if their generation, assuming they agree on what this might be, possesses any independent value.

Nevertheless, the crux of the Brown Weiss view is worthy of exploration if we apply it to cultural groups rather than generations. The idea is that appeals to holistic rights avoid problems of non-identity because the conditions of group existence are more fixed than those of their individual members: they typically endure for a much longer time-span, for example, and their formation does not depend upon the coming together of a particular sperm and egg. It could, therefore, be irrelevant, on this view, that no particular future islander in the above case will be harmed by Kyoto Lite's adoption, for it may still remain the case that the islanders as a group are harmed. Here there is a direct link between the fact that group existence is not as precarious as individual existence, and the possibility that the interests of groups qua groups may be disadvantaged by the social policies adopted at earlier moments in time.

For illustration, recall the four beliefs that seem to be inconsistent in circumstances of non-identity. The response to this inconsistency is to retain unaltered beliefs (1) and (4) – and to revise beliefs (2) and (3) to incorporate groups as being fully-fledged ethical entities. This response is consistent with the identity-dependent view of ethics, because it is *particular* groups that possess an interest in (and thus rights to) the maintenance of an undamaged heritage of cultural goods. The value of cultural preservation, on this view, is not owed 'to the world' abstracted from the way it connects to the flourishing, and continued survival, of human life. Indeed, both individual and group-rights share at least this one feature, namely, that they can be held only by particular, unified, entities.

Because it retains an identity-dependent structure, one merit of the group-centred view is that it is readily reconcilable with the contractualism of both Barry and Scanlon. Recall that, for Scanlon, an act is wrong only if its performance 'would be disallowed by any system of rules for the general regulation of behaviour which no one could reasonably reject as a basis for informed, unforced general agreement'.[75] It was argued above that contractualism seems problematic in the context of non-identity cases such as Kyoto II, since the Kyoto Lite people, taken one by one, do not appear to have a legitimate complaint against Kyoto Lite.

Contractualists, however, need not be committed to the claim that the complaints viewed as unanswerable must be restricted to those arising from harms, or wrongs, done to particular persons. This is demonstrated by Scanlon's understanding of the scope of contractualism, according to which ethically considerable entities must (1) possess a good in the sense that 'there be a clear sense in which things can be said to go better or worse for that being', and (2) 'constitute a point of view; that is there be such a thing as what it is like to be that being'.[76] These two conditions must hold, Scanlon thinks, for the notion of justification to be applied to an entity. But while there are certainly differences between the 'points of view' of particular human beings on the one side, and groups of human beings on the other, it is at least possible that there can be such a thing as a group perspective on things or that things can go better or worse for some groups.

While I have not the space here to construct a more positive defence for this line of thought, it is worth mentioning the fact that many people's ethical convictions certainly point in this direction. Consider, once more, the widespread conviction that the deaths of large numbers of persons from small indigenous communities (which result in the deaths of these communities) are more regrettable from the ethical point of view than equivalent numbers of deaths of unrelated individuals. In the spirit of this conviction, the suggestion is that we revise Scanlon's account of moral reasoning to read that 'an act is wrong only if it affects some particular individual *or group* in a way that cannot be justified'.

There is one problem with the group-centred approach that suggests that it could only provide a partial solution to the non-identity problem. Suppose that a course of action that we think will harm a certain future group's interests would also be a necessary condition of that group coming into existence in the first place. In such cases, the approach seems open to a new group-centred puzzle which we might call the *extended non-identity problem.*

An interesting historical example of how the extended non-identity problem could arise is grounded in the experience of the descendants of historically abused groups, such as the West Africans who were transported to North America to live as slaves in previous centuries.[77] An African American, on this view, is instantly enmeshed in conceptual difficulties on arguing that they, as a descendant of a disadvantaged population, deserve both an apology and compensation for the social stigma of being born into a community which had been created by injustice many decades or centuries before. The extended non-identity problem suggests that this complaint could not be upheld as this person owed her existence, in part, to the very actions and policies that generated the stigma she suffers.

Suppose, however, that the complaint had been made on behalf of the present-day African American community, rather than on behalf of a present-day African American individual. The enslavement seems to have been a necessary condition of the existence of the present-day African American community. Let me explain. If this grave injustice – or series of injustices – had never occurred, there would be no African American community in quite the same sense as there is today. There would no doubt be some Africans who had emigrated to the United States, for example, but it is unlikely that there would be the rich diversity of African American linguistic and cultural heritage that there is today. As a result, according to the extended version of the non-identity problem, the representative of this present-day community could not plausibly argue that her present-day *community* had been harmed by the original enslavements. The appeal to group rights, then, like the appeal to specific interests, solves the non-identity problem only in some cases.

6.5   CHAPTER SUMMARY

In this chapter, I have dealt with some of problems with applying harm-based theories of distributive justice to the intergenerational domain. I began by outlining what I called the non-identity problem. I then explored several ways in which the problem might be solved. As I explained, all of the responses that remain within an identity-dependent ethical paradigm are subject to serious objections, but each, and particularly the group-based approach, seemed to generate at least some duties on the part of existing persons not to damage the environment that our remote descendants will inherit form us. This is an important result since, as we have seen, the ethical case for a stringent climate regime is strongest when it can appeal to the importance of avoiding predictable harms to our descendants as well as to the importance of bringing about an impersonal pattern of benefits in the future that is just and equitable.

NOTES

1.   O'Neill, 1996, p. 116.
2.   Parfit, 1984, p. 361.
3.   See, for example, Parfit, 1976, and 1984, pp. 351ff; Schwartz, 1978; and Adams, 1979.
4.   These, and a number of alternative options, are discussed in Fred Pearce, 2005b.
5.   The Contraction and Convergence option was pioneered by the Global Commons Institute (http://www.gci.org.uk) and is defended in, amongst others, Athanasiou and Baer, 2002, pp. 47ff.
6.   Parfit, 1984, p. 359.
7.   Barry, 1996, pp. 372–3; see also 1995, pp. 86ff.
8.   Scanlon, 1981, p. 116.
9.   Scanlon, 1981, p. 110, and 1999, pp. 189ff. Brian Barry endorses Scanlon's contractualist approach in Barry 1995, pp. 67–72; and 1996.
10.   For a contrary view, see Kumar, 2003, especially pp. 105ff; Meyer, 2004, pp. 20ff.
11.   See, for example, Scanlon, 1981, p. 115, p. 128.
12.   Scanlon, 1981, p. 115n.
13.   This case is discussed briefly in Fishkin, 1991, pp. 91ff.
14.   For a contrary view, see Thompson, 2000, pp. 473–5; and Levy, 2002.
15.   Figures from the UN global population database: <http://esa.un.org/unpp/p2k0data.asp>.
16.   Heyd, 1992, pp. 80ff.
17.   Schwartz, 1978, p. 3.
18.   Goodin, 1992, pp. 42–3.

19. World Commission on Environment and Development, 1987, p. xiv.
20. See Routley and Routley, 1995.
21. Elliot, 1995b, p. 9.
22. Peter Singer, 1993, p. 55.
23. Regan, 2004, p. 243.
24. Rolston III, 1988, pp. 98ff.
25. Taylor, 1986.
26. Elliot, 1995a.
27. Leopold, 1949, p. 262; see also Callicott, 2003.
28. Consider the following three statements contained in the UN Framework Convention on Climate Change: (1) 'The ultimate objective of this Convention . . . is to achieve . . . stabilization of greenhouse gas concentrations in the atmosphere at a level that would prevent dangerous anthropogenic interference with the climate system' (Article 2); (2) 'The Parties should protect the climate system for the benefit of present and future generations of humankind, on the basis of equity and in accordance with their common but differentiated responsibilities and respective capabilities' (Article 3); and (3) 'The specific needs and special circumstances of developing country Parties, especially those that are particularly vulnerable . . . should be given full consideration' (Article 3).
29. See Parfit, 1984, pp. 381ff.
30. The classic source of this view is John Stuart Mill's 'simple principle', according to which 'the sole end for which mankind are warranted, individually or collectively, in interfering with the liberty of action of any of their number is self-protection. That the only purpose for which power can be rightfully exercised over any member of a civilised community, against his will, is to prevent harm to others' (Mill, 1974, p. 68).
31. Baer et al., 2001.
32. Jamieson, 2003, p. 293.
33. See Shue, 1995, pp. 245–6; 2001, pp. 449ff.
34. I prefer to think in terms of climate 'regime' over climate 'policy' as the former hints at the complexity of the choices faced by climate negotiators, which concern not simply choices between rival climate policy but the adoption of a whole set of aims, objectives, and mechanisms.
35. See Steiner, 1983, pp. 154–5; 1994, pp. 259–61; and 1991, pp. 49–52.
36. Waldron, 1988, p. 95.
37. Steiner, 1991, p. 52.
38. Raz, 1984, p. 183; see also Raz, 1986, pp. 166ff.
39. See Feinberg, 1980, pp. 180–84; Partridge, 1990; and Elliot, 1989, pp. 159–60.
40. Feinberg, 1980, p. 181.
41. See McMahan, 1981, pp. 124ff; and Smolkin, 1994, pp. 316ff.
42. See Parfit, 1984, p. 384; Woodward, 1986, p. 821.
43. See McMahan, 1981, p. 127; and Parfit, 1984, p. 365.
44. It is worth noting that some writers have denied this claim. David Heyd holds, for example, that no meaningful comparison can be made between existence and non-existence. As a result, he denies that it can be worse for a person to exist than for them never to have been born no matter how miserable their life is in actuality (Heyd, 1992, pp. 80ff).
45. See Parfit, 1984, p. 365. Note that Parfit uses a broader choice between environmental programmes of 'Conservation' versus 'Depletion' to make this point, although nothing substantially turns on this.
46. Note that the distinction made in the text between general and specific rights should not be confused with H.L.A. Hart's influential distinction between 'general' and 'special' rights, where the former are 'general' in the sense that they are possessed by all human persons, and the latter are 'special' in the sense that they are grounded in some unique feature of their owner, or their relations to others, rather than their owner's humanity. See Hart, 1955, pp. 183–8.
47. Woodward, 1986, p. 809.
48. I focus here on the issues raised in the exchange between Woodward and Parfit in the Journal *Ethics*, as well as those raised by Parfit's discussion of these issues in *Reasons and Persons*. See Woodward, 1986, pp. 810ff; 1987, p. 802; Parfit, 1986, pp. 854–62; 1984, pp. 364–66.

49. Raz, 1994, p. 46.
50. Raz, 1994, p. 46.
51. As suggested by Larry Temkin, 1993, pp. 248ff.
52. See Carter, 2002, pp. 92ff; and Page, 1999. See also Carter, 2001.
53. A similar view has been defended by Lukas Meyer, who claims that there could be a harm-based complaint in non-identity cases since the future persons concerned are harmed in the sense that they were brought into existence worse off than they *were entitled to be* even if they are were not thereby made worse off than they *would, or could, have been*. The former, 'subjunctive', conception of harm can be developed in a number of ways. Meyer's idea is that people are entitled to a minimum level of well-being that enables them to lead a satisfactory life. Acts or policies that predictably result in future people being driven below this threshold of well-being are harmful, for Meyer, because they violate a sufficiency-type principle even if they are not thereby made worse off all things considered. See Meyer, 2004.
54. Parfit, 1984, p. 364.
55. Woodward, 1986, p. 823.
56. See Thompson, 2000, pp. 474–5; and Kumar, 2003, pp. 116ff.
57. See Feinberg, 1988, pp. 25ff.
58. Raz, 1986, p. 166.
59. The distribution of benefits of inherent public goods are 'not subject to voluntary control by anyone other than each potential beneficiary controlling his share of the benefits' and this is the case irrespective of technological factors (see Raz, 1986, pp. 198–9).
60. Raz, 1986, p. 208.
61. Raz, 1986, p. 187; see also Hartney, 1995, p. 209.
62. Kymlicka, 1989, pp. 135ff; and 1995, pp. 49ff. Kymlicka's view has a number of close cousins, most prominent of which is the account defended by Allen Buchanan. See Buchanan, 1991, pp. 52ff and pp. 74ff; and 1994, pp. 7ff.
63. See Peter Jones, 1994, pp. 184–5. See also Jones, 1999.
64. For a contrary view, see Johnson, 2003.
65. Van Dyke, 1985, pp. 31–3.
66. Van Dyke, 1982, p. 33.
67. Onora O'Neill, 2000, p. 192.
68. See Bijlsma et al., 1996.
69. Nurse et al., 2001, pp. 854–5.
70. Kymlicka, 1989, p. 208; and 1995, pp. 80ff.
71. See Kymlicka, 1995, pp. 34ff.
72. Brown Weiss, 1990, p. 203; and 1992, pp. 114–15.
73. Brown Weiss, 1990, p. 205.
74. Brown Weiss, 1990, p. 205.
75. Scanlon, 1981, p. 110.
76. Scanlon, 1981, pp. 113–14.
77. Fishkin, 1991, pp. 91ff; Page, 1999, p. 66.

7. Concluding chapter

Understand that in a world beset by ecological crisis, distributive justice must mean more than it did in the past. It must include not only the fair distribution of wealth, resources, and opportunities, but the fair distribution of 'impacts' as well. Because the elemental truth is that as storms become more violent and the droughts more fierce, some of us will be hurt far, far more, and far earlier, than others.[1]

Tom Athanasiou and Paul Baer

Justice delayed, is justice denied.[2]

William Gladstone

7.1   INTRODUCTION

There now exists a broad consensus that climate change, or global warming, to use its popular title, raises a number of important questions of justice. In this book, the tools of analytical philosophy have been harnessed to investigate some of these questions, in particular those that concern the duties we have to avoid activities that will bring about dangerous changes in global climate in the future. In order to function as a focus for discussion, an argument underpinning our duties to future generations was presented. This was called the *intergenerational responsibility argument*. This argument went as follows:

P1. The changes in the climate system that are being brought about by human action threaten the well-being of members of future generations.
P2. Human action that threatens the well-being of members of future generations is unjust.
C. The changes in the climate system that are being brought about by human action are unjust.

We saw that the truth of this argument, which appeared to be valid in the technical sense, could be questioned on a number of grounds, and that the notion of justice it invokes, which transcends the usual focus on duties that hold between contemporaries, needed further analysis. This analysis became the focus of subsequent chapters of the book. After an introductory chapter that explored a number of general and methodological questions, Chapter 2 addressed the evidence for, and against, premise P1. Chapters 3 and 4 investigated in more detail what it means to distribute benefits and burdens for the sake of justice and suggested ways in which alternative theories, which were limited to those that give prominence to equality or a related distributive ideal, might be applied to the further future. Chapters 5 and 6 addressed, and partially rebutted, some objections to P2 grounded in the notions of non-reciprocity and non-identity.

The intergenerational responsibility argument was constructed in terms of justice and entitlement as opposed to other ethical values such as charity, humanity, altruism or emotion. The use of the language of entitlement and justice is important: although there is a range of alternative reasons for preserving environmental goods for present and future generations, justice appears to provide a more compelling and urgent defence of environmental and intergenerational duties than rival approaches. Justice is often taken to be superior, for example, in terms of its ability to motivate people to act for the sake of others, as well as comply with such motivations when there are counter-motivations grounded in individual self-interest. The bonds of justice are, in addition, often viewed to be weightier than other considerations from the ethical perspective quite apart from their motivational force.

Despite the fact that climate change will result in a wide range of generally adverse impacts on future human well-being, some have questioned whether existing persons and institutions are bound by duties of justice to manage the climate system for the sake of their successors. It has been suggested, for example, that members of future generations lack the ethical status possessed by existing people.[3] Others have claimed that climate change, as a matter of empirical fact, threatens the well-being of a limited number of future individuals.[4] Still others have claimed that, although the not-yet-born possess some degree of ethical status, our duties to them attenuate rapidly as they become more remote in time from us.[5] On any particular one (or combination) of these three views, the generally adverse impacts of climate change matter much less than they would if they were to be experienced solely by our contemporaries.

One of the clear messages of the book is that there is little to be said in favour of any of these three justifications of a sceptical approach to intergenerational justice. However, an analysis of each has led us in the direction of fairly serious modifications in the way traditional distributive theories are conceived in order for them to be rendered consistent with extensive duties to future generations. Nevertheless, such revisions should be made in light of the fact that future persons will possess interests broadly comparable to our own when they come into existence and at least some of these interests will be vulnerable, either individually or collectively, to the behaviour of prior generations. The modifications required, which the book only considers in outline, concern the importance of finding space for both considerations of the interests of particular future people and other, impersonal, considerations which are not easily reduced to matters of personal or collective interest.

In what follows, the main theoretical claims made in the book will first be presented before the discussion is widened in order to explore two important issues of climate justice that have not yet been addressed. The first of these concerns the identities of those who should bear the burden of mitigating adverse climate impacts that can reasonably be avoided or of adapting to the dangerous climate change that cannot reasonably be avoided. The second concerns which, of the many possibilities, would be the most equitable approach to climate mitigation and adaptation after the Kyoto Protocol expires at the end of 2012.

7.2 SUMMARY OF THE BOOK

In recent years, an enormous amount of effort has been devoted to the exploration of the scientific basis of global climate change, as well as its likely impacts on human life. Three key claims have emerged from this effort. First, 'the balance of evidence', to quote the IPCC, 'suggests discernible human influence on climate change'.[6] Second, climate change will impact significantly on the distribution of benefits and burdens within and between generations.[7] Third, climate impacts will be generally, if not uniformly, adverse.[8]

In Chapter 2, I summarised the salient evidence both for, and against, these three claims. It was found that the evidence in favour of them was overwhelming: climate change is set to have a devastating impact on the health of many human populations in the future, as well as on the cultural and socioeconomic structures handed down to future generations. It was also shown that climate change will have more adverse effects for vulnerable populations, such as those located in coastal areas of developing nations and for small-island communities. The balance of evidence, then, is that P1 of the intergenerational responsibility argument is true: human activities are changing the climate system in ways that threaten the well-being of both present and future persons.

Despite the growing interest in ethical dimensions of climate change, there have been few systematic attempts to test the significance of its likely impacts for pre-eminent theories of distributive justice. The possibility that such theories might not be suitable for extension to the climate change problem, for example, has rarely been discussed. In order to fill this gap in the literature, I discussed, in Chapters 3 and 4, a variety of distributive theories in order to establish whether the findings of the IPCC raise issues which these theories would regard as significant.

In Chapter 3, I found that the likely impacts of climate change would be of genuine concern for a variety of theories of what it is that should be distributed according to the demands of justice, such as theories of welfare, resources, basic capabilities, and midfare. This is essentially because human well-being is intimately connected to adequate access to the absorptive properties of the atmosphere, as well as the life-supporting systems that the atmosphere sustains. In Chapter 4, I found that future climate impacts would also be of concern for competing theories of the profile of justice, of how shares of any given currency of justice should be distributed amongst a given population, such as equality, priority and sufficiency. This is because climate change will modify the profile of benefits and burdens across space and time.

One question that arose from Chapters 3 and 4 was whether theories of distributive justice, as premise P2 of the intergenerational responsibility argument assumes, can be extended beyond the context of the present generation without incoherence. In Chapters 5 and 6, two much discussed arguments were presented that suggest that many familiar principles, and theories, of distribution cannot be so extended. According to the first argument, the lack of reciprocity between persons belonging to different generations undermines the claims of future persons to resources currently at the disposal of existing persons. I called this the *non-reciprocity problem*. In Chapter 5, I discussed the non-reciprocity problem in some detail and showed how it seems to undermine the intergenerational extension of a cluster of theories which assume that the scope of justice is determined by the notion of reciprocal benefit (these were called 'reciprocity-based' theories). It was later argued, however, that even if distributive justice is in some sense reciprocity-based, a natural broadening of the notion of reciprocity would allow us quite naturally to talk of 'intergenerational justice'. Two ways in which such a broadening might work were discussed under the rubrics of 'indirect' and 'posthumous' reciprocity.

Indirect reciprocity was developed in terms of two 'models' of intergenerational obligation: the 'chain of concern' and 'trusteeship' models. It was found that, although there are problems with each, the duties they define seem defensible when the correct pre-conditions obtain. The notion of posthumous reciprocity was introduced in relation to a prior analysis of human well-being. The idea was that, while present persons can either enhance or diminish the well-being of future persons through standard causal pathways, future persons will often find themselves in a position where they can increase or diminish the well-being of their ancestors through the avenue of posthumous harm. Although the notion of posthumous harm is contentious, I argued that a number of objections to it that have been raised in the philosophical literature were flawed, and that two popular theories of well-being (based on desire-fulfilment and the possession of objectively valuable goods) seem consistent with it. One note of caution lay in the consideration that the reciprocity created by posthumous harm is somewhat limited. However, since posthumous and indirect reciprocity are reconcilable, I suggested that, when taken together, they represent a powerful response to the non-reciprocity problem. I concluded that considerations of reciprocity do not, after all, pose a serious threat to the intergenerational responsibility argument.

According to the second challenge to premise P2, activities which damage the well-being of future humans by degrading the environment they inherit cannot be said to be unjust because these activities function as necessary, if remote, conditions of the vast majority of future persons coming into existence. As a result, they can only be said to worsen the prospects, or to harm the interests, of a very small number of those who will later live. This argument, which trades on what has become known as the 'non-identity problem', has important implications for how climate change should be managed. For, if we assume that justice protects the interests of particular persons (that is we think that justice has a 'person-affecting' structure) we seem forced to abandon the view that environmental interventions that predictably lower the quality of life in the future are unjust because of their bad effects on particular people.

There is a large, and expanding, literature on the non-identity problem, and there exists great disagreement as to its implications for intergenerational justice. Like many, I hold what has become known as the 'no difference view'. That is to say, I do not believe that the problem shows us that we have less responsibility than we previously believed to protect environmental and other goods for the sake of future generations. Rather, I believe that the problem should inspire us to think seriously about the theoretical basis for the responsibilities to which many of us are already intuitively committed.

It was also suggested that there were at least two person-affecting, or more accurately 'identity-dependent', responses to the non-identity problem. According to the first, many of the obligations violated when we despoil the environment, or worsen the greenhouse effect, are grounded in the specific, rather than the general, interests and rights possessed by future individuals. Such interests and rights can be violated by the actions of others even if their owners are not thereby rendered worse off 'all things considered' (that is, worse off than they would have been). So, if such rights and interests exist, they seem invulnerable to the non-identity problem. I found that, despite there being some mileage in the appeal to specific rights and interests, theories that appeal solely to considerations of individual interest seem unlikely to explain more than a small part of our responsibility to future generations. It could not easily explain, for example, how the specific interests of future persons could be balanced against the specific and general interests of existing persons.

According to the second identity-dependent response, many of the obligations we violate by damaging the environment are grounded in the interests and rights of future human groups. I noted that the idea of group rights has been interpreted in several, often incompatible, ways and that the whole notion of rights which protect the interests of collective units needs clarification. It was suggested that, as in the case of the appeal to the specific rights of individuals, the appeal to group rights appeared to provide some explanation of our intergenerational responsibilities. However, I also found that a new version of the non-identity problem would arise in many circumstances that limited the scope of the appeal because many future groups – for example, those that are created from refugee crises caused by climate events – will owe their existence to the environmentally profligate acts performed by previous generations. It could not coherently be claimed in such cases that these groups had been harmed 'all things considered' by acts or policies that were necessary for their later existence.

Because the appeals to specific rights and group rights could not, even if they were combined, explain the depth of the injustice associated with adopting policies that predictably lower the future quality of life, it seems that a complete account of intergenerational justice must appeal, at least in part, to 'identity-independent' principles. Identity-independent principles evaluate acts and policies according to the extent that they promote the quality and quantity of life independently of how particular individuals fare in alternative scenarios (when focused solely on human life, they are referred to as 'impersonal' principles). It was suggested that intergenerational justice is usefully viewed as being 'pluralistic' not merely in the sense that no account of its currency, or profile, can be constructed that does not appeal to a combination of superficially incompatible principles, but in the deeper sense that it contains elements that can, and elements that cannot, be reduced to the well-being of particular entities; and that the relationship between these elements is complex.

In an influential essay on the ethics of climate change, Dale Jamieson has recently claimed that there is a need for new ethical values, and new conceptions of justice and responsibility, to capture the extent of our environmental duties as well as to motivate people to respect them.[9] In particular, he points to the fact that traditional theories of ethics – which assumed that activities and their harmful impacts were not remote in time or space and that seemingly insignificant actions could not add up to inflict grave damage on non-compatriots and non-contemporaries – are flawed in the context of climate change. A similar call for an adjustment of our ethical theorising to make sense of the complexity of human–environmental relations is made by Peter Singer.[10] In many ways, the tentative proposal for greater pluralism outlined above is in tune with the analyses of Jamieson and Singer and yet it also suggests that these writers underestimate what can be achieved to explain our environmental and intergenerational duties by bringing together values that already command widespread allegiance but which are usually viewed as being incompatible. The suggestion is that we do not so much need new values to the climate change problem as new methods to help us use the values we already have more creatively.

7.3   THE BEARERS OF GLOBAL CLIMATE JUSTICE

In previous chapters, the focus of our discussion of the relations amongst justice, future generations and climate change has been the recipients of justice. However, discussions of who the recipients of justice are, what they are entitled to receive, and which of the many units of currency should be adopted leaves unaddressed the question of who bears the responsibilities of justice. This aspect of the scope of justice is, in many ways, more complicated than those we have already examined when developed in the context of climate change. On the one hand, it might seem obvious that it is existing humans that bear this responsibility: they are the only agents who can act now to reduce emissions or adopt policies that will facilitate adaptation. On the other hand, there is a wide range of human agents other than individual persons to which responsibilities of justice might be allocated. These include individual countries, supranational organisations, national and multinational corporations, international and domestic institutions, and, most abstractly, the present generation as a whole.

Faced with the problem of which level of human agency is responsibility for combating climate change, much of the literature focuses on the unique political and ethical responsibilities of the developed countries.[11] This idea is a key principle of the Framework Convention on Climate Change, which endorses a principle of 'common but differentiated responsibilities' according to which 'the developed country Parties should take the lead in combating climate change and the adverse effects thereof'.[12] However, despite the fact that a number of arguments have been proposed to give this principle wider ethical foundation, no one argument seems to bear its weight. In this section, we take a closer look at two prominent arguments for the view that the developed countries are the primary duty-bearers of climate justice.

7.3.1   Contribution to the Problem

There is little doubt that developed countries are responsible for the bulk of anthropogenic greenhouse gases currently being released into the atmosphere. The simple idea behind the 'contribution to problem' argument is that, like other polluters, the developed world should internalise the long-term costs of the activities that caused, and later exacerbated, the enhanced greenhouse effect. Only in this way can they compensate those in the present generation who have been made worse off by climate change, as well as preventing the interests and rights of future users of the atmosphere from being violated.[13]

The empirical basis of the 'contribution to problem' argument is, in many ways, undeniable. Since one tonne of any greenhouse gas has an equal climate-forcing effect wherever it is emitted, and since scientists have developed clear protocols for measuring the source and quantity of greenhouse emissions, it is relatively straightforward to assign responsibility for current and recent emissions. To match the overriding primacy given to nation states in international and environmental politics, the statistics almost exclusively focus on country-by-country emissions. The SAR reported that the developed countries (defined as OECD, North America and Europe, Eastern Europe, former USSR, Japan and Oceania), with roughly 20 per cent of the global population, accounted for roughly two-thirds of global carbon emissions from fossil fuel use in 1993, with the remaining third coming from the developing world.[14]

Moving on to the issue of emissions in the past, as we saw in Chapter 2, greenhouse gases have long atmospheric lifetimes. CO_2, which is by far the most common greenhouse gas, continues to contribute to global warming up to 200 years after being emitted, whereas sulphur hexafluoride, which is thankfully rare, contributes for 3000 years or more and is roughly 22 000 times more effective than CO_2 at warming the atmosphere.[15] The quantity and source of emissions over a longer time-period, then, is highly relevant for assigning responsibility for both present and future climate change.

Figures from the respected World Resources Institute for the period 1800–2000, which represents the most significant period of greenhouse gas growth, show that the USA emitted 301 279 million metric tonnes of CO_2 between 1800 and 2000, which is roughly four times as much as the next biggest emitters, Russia (86 705) and Germany (75 606).[16] The cumulative contribution of developing countries over this period is, by contrast, very small. Between 1800 and 2000, the whole of Sub-Saharan Africa emitted just 17 665, and Central America and the Caribbean just 13 376, million metric tonnes of CO_2.[17] Figures published by the IPCC tell a similar story, and estimate that developed countries were responsible for 67.8 per cent of total CO_2 emissions between 1900 and 1988.[18] In the light of these figures, Singer seems fully justified in claiming that:

> to put it in terms a child can understand, as far as the atmosphere is concerned, the developed nations broke it. If we believe that people should contribute to fixing something in proportion to their responsibility for breaking it, then the developed nations owe it to the rest of the world to fix the problem with the atmosphere.[19]

Nevertheless, the normative case for linking present responsibility with past emissions is actually much more contentious than it might seem. One reason for this is that 'contribution to problem' arguments seem to rely on 'deontic' principles of justice (these are sometimes referred to in the literature as 'historical' principles, but the equivalence is not exact). Such principles, which we met earlier, evaluate distributions of benefits and burdens in terms of how they came about. If their origins involved no wrong-doing, then they are just; if their origins involved wrong-doing, then they are unjust and redistribution is justified to re-establish justice.

Deontic principles undoubtedly capture something important about justice, but they are limited in the present context as they do not appear to explain the ethical basis of all of our duties to future generations. Imagine for a moment that the problem of global climate change turned out to be a real, but natural, phenomenon (as we saw in Chapter 1, there have been great changes in climate during the evolution of the human species, and each, though entirely non-anthropogenic in origin, had significant impacts on human well-being). In such circumstances, 'contribution to problem' arguments cannot be appealed to in order to explain why we should not simply abandon future generations to their fate, rather than adopting stringent climate policies for their benefit. Moreover, the problem is not merely that these principles cease to apply in the absence of wrong-doing, but also that they seem to clash with other sorts of principles that can explain why significant comparative or absolute disadvantage should be corrected.

'Contribution to problem' arguments are prone to further problems.[20] First, past activities that have contributed to the enhanced greenhouse effect also seem to have brought many benefits to present members of developing countries, even though these benefits are in no way as great as those gained by the developed countries. This suggests that the responsibilities of present members of developed countries to rectify the damage done by their compatriots to the lives of members of developing countries should be discounted somewhat to take account of these benefits. Second, the injustice perpetrated on the developing world by the developed world's refusal to internalise all of the costs of industrialisation are at least tempered by widespread ignorance of the enhanced greenhouse effect's nature and scale until the 1990s. Again, it seems fair to discount any contribution-based responsibilities in line with the principle that one cannot be held responsible for impacts which one cannot reasonably foresee. Third, those responsible for much of the greenhouse effect are now dead and it seems unfair to shoulder their descendants with both the responsibility for their own environmental behaviour and that of their ancestors.

Like most commentators, I am far from convinced that the above considerations reduce the responsibility of existing members of developed world, or the countries they inhabit. However, there is a further problem that suggests that 'contribution to problem' arguments cannot alone bear the burden of the claim that developed countries, and their inhabitants, possess a special duty to take the lead in combating climate change. This is that, as argued in

Chapter 6, the emissions that contributed to the emergence of climate change as a global problem originated in acts and policies that have affected the size and composition of subsequent generations, such that very few members of the present generation can plausibly argue that they have been harmed, or made worse off, by the historical greenhouse emissions associated with industrialisation.

As we saw in the earlier analysis of the non-identity problem, there are a number of ways in which we might retain the language of justice to condemn past and present carbon-emitting behaviour. We might argue that many present people lead, and future people will lead, lives that are *not* worth living as a result of the developed world's carbon-rich lifestyles; or that impersonal values, such as the perfection of the human species, have been set back by these lifestyles. Neither of these moves, however, can fully justify the robust duties of mitigation and adaptation that proponents of 'contribution to problem' arguments seek. This is because such considerations possess limited scope, and even where they do apply they are not weighty enough to ground the huge efforts that are needed to mount the necessary global assault on the causes and effects of climate change.

Next, we could argue that the developed world's past emissions violate the 'specific interests' of present members of developing world to make use of their fair share of the atmospheric commons.[21] This violation might not involve any particular person leading a life that is not worth living, or being harmed all things considered, but it would be a sort of 'harmed condition' where the dignity of the person is damaged.[22] Or, it could be argued that the rights and interests of many developing world groups, or cultures, have been harmed by the build-up of greenhouse gases in the atmosphere. Many groups, or cultures, would have existed even on the scenario that alternative, climate-neutral, methods of industrialisation had been adopted and therefore could, through some party, argue that they had been harmed, 'all things considered', by climate change.

Quite apart from the limitations of both responses, which were discussed in Chapter 6, it seems problematic to assign the responsibility for rectifying past climate injustices to existing members, or groups of members, of developed countries since they were not responsible for the suggested specific interests, or group rights, violations; and to ground their responsibility in the benefits they have unwittingly received from their descendants seems itself unjust. This suggests that no ethical explanation of the duties of climate justice, or where they lie, should lean too heavily on 'contribution to problem' arguments.

7.3.2 Ability to Pay

The second type of argument for differentiated responsibility holds that the developed countries and their inhabitants should shoulder the burden of climate justice because their greater comparative and absolute wealth means that they are uniquely able to undertake the action required. As Shue explains, 'ability to pay' arguments rest on the fundamental principle of equity that 'among a number of parties, all of whom are bound to contribute to some endeavour, the parties who have the most resources should contribute the most to the endeavour'.[23]

One objection to 'ability to pay' arguments is that they may ultimately prove counter-productive to the common good by discouraging people, or the countries they belong to, from activities that result in greater wealth creation since the resulting wealth risks being redistributed to those who are worse off. George W. Bush, for example, seemed to be invoking this sort of consideration when he observed in 2002 that:

> Addressing global climate change will require a sustained effort over many generations. My approach recognizes that economic growth is the solution, not the problem. Because a nation that grows its economy is a nation that can afford investments and new technologies.[24]

I assume that we should ignore this sort of objection, however. We are concerned, here, with what a just distribution of responsibilities for climate change might be and not with what would be the most efficient distribution of rights and duties from the point of view of maximising utility in a world of rational egoists. Nevertheless, further objections to 'ability to pay' arise concerning the implications of its use, as well as its conceptual underpinnings.

It might be argued, for example, that those who enjoy the greatest well-being are not bound to cover the costs of climate mitigation and adaptation *because* they are the best off. Having more than others does not confer any responsibility on a person to improve the lot of others, for the best off might themselves, though possessing a greater capacity than others, be quite badly off. They might, for example, have just enough wherewithal to lead a decent life. This suggests that Shue's articulation of the argument needs amending: it is not 'the parties who have the most resources' that are responsible for addressing the climate problem, but rather 'the parties with more than enough resources.' The idea, which is grounded in a sufficientarian approach to justice, is that the basis for allocating the responsibility for action on climate change to the developed world is that its inhabitants generally possess more than they need to lead a decent life, so they also possess a duty to come to the aid of others so long as this will not reduce them to below the threshold where they lead a decent life. If the best off are only just above the point where they have enough, though, these duties cease to operate as does the 'ability to pay' justification of differentiated responsibility.

Interestingly, Shue himself goes on to defend a sufficiency-based restriction on 'ability to pay.' However, this defence sets the threshold of the life a person is entitled to at a relatively low level. Having enough, he argues, means having 'the essentials for at least a bit more than mere physical survival – for at least a distinctive human, if modest, life'.[25] Regardless of whether we embrace a minimal, modest or generous conception of sufficiency, however, it seems that there is some reason to hold that the developed countries, and their typical citizens, are the main bearers of climate justice. They have it clearly within their reach to do much more about climate change; for every day that the developed world delays the adoption of a longer-term, and more stringent, climate framework, large numbers of people in the developing world will be dragged below the point where they have enough. In short, the capacity of the developed world indicates that the requirements of justice can be achieved; but it is the principle of sufficiency that explains what these requirements are and how they arise.

The sufficiency view, as I have presented it, is not uncontroversial. So it is important to note that rival theories of what I have called 'broad egalitarianism' also pull us in the direction of viewing the developed world, and its inhabitants, as the main bearers of justice, albeit for subtly different reasons. Other things being equal, equality principles will require interventions, in the form of preventative and compensatory transfers for the sake of developing countries, as climate change will exacerbate their undeserved inequality relative to developed countries; priority principles require intervention in order to improve the prospects of the worse off, who will almost certainly be rendered worse off by climate change and who will reside in developing countries; and 'pluralist' theories, for example those that apply a sufficiency principle when at least some are below the threshold and a priority principle when all are above it, will follow suit.

Ability to pay arguments, as they do not assume that those encumbered by duties are responsible for outcomes that need addressing, are not obviously prone to problems of non-identity. But they do need grounding within some wider approach to justice or they begin to seem rather arbitrary. Suppose, again, that climate change, though real, had entirely non-anthropogenic origins. As we saw, this assumption would create problems for anyone who affirms only deontic principles. But it also raises problems for 'ability to pay' views since the duty of the developed world, here, will be equally as strong as if they were totally responsible. But should there not be some 'discount' in what is required of the better off when their behaviour is not cause of the problem?

Imagine, next, that climate change was a much more localised problem for human well-being in that those who emitted the most, the developed countries, also suffered the most from its adverse effects. After several centuries, the consequence might be that the prospects of the developed and developing world completely reversed. Would the new developed world be under a strong obligation of justice to aid the old, now poor, developed world despite the fact that the latter brought their misery on themselves? Suppose we thought that they would be. Would this duty be as strong as the duty we intuitively believe the present-day developed countries have to address the climate problem that has, and will have, such adverse effects on their developing country neighbours? So long as we hold that the intensity, and possibly the content, of the duties in these two cases do not converge, it seems that at 'ability to pay' arguments gain at least some of their plausibility from the implicit assumption that those who have the ability to solve environmental problems are generally those responsible for them.

The fact that considerations of historical responsibility can sometimes underpin, and sometimes undermine, 'ability to pay' arguments suggests that some weight should be given to both within a pluralist approach. It also suggests that the fundamental basis for ascribing duties of climate mitigation and adaptation lies in terms of what profile of distribution we are seeking to bring about. This suggests that the search for clear-cut answers to the question of who the bearers of climate justice are, and why, is to a certain extent misguided. The really pressing question is not who possesses most capacity, or is most to blame for the problem, but who has what entitlements. The bearers of climate justice, on this view, are not identifiable by virtue of their past behaviour or comparative wealth, but rather by the fact that they alone have enough to contribute to climate change policies without jeopardising their own sufficiency. These persons, for it is persons who can lead decent lives and not the countries they belong to, are the ultimate bearers of climate responsibilities, and they are not located solely in the developed world. Allocating the primary responsibility for climate change management to developed countries, as well as adopting the nation state as the basic unit of climate politics in general, is at bottom a pragmatic, not an ethical, decision.

7.4 THE FUTURE FOR KYOTO

Assuming that the developed countries should take the lead in combating climate change for the sake of existing and future persons, what sort of climate regime should be brought into effect after the present arrangement concludes in 2012? As one commentator has put it, should we 'Tear up Kyoto or make it tougher?'[26] In this section, I examine the present regime and three possible replacements from the point of view of distributive justice.

The Kyoto Protocol, which entered into force on 16 February 2005, requires 39 developed countries to bring about an average of a 5.2 per cent cut in greenhouse emissions by 2012 relative to their 1990 levels. An important aspect of the Protocol was the provision for three 'flexibility mechanisms' to lower the costs of achieving emissions reductions.[27] These were *joint implementation*, which provides emissions credits for developed countries that implement cooperative emissions projects or remove carbon from the atmosphere; a *clean development mechanism*, which allows developed countries to implement projects that reduce emissions in developing countries in order to meet their commitments; and *emissions trading*, which enables developed countries to buy carbon credits from other countries with spare capacity to help meet their commitments. The emissions cuts required by the Protocol varied from country to country. The EU, for example, which accounts for 21 per cent of current global emissions, must reduce its emissions by 8 per cent; whereas Russia, which accounts for 17 per cent of global emissions, is permitted to emit the same amount in 2012 as it did in 1990.

Although hailed by many as a landmark in international environmental politics, the measures agreed at Kyoto, and subsequently modified at subsequent Conferences of the Parties in Bonn and Marakesh in 2001, have attracted widespread criticism.[28] First, real participation in the Protocol, despite the fact that it has been ratified by over 140 countries, is limited in important ways. One problem is that the emissions reductions negotiated were not designed to apply to developing countries. This is a problem because a number of developing countries – notably China, India and Brazil – have rapidly expanding economies and greenhouse emissions to match. China, for example, is now the world's third largest greenhouse emitter if the EU, in second place, is counted as one country. Key developed countries, such as the USA[29] and Australia,[30] have withdrawn from the process at least partly because it is neither economically feasible nor equitable in the absence of full developing country participation.

Second, research indicates that the Kyoto Protocol, assuming that it is extended to cover emissions over the course of this century, would only achieve very modest reductions in greenhouse emissions. Research suggests that, as a consequence, it would only effect a reduction in global temperature of between 0.02°C and 0.28°C by the year 2050 compared to the mid-range increase projected by the SAR.[31] Lomborg points out that the most optimistic figure would amount to just a six-year postponement in the warming that would have occurred in 2094 in the absence of Kyoto to 2100.[32] The Kyoto Protocol would not, even on the most optimistic scenario, prevent more than a small proportion of the extreme weather events, health impacts, and socio-economic stresses discussed in Chapter 2.

Third, the complexity of the climate mechanisms introduced by the Protocol have opened up various possibilities for the developed countries to meet their targets in ethically dubious ways, for example by reducing their commitments by buying emissions credits from countries that will meet their targets as a result of contingent socio-economic factors or by exploiting the fortuitous location of greenhouse sinks, such as forests, within their territory. The main beneficiaries of the inclusion of sinks, which was necessary to secure the future of the regime as whole, are countries associated with high standards of living and high historical emissions, such as Japan, Russia, Canada and Australia. It is thought that, far from bringing about a 5 per cent decrease in global emissions by 2012, the inclusion of sinks and other mechanisms means that the regime will at best bring about a 2 per cent or so cut in CO_2 emissions on 1990 levels by 2012.[33]

Putting aside the possibility that the existing regime will expire in 2012 with no replacement, there appear to be three main possibilities for a post-Kyoto regime. It is useful to think of each of these as a complex combination of aims, objectives and mechanisms. Some of these will be endorsed by all three regimes, whereas others will be more unique selling points (or flaws, depending on one's view). Each of the candidate regimes, for example, claims to share a commitment to the central aims of the Framework Convention on Climate Change, which, to recap, are: (1) to 'prevent dangerous anthropogenic interference with the climate system' and (2) to 'promote sustainable development'.[34] However, much more diversity surrounds the selection of *objectives*, which can be understood as concrete targets adopted by the regime, such as keeping CO_2 emissions, or global rises in temperature, below a certain threshold and *mechanisms*, which are adopted as means to meet aims and objectives as efficiently as possible, such as incentives to encourage greater use and development of specific carbon reduction technologies.

The 'Kyoto Lite' approach, which is being driven by the US administration under the rubric of its Clear Skies, Global Climate Change and FutureGen initiatives, seeks to provide voluntary targets for national emissions based on the ratio of national carbon emissions to economic output. At the time of writing, six states had signed up to the approach: the USA, Australia, China, India, South Korea and Japan, which together account for more than 50 per cent of current global emissions.[35] The approach – which focuses on the setting of voluntary targets to reduce greenhouse emissions, incentives to businesses to move away from carbon intense technologies, and technology transfer to the developing world – has the objective of reducing the carbon intensity of developed and developing world economies. Because there would be no mandatory emissions targets, however, the approach would almost certainly fail to halt the rise of greenhouse emissions, though it might reduce it relative to the scenario that no replacement for Kyoto is adopted.

One problem with Kyoto Lite, even if it is evaluated according to its own modest aims and objectives, is that, as economies become more efficient, they may experience a downward drift in their carbon intensity indices while emitting more and more carbon into the atmosphere. The consequence, as one commentator has argued, is that the approach 'might encourage innovation, but would not necessarily lead to real reductions. The world might simply head for the abyss more efficiently'.[36] The implementation of Kyoto Lite, as was suggested in Chapter 6, is likely to be of little benefit to future generations of all countries, but may bring beneficial outcomes for existing and proximate generations in developed countries who will gain from very modest reductions in climate risks and relatively uncompromised economic growth.

The 'Kyoto Plus' regime (also known as 'son of Kyoto') is supported by the European Union and a range of other developed countries and non-governmental organisations, such as the International Climate Change Taskforce.[37] It would build on the existing architecture of the Kyoto Protocol – and the political, institutional, and intellectual resources that secured it – whilst making a range of modifications. It would, for example, require much deeper cuts of developed country parties (up to 30 per cent by 2030) and introduce a new system of mandatory, and voluntary, first-time targets for many developing countries, including the bigger emitters such as Brazil, China and India. The approach will also involve technology and financial resource transfer to developing countries.

The Kyoto Plus regime would come into effect as the present regime expires in 2012, and would initially cover emissions until at least 2030. Beyond this point, a set of longer-term objectives and mechanisms would be adopted congruent with the aim of avoiding dangerous climate change, and informed by the regular assessments of the IPCC. A crucial ingredient in the long-term development of the regime would be a move towards the principle that each person on the planet possesses an equal right to use the absorptive capacity of the atmosphere. However, this principle, which was first proposed by Anil Argawal and Sunita Narain,[38] is not intrinsic to the initial architecture of Kyoto Plus, which attempts to achieve cuts in greenhouse emissions based on an eclectic range of mechanisms and targets with no overriding ethical foundation other than avoiding dangerous climate change. Because the approach, on all interpretations, will involve significant cuts in developed country emissions, and real engagement of developing countries, it can be assumed that it would have a range of beneficial effects on human well-being relative to Kyoto Lite and would entice a number of critics of its predecessor back into the international climate regime.

The main problem with the Kyoto Plus proposal is its long-term efficacy. Because it would retain many structural features of the original Protocol – including provision for carbon trading and carbon sinks, as well as the setting of national emissions targets on the basis of case-by-case negotiation, rather than by scientifically led analyses of what levels of emissions the atmosphere can withstand – it is doubtful that it will significantly reduce the risks of dangerous climate change. It is, therefore, inconsistent with a broad range of distributive duties to future generations since much more could clearly be done to limit climate change. Moreover, while the approach maintains a much more even balance between considerations of equity and efficiency than Kyoto or Kyoto Lite, the emissions allocation process is designed to be open to adjustment by parties who enjoy radically unequal negotiating positions, with the result that the approach has intrinsically inequitable foundations. By contrast, what is needed is an architecture that does not delay the adoption of principles of equity or justice until more favourable conditions emerge, but rather adopts them in the first instance, albeit in the knowledge that it may take some time before a truly just distribution emerges.[39]

The third approach, 'contraction and convergence', is supported by a range of non-governmental organisations, such as the Global Commons Institute and EcoEquity, as well as a broad group of developing and developed countries, such as Switzerland and Mexico.[40] The approach, which we first met in Chapter 6, has three main components. First, each person on the planet is granted an equal right to emit carbon by virtue of their equal right to use the benefits provided by a shared atmosphere. This principle is treated as intrinsic to the architecture of the approach and not a longer-term aspiration as in the case of Kyoto Plus. Second, a 'global ceiling' for greenhouse emissions is set based on a calculation of the amount the global environment can withstand without dangerous climate change taking place. Third, each country is allocated a yearly 'carbon emissions budget' consistent with the global ceiling not being exceeded, and calculated according to each country's population size relative to an agreed base year.

The name of the approach comes from the notion that, over time, it aims to bring about a stabilisation, and later a *contraction*, in global greenhouse emissions so that they stay below a safe level; and that, in the longer term, developed and developing countries will *converge* on a roughly equal level of per capita emissions. Within this overall approach, a country that wants to emit more than its yearly quota must buy credits from countries that have spare capacity. The country selling the credits is then free to invest the receipts in activities enabling it to develop sustainably. An emissions mechanism is a key feature of all of the proposed successors to Kyoto, but in this version the trading zone covers the whole planet from the outset. The consequence is that Contraction and Convergence offers a unique mixture of equity and flexibility which does not seek a literal convergence in greenhouse emissions, but rather a convergence in the rights of all countries to make use of the atmospheric commons.[41]

Unlike a number of competing approaches, contraction and convergence, if fully implemented and complied with, could be expected to reduce the risks of dangerous climate change substantially, although it will not prevent many adverse impacts in the short- to medium-term. It also has the merit that, because it adopts emissions targets based on scientific criteria for protecting the atmosphere, it reduces the role of power politics in determining the structure of the regime. There is still a certain amount of political horse-trading associated with the selection of the base year – as well as with the specific details of mechanisms concerned with emissions trading, the role of sinks, and acceptable methods of taking CO_2 out of the atmosphere – but much less than with rival views.

It is not an easy matter to apply the distributive theories that have been examined in the book to the choice amongst Kyoto Lite, Kyoto Plus and Contraction and Convergence (or variations on these approaches). These theories are designed to operate in a wide range of, possibly all, circumstances and are constructed at a rather abstract level. Regimes designed to combat climate change, on the other hand, are neither abstract nor developed to solve all problems of distribution either within, or between, generations. Nevertheless, it is important to locate alternative climate regimes in the broader context of distributive justice since only a truly just regime will secure popular legitimacy and support in the longer term. There would be little point, then, of implementing a regime that proved to be effective at reducing the risks of dangerous climate change if the price for this was greater injustice within, or between, generations. In the following brief remarks, it is suggested that, at present, Contraction and Convergence is the most attractive approach to the climate problem. It is attractive on a large number of theories of the profile and currency of justice and raises no more problems than its rivals in terms of the scope of justice.

First, the Contraction and Convergence approach seems congruent with both 'contribution to problem' and 'ability to pay' arguments for differential responsibility, yet it does not depend on either of these for its essential justification. The approach does not assume that those that must make the biggest changes in their environmental practices were responsible for the climate problem either historically or contemporarily. Rather, it distributes the responsibilities of climate change abatement in terms of a scientific analysis of a sustainable future where dangerous climate change is avoided (the IPCC refers to this as 'Backcasting'[42]) and a principle of equality of usage of the atmosphere. Neither idea, however, is wholly reducible to the 'ability to pay' or 'contribution to problem' principles.

Second, the approach is at least as comfortable as its rivals with any of the plausible theories of the currency of justice that were examined in Chapter 3. Although much further research is needed in terms of the impact of climate change on the components of well-bring such as human health, Contraction and Convergence seems well suited to the promotion of existing and future welfare, resources, basic capabilities and midfare.

Third, the approach seems consistent with a range of theories of the profile of justice. It will be attractive to egalitarians, for example, as it will reduce inequalities between developing and developed countries, and between generations, relative to its rivals. It will also tend to improve, relative to rival approaches, the position of the worst off since research suggests strongly that very many of the worst off will be members of developing countries in a future world blighted by climate change.[43] Finally, it will be attractive to those who wish to bring as many people as possible to the point where they have enough since the measures it will introduce will benefit many millions of people in developed and developing countries who lead, or will lead, lives lacking in what is needed for a decent life without bringing more than a very limited number of people below the sufficiency level. There may, of course, be some members of developed countries who, for whatever reason, fall below the baseline of a dignified life as an indirect result of this tough approach to climate change. But this will be a feature of any approach to climate change, including doing nothing at all.

NOTES

1. Athanasiou and Baer, 2002, p. 41.
2. http://www.quotationspage.com/quote/28904.html
3. See, for example, Schwartz, 1978; Heyd, 1992, pp. 80ff.
4. See Fred Singer, 2000; Lomborg, 2001, pp. 300ff; and Michaels, 2004.
5. See, for example, de Shalit, 1995, pp. 13–50.
6. 'Summary for policymakers', IPCC, 1996a, p. 5.
7. See, for example, 'Technical summary', in IPCC, 2001b, pp. 21ff.
8. See, for example, McMichael et al., 1996a, pp. 561–84.
9. Jamieson, 2003, pp. 292–5.
10. Peter Singer, 2002, pp. 18–19.
11. See, for example, Peter Singer, 2002, pp. 32ff; Shue, 1999, pp. 531–45; Gardiner, 2004a, pp. 23–39; DeSombre, 2004, pp. 41–6; Gardiner, 2004b.
12. United Nations, 1995, Article 2, p. 5.
13. The argument has been developed recently by Shue, 1999, pp. 533–7; Peter Singer, 2002, pp. 27–34; and Gardiner, 2004b, pp. 578–83.
14. Banuri et al., 1996, pp. 94–5.
15. Prather et al., 2001, pp. 244–5.
16. World Resources Institute, 2003, p. 258.
17. World Resources Institute, 2003, p. 259.
18. Banuri et al., 1996, p. 94.
19. Singer, 2002, pp. 33–4.
20. A number of these are discussed in Shue, 1999, pp. 534ff; and Gardiner, 2004b, pp. 581ff; Beckerman and Pasek, 2001, pp. 180ff.
21. Singer, 2002, pp. 31–2; Gardiner, 2004b, pp. 579–80.
22. The distinction between a person 'being harmed' (which requires that they were made worse off than they would have been) and their experiencing a 'harmful condition' (which does not require this counterfactual test being met) is suggested in Feinberg, 1988, pp. 25ff. The idea of specific interests, which appeals to a notion of 'harmful condition' to solve non-identity cases, was first developed in Woodward, 1986.
23. Shue, 1999, p. 537.
24. Speech to the National Oceanic and Atmospheric Administration, Silver Spring, Maryland, 14 February 2002 (available at: http://www.whitehouse.gov/news/releases/2002/02/20020214-5.html).

25. Shue, 1999, pp. 540–41.
26. Fred Pearce, 2005b, p. 12.
27. These are usefully summarised in Grubb et al., 1999, pp. 155ff.
28. Gardiner provides a useful critical review of Kyoto in Gardiner, 2004a, pp. 23–39.
29. The continued hostility of the US administration to the Kyoto Protocol was underlined at July 2005 Gleneagles G8 summit. The summit, which involves countries responsible for 65 per cent of global GDP and 47 per cent of current global CO_2 emissions, failed to generate a roadmap towards a replacement for Kyoto or even a strong statement of support for the limited greenhouse reduction measures required by it. Instead, the Protocol was mentioned just once in the G8's final communiqué which commented merely that 'Those of us who have ratified the Kyoto Protocol welcome its entry into force and will work to make it a success' (The Gleneagles Communiqué (Gleneagles, G8, 2005), p. 2 (available online at: http://www.g8.utoronto.ca/summit/2005gleneagles/communique.pdf).
30. For a discussion of the Australian Government's approach to Kyoto, see McDonald, 2005.
31. Wigley, 1998.
32. Lomborg, 2001, p. 302.
33. Gardiner, 2004a, p. 34.
34. Article 2, *Kyoto Protocol to the United Nations Framework Convention on Climate Change*, in Grubb et al., 1999, p. 281; and United Nations, 1995, Article 2, p. 4.
35. See Richard Black, 'New climate plan "to rival Kyoto"', *BBC News Online*, Wednesday 27 July 2005 (http://news.bbc.co.uk/1/hi/sci/tech/4721449.stm).
36. Fred Pearce, 2005b, p. 13.
37. See, for example, Hamilton et al., 2005, pp. 1–14; and International Climate Change Taskforce, 2005, pp. 1–26.
38. Argawal and Narain, 1991.
39. Shue, 1992; and Paterson, 1996.
40. See, for example, Athanasiou and Baer, 2002, pp. 47ff; Meyer, 2000, pp. 56ff; Baer et al., 2001, p. 828.
41. Athanasiou and Baer, 2002, p. 84.
42. Banuri and Weyant, 2001, p. 96.
43. See 'Technical summary: impacts, adaptation and vulnerability', IPCC, 2001b, pp. 44ff; and Banuri et al., 1996, pp. 97ff.

References

Adams, Robert M. (1979) 'Existence, self-interest, and the problem of evil', *Nous*, **13**, pp. 53–65.

Addison, Joseph (1714) *The Spectator*, Friday 20 August, reprinted in Donald F. Bond (ed.) (1968) *The Spectator* (Oxford: Clarendon Press), pp. 592–5.

Agarwal, A.A. and Narain, S. (1991) *Global Warming in an Unequal World: A Case of Environmental Colonialism* (New Delhi: Centre for Science and Environment).

Aguado, Edward and Burt, James E. (1999) *Understanding Weather and Climate* (New Jersey: Prentice Hall).

Ahrens, C. Donald (2000) *Meteorology Today: An Introduction to Weather, Climate and the Environment* (Pacific Grove, CA: Brooks/Cole).

Anderson, Elizabeth (1999) 'What is the point of equality?', *Ethics*, **109**, pp. 287–337.

Arendt, Hannah (1961) *Between Past and Future: Six Essays on Political Thought* (London: Faber).

Aristotle (1953) *Nichomachean Ethics* (translated by J. Thomson) (London: Penguin).

Aristotle (1962) *Meteorologica* (translated by H.D.P. Lee) (Cambridge, MA: Loeb).

Arnell, Nigel and Liu, Chunzhen (2001) 'Hydrololgy and water reources', in James J. McCarthy et al. (eds) *Climate Change 2001: Impacts, Adaptation, and Vulnerability* (Cambridge: Cambridge University Press), pp. 191–233.

Arneson, Richard (1982) 'The principle of fairness and free-rider problems', *Ethics*, **92**, pp. 616–33.

Arneson, Richard (1989) 'Equality and equal opportunity for welfare', *Philosophical Studies*, **56**, pp. 77–93.

Arneson, Richard (1995) 'Equality', in Robert E. Goodin and Philip Petit (eds) *A Companion to Contemporary Political Philosophy* (Oxford: Blackwell), pp. 489–507.

Arneson, Richard (1997) 'Egalitarianism and the undeserving poor', *The Journal of Political Philosophy*, **5**(4), pp. 327–50.

Arneson, Richard (1999) 'Human flourishing versus desire satisfaction', *Social Philosophy and Policy*, **16**(1), Winter, pp. 113–42.

Arneson, Richard (2000a) 'Luck, egalitarianism and prioritarianism', *Ethics*, **110**, January, pp. 339–49.

Arneson, Richard (2000b) 'Perfectionism and politics', *Ethics*, **111**, pp. 37–63.

Arneson, Richard (2002) 'Review of sovereign virtue', *Ethics*, **112**, pp. 367–71.

Arrhenius, Svante (1896) 'On the influence of carbonic acid in the air upon the temperature of the ground', *Philosophical Magazine*, **41**, pp. 237–76.

Arrow, K.J., Cline, R., Maler, K-G. Munasinghe, M., Squitieri, R. and Stigliz, J.E. (1996) 'Intertemporal equity, discounting, and economic efficiency', in James Bruce et al. (eds) *Climate change 1995: Economic and Social Dimensions of Climate Change* (Cambridge: Cambridge University Press), pp. 125–44.

Athanasiou, Tom and Baer, Paul (2002) *Dead Heat: Global Justice and Global Warming* (New York: Seven Stories Press).

Attfield, Robin (2003) *Environmental Ethics* (Oxford: Polity).

Azar, Christian and Lindgren, Kristian (2003) 'Catastrophic events and stichastic cost–benefit analysis of climate change', *Climatic Change*, **56**, pp. 245–55.

Baer, Paul et al. (2000) 'Equity and greenhouse gas responsibility', *Science*, **289**, 29 September, p. 2287.

Baer, Paul et al. (2001) 'Response to Arthur H. Westing', *Science*, **291**, 2 February, p. 828.

Baier, Annette (1981) 'The rights of past and future persons', in E. Partridge (ed.) *Responsibilities to Future Generations*, (Buffalo: Prometheus Books), pp. 171–83.

Banuri, T., Göran-Mäler, K., Grubb, M., Jacobson, H.K. and Yamin, F. (1996) 'Equity and Social Considerations', in James Bruce et al. (eds) *Climate Change 1995: Economic and Social Dimensions of Climate Change* (Cambridge: Cambridge University Press), pp. 79–124.

Banuri, Tarqi and Weyant, John (2001) 'Setting the stage: climate change and sustainable development', in Bert Metz, Ogundlade Davidson, Rob Swart and Jiahua Pan (eds) (2001) *Climate Change 2001: Mitigation* (Cambridge: Cambridge University Press), pp. 73–114.

Barnett, J. and Adger, W.N. (2003) 'Climate dangers and atoll countries', *Climate Change*, **61**, pp. 321–37.

Barry, Brian (1977) 'Justice between generations', in P.M.S. Hacker and J. Raz (eds) *Law, Morality and Society: Essays in Honour of H.L.A. Hart* (Oxford: Clarendon Press), pp. 268–84.

Barry, Brian (1989a) 'Justice as reciprocity', in B. Barry *Democracy, Power and Justice* (Oxford, Clarendon), pp. 463–93.

Barry, Brian (1989b) 'The ethics of resource depletion', in B. Barry *Democracy, Power and Justice* (Oxford, Clarendon), pp. 511–28.

Barry, Brian (1989c) *Theories of Justice* (Hemel Hempstead: Havester-Wheatsheaf).

Barry, Brian (1995) *Justice as Impartiality* (Oxford: Oxford University Press).

Barry, Brian (1996) 'Contractual justice: a modest defence', *Utilitas*, **8**, pp. 357–80.

Barry, Brian (1999) 'Sustainability and intergenerational justice', in Andrew Dobson (ed.) *Fairness and Futurity* (Oxford: Oxford University Press), pp. 93–107.

Barry, Brian (2005) *Why Social Justice Matters* (London: Polity).

Barry, John (1999) *Environment and Social Theory* (London: Routledge).

Beck, Ulrich (1992) *Risk Society: Towards a New Modernity* (London: Sage).

Becker, Lawrence (1986) *Reciprocity* (London: Routledge).

Beckerman, Wilfrid (1995) *Small is Stupid: Blowing The Whistle on the Greens* (London: Duckworth).

Beckerman, Wilfrid, (1999) 'Sustainability and intergenerational equality', in Andrew Dobson (ed.) *Fairness and Futurity* (Oxford: Oxford University Press), pp. 71–92.

Beckerman, Wilfrid and Pasek, Joanna (2001) *Justice, Posterity and the Environment* (Oxford: Oxford University Press).

Beckett, Margaret (2003) 'A stitch in time: UN action to tackle climate change', *New Economy*, **10**(3), September, pp. 155–60.

Bell, Derek (2002) 'How can political liberals be environmentalists', *Political Studies*, **50**(4), pp. 703–24.

Bentham, Jeremy (1962) 'An introduction to the principles of morals and legislation', Chapters 1–5 in Mary Warnock (ed.) *Utilitarianism* (London: Fontana), pp. 33–58.

Berlin, Isaiah (1969) *Four Essays on Liberty* (Oxford: Oxford University Press).

Bernstein, L. et al. (2002) *Climate Science and Policy: Making the Connection* (Cambridge: European Science and Environment Forum).

Bijlsma, L. et al. (1996) 'Coastal zones and small islands', in R.T. Watson et al. (eds) *Climate Change 1995: Impacts, Adaptations, and Mitigation of Climate Change* (Cambridge: Cambridge University Press), pp. 289–324.

Binmore, Kenneth (1998) *Game Theory and the Social Contract Volume 2: Just Playing* (London: MIT Press).

Bowles, Samuel, Boyd, Robert and Fehr, Ernst (2005) *Moral Sentiments and Material Interests: The Foundations of Cooperation in Economic Life* (Boston: MIT Press).

Brighouse, Harry (2004) *Justice* (Oxford: Polity).

Brown Weiss, Edith (1990) 'Our rights and obligations to future generations for the environment', *The American Journal of International Law*, **84**(1), January, pp. 198–207.

Brown Weiss, Edith (1992) *In Fairness to Future Generations: International Law, Common Patrimony* (Tokyo: United Nations University).

Brown, Campbell (2003), 'Giving up levelling down', *Economics and Philosophy*, **19**, 2003, pp. 111–34.

Bruce, James P., Lee, Hoesung and Haites, Erik F. (eds) (1996) *Climate Change 1995: Economic and Social Dimensions of Climate Change* (Cambridge: Cambridge University Press).

Buchanan, Allen (1990) 'Justice as reciprocity versus subject-centred justice', *Philosophy and Public Affairs*, **19**(3), Summer, pp. 227–52.

Buchanan, Allen (1991) *Secession* (Oxford: Westview Press)

Buchanan, Allen (1994) 'Liberalism and group rights', in Jules L. Coleman and Allen Buchanan (eds) *In Harm's Way: Essays in Honour of Joel Feinberg* (Cambridge: Cambridge University Press), pp. 1–15.

Buchanan, Allen, Brock, Dan W., Daniels, Norman and Wikler, Daniel (2002) *From Chance to Choice: Genetics and Justice* (Cambridge: Cambridge University Press).

Burke, Edmund (1968) *Reflections on the Revolution in France* (London: Penguin).

Burley, Justine (ed.) (2004) *Dworkin and His Critics* (Oxford: Blackwell).

Cabasch, U. and Meehl, G.A. et al. (2001) 'Projections of future climate change', in John T. Houghton et al. (eds) *Climate Change 2001: The Scientific Basis* (Cambridge: Cambridge University Press), pp. 525–82.

Callahan, Joan C. (1987) 'On harming the dead', *Ethics*, **97**, pp. 341–52.

Callendar, G.S. (1938) 'The artificial production of carbon dioxide and its influence on climate', *Quarterly Journal of the Royal Meteorological Society*, **64**, pp. 223–40.

Callicott, John B. (1989) *In Defense of the Land Ethic* (Albany: State University of New York Press).

Callicott, John B. (2003) 'The land ethic', in Dale Jamieson (ed.), *A Companion to Environmental Philosophy* (Oxford: Blackwell), pp. 204–17.

Caney, Simon (2005) *Justice Beyond Borders* (Oxford: Oxford University Press).

Carter, Alan (2001) 'Can we harm future people?', *Environmental Values*, **10**, pp. 429–54.

Carter, Alan (2002) 'On harming others: a response to Partridge', *Environmental Values*, **11**, pp. 87–96.

Casal, Paula (1999) 'Environmentalism, procreation, and the principle of fairness', *Public Affairs Quarterly*, **13**, pp. 363–76.

Casal, Paula and Williams, Andrew (2004) 'Equality of resources and procreative justice', in Justine Burley (ed.) *Dworkin and His Critics* (Oxford: Blackwell), pp. 150–69.

Cohen, G.A. (1989) 'On the currency of egalitarian justice', *Ethics*, **99**, July, pp. 906–44.

Cohen, G.A. (1993) 'Equality of what? On welfare, goods, and capabilities', in Martha Nussbaum and Amartya Sen (eds) *The Quality of Life* (Oxford: Oxford University Press), pp. 9–29.

Cohen, G.A. (2001) *If You're an Egalitarian, How Come You're So Rich* (Cambridge, MA: Harvard University Press).

Cohen, G.A. (2004) 'Expensive taste rides again', in J. Burley (ed.) *Dworkin and His Critics* (Oxford: Blackwell), pp. 3–29.

Commonwealth Secretariat (1997) *A Future for Small States: Overcoming Vulnerability* (London: Commonwealth Secretariat).

Cotton, William R. and Pielke, Roger A. (1995) *Human Impacts on Weather and Climate* (Cambridge: Cambridge University Press).

Cox, Peter M. et al. (2000) 'Acceleration of global warming due to carbon-cycle feedbacks in a coupled climate model', *Nature*, **408**, 9 November, pp. 184–7.

Crisp, Roger (2003a) 'Egalitarianism and compassion', *Ethics*, **114**, October, pp. 119–26.

Crisp, Roger (2003b) 'Equality, priority, and compassion', *Ethics*, **113**, July, pp. 754–63.

Cullity, Garett (1995) 'Moral free-riding', *Philosophy and Public Affairs*, **24**, pp. 3–34.

Daniels, Norman (1996) *Justice and Justification: Reflective Equilibrium in Theory and Practice* (Cambridge: Cambridge University Press).

Dasgupta, Partha (2001) *Human Well-Being and the Natural Environment* (Oxford: Oxford University Press).

De George, Richard T. (1979) 'The environment, rights and future generations' in E. Goodpaster and K.M. Sayre (eds) *Ethics and Problems of the 21st Century* (Notre Dame: University of Notre Dame Press), pp. 93–105.

del Ninno, C., Derush, P.A., Smith, L.C. and Roy, P.K. (2001) *The 1998 Floods in Bangladesh: Disaster, Impacts, Household Coping Strategies, and Responses* (Washington DC: International Food Policy Research Institute).

Department of the Environment (1996) *Review of the Potential Effects of Climate Change in the United Kingdom* (London: HMSO Books).

Department of the Environment (1997) *Climate Change: The UK Programme* (London: HMSO Books) February.

Department of Health (2001) *Health Effects of Climate Change in the United Kingdom* (London: Department of Health), pp. 70ff.

de Shalit, Avner (1990) 'Bargaining with the not-yet-born', *International Journal of Moral Social Studies*, **5**(3), Autumn, pp. 221–34.

de Shalit, Avner (1992) 'Community and the rights of future generations', *Journal of Applied Philosophy*, **9**(1), pp. 105–15.

de Shalit, Avner (1995) *Why Posterity Matters* (London: Routledge).

DeSombre, Elizabeth R. (2004) 'Global warming: more common than tragic', *Ethics and International Affairs*, **18**(1), pp. 41–6.

Douglas, Mary et al. (1998) 'Human needs and wants', in Steve Rayner and Elizabeth Malone (eds) *Human Choices and Climate Change Volume 1: The Societal Framework* (Columbus: Batelle Press), pp. 195–264.

Dworkin, Ronald (1981a) 'What is equality? Part 1: equality of welfare', *Philosophy and Public Affairs*, **10**(3), pp. 185–246.

Dworkin, Ronald (1981b) 'What is equality?: Part 2: equality of resources', *Philosphy and Public Affairs*, **10**(4), pp. 283–345.

Dworkin, Ronald (2000) *Sovereign Virtue: The Theory and Practice of Equality* (Cambridge, MA: Harvard University Press).

Dworkin, Ronald (2002) '*Sovereign Virtue* Revisited', *Ethics*, **113**, October, pp. 106–43.

Elliot, Robert (1989) 'The rights of future people', *Journal of Applied Philosophy*, **6**(2), pp. 159–69.

Elliot, Robert (1995a) 'Faking nature', in Robert Elliot (ed.) *Environmental Ethics* (Oxford: Oxford University Press), pp. 76–88.

Elliot, Robert (1995b) 'Introduction', in Robert Elliot (ed.) *Environmental Ethics* (Oxford: Oxford University Press).

Elliot, Robert (2001) 'Normative ethics', in Dale Jamieson (ed.) *A Companion to Environmental Philosophy* (Oxford: Blackwell), pp. 177–91.

English, Jane (1977) 'Justice between generations', *Philosophical Studies*, **31**, pp. 91–104.

European Environment Agency (2004) *Impact of Europe's Changing Climate* (Luxembourg: Office for Official Publications of the European Union).

Fagan, Brian (2002) *The Little Ice Age: How Climate Made History 1300–1850* (New York: Basic Books).

Fagan, Brian (2004) *The Long Summer: How Climate Changed Civilization* (London: Granta Books).

Feinberg, Joel (1980) 'The rights of animals and unborn generations' in J. Feinberg (ed.) *Rights, Justice and The Bounds of Liberty* (Princeton: Princeton University Press), pp. 159–84.

Feinberg, Joel (1988) *Harmless Wrongdoing* (Oxford: Oxford University Press).

Ferguson, Kitty (2002) *Tycho and Kepler: The Strange Partnership that Revolutionised Astronomy* (London: Review).

Fishkin, James S. (1991) 'Justice between generations', in John Chapman (ed.) *Nomos XXXIII: Compensatory Justice* (New York: New York University Press), pp. 85–96.

Foster, K.R. (2000) 'Science and the precautionary principle', *Science*, 12 May, pp. 979–81.

Fourier, Jean Baptiste (1824) 'Remarques Générales Sur Les Températures Du Globe Terrestre Et Des Espaces Planetaire', *Annales de Chemie et de Physique*, **27**, pp. 136–67.

Frankfurt, Harry (1987) 'Equality as a moral ideal', *Ethics*, **98**, October, pp. 21–43.

Frankfurt, Harry (1997) 'Equality and respect', *Social Research*, **64**, pp. 3–13.

Friis-Christensen, E. and Lassen, K. (1991) 'Length of the solar cycle: an indicator of solar activity closely associated with climate', *Science*, **254**, pp. 698–700.

Gardiner, Stephen M. (2004a) 'The global warming tragedy and the dangerous illusion of the Kyoto Protocol', *Ethics and International Affairs*, **18**(1), pp. 23–39

Gardiner, Stephen M. (2004b) 'Ethics and global climate change', *Ethics*, **114**, pp. 555–600.

Gauthier, David (1986) *Morals by Agreement* (Oxford: Clarendon Press).

Gauthier, David (1990a) *Moral Dealing: Contract, Ethics, and Reason* (Ithaca: Cornell University Press).

Gauthier, David (1990b) 'Thomas Hobbes: moral theorist', in D. Gauthier *Moral Dealing: Contract, Ethics, and Reason* (Ithaca: Cornell University Press), pp. 11–23.

Gintis, Herbert (2000) 'Strong reciprocity and human sociality', *Journal of Theoretical Biology*, **206**, pp. 169–79

Gitay, Habiba, Brown, Sandra, Esterling, William and Jallow, Bubu (2001) 'Ecosystems and their goods and services', in James J. McCarthy et al. (eds) *Climate Change 2001: Impacts, Adaptation, and Vulnerability* (Cambridge: Cambridge University Press), pp. 235–342.

Glover, Jonathan (1977) *Causing Death and Saving Lives* (London: Penguin).

Goodin, Robert (1985) *Protecting the Vulnerable* (Chicago: University of Chicago).

Goodin, Robert (1992) *Green Political Theory* (Cambridge: Polity).

Griffin, James (1986) *Well-Being* (Oxford: Oxford University Press).

Griffin, James (1996) *Value Judgement* (Oxford: Oxford University Press).

Grove, Jean M. (1988) *The Little Ice Age* (London: Methuen).

Grover, Dorothy (1987) 'Posthumous harm', *The Philosophical Quarterly*, **39**, (156) pp. 334–53.

Grubb, Michael, with Christian Vrolijk and Duncan Brack (1999) *The Kyoto Protocol* (London: Earthscan).

Haines, A. and Patz, J. (2004) 'Health effects of climate change', *Journal of the American Medical Association*, **291**, pp. 99–103.

Hales, S., Edwards, S.J. and Kovats, R.S (2003) 'Impacts on health of climate extremes' in A.J. McMichael et al. (eds) *Climate Change and Human Health: Risks and Responses* (Geneva: World Health Organisation), pp. 79–102.

Hamilton, Clive, Sherrard, Justin and Tate, Alan (2005) *Climate Change Policy Beyond Kyoto: A New Global Plan* (Canberra: Australia Institute).

Hardy, John T. (2004) *Climate Change: Causes, Effects, and Solutions* (Chichester: Wiley).

Harremoës, Paul et al. (2002) *The Precautionary Principle in the 20th Century* (London: Earthscan).

Hart, H.L.A. (1955) 'Are there any natural rights', *Philosophical Review*, **64**(2), April, pp. 175–91.

Hartney, Michael (1995) 'Some confusions concerning collective rights', in Will Kymlicka (ed.) *The Rights of Minority Cultures* (Oxford: Oxford University Press), pp. 202–27.

Hecht, Jeff (2005) 'Record-breaking fourth hurricane hits Florida', *New Scientist*, 27 September (http://www.newscientist.com/article.ns?id=dn6446).

Heyd, David (1992) *Genethics* (Berkeley: University of California Press).

Hobbes, Thomas (1968) *Leviathan* (London: Penguin).

Honderich, Ted (1976) *Three Essays on Political Violence* (Oxford: Blackwell).

Honderich, Ted (1989) *Violence for Equality* (London: Routledge).

Houghton, John (2004) *Global Warming: The Complete Briefing (3rd edition)* (Cambridge: Cambridge University Press).

Houghton, J., Jenkins, G.J. and Ephraums, J.J. (eds) (1990) *Climate Change: The IPCC Assessment* (Cambridge: Cambridge University Press).

Houghton, J.T., Ding, Y., Griggs, D.J., Noguer, M., van der Linden, P.J., Dai, X., Maskell, K. and Johnson, C.A. (eds) (2001) *Climate Change 2001: The Scientific Basis* (Cambridge: Cambridge University Press).

Houghton, J.T., Meira-Filho, L.G., Callander, B.A., Harris, N., Kattenberg, A. and Maskell, K. (eds) (1996) *Climate Change 1995: The Science of Climate Change* (Cambridge: Cambridge University Press).

Howarth, Richard B. (1992) 'Intergenerational justice and the chain of obligation', *Environmental Values*, **1**, pp. 133–40.

Hubin, D. Clayton (1976) 'Justice between generations', *Philosophy and Public Affairs*, **6**, Summer, pp. 70–83.

Hulme, M., Turnpenny, J. and Jenkins, G. (2002) *Climate Change Scenarios for the United Kingdom: The UKCIP02 Briefing Report* (Norwich: Tyndall Centre for Climate Change Research)

Hurka, Thomas (1993) *Perfectionism* (New York: Oxford University Press).

International Climate Change Taskforce (2005) *Meeting the Climate Challenge* (London: Institute for Public Policy Research).

IPCC (Intergovernmental Panel on Climate Change) (1996a), see J.T. Houghton et al. (1996).

IPCC (1996b), see Robert T. Watson et al. (1996).

IPCC (1996c), see James P. Bruce et al. (1996).

IPCC (2001a), see J.T. Houghton et al. (2001).

IPCC (2001b), see James J. McCarthy et al. (2001).

IPCC (2001c), see Bert Metz et al. (2001).

James, Oliver (1997) *Britain on the Couch* (London: Century).

Jamieson, Dale (1993) 'Method and moral theory', in Peter Singer (ed.) *A Companion to Ethics* (Oxford: Blackwell), pp. 476–87.

Jamieson, Dale (2001) 'Climate change and global environmental justice', in Clark Miller and Paul N. Edward (eds) *Changing the Atmosphere: Expert Knowledge and Environmental Governance* (Boston: MIT Press), pp. 287–308.

Jamieson, Dale (2003) 'Ethics, public policy, global warming', in *Morality's Progress: Essays on Humans, Other Animals, and the Rest of Nature* (Oxford: Clarendon Press), pp. 282–95.

Johnson, Lawrence E. (2003) 'Future generations and contemporary ethics', *Environmental Values*, **12**, pp. 471–87.

Jones, Nicola (2003) 'Europe's weird weather warms debate', *New Scientist*, 5 August.

Jones, Peter (1994) *Rights* (London: Macmillan).

Jones, Peter (1999) 'Human rights, groups, rights and people's rights', *Human Rights Quarterly*, **2**(1), pp. 80ff.

Kavka, Gregory (1986) *Hobbesian Moral and Political Theory* (Princeton: Princeton University Press).

Keeling, C.D. and Whorf, T.P. (2004) 'Atmospheric CO_2 records from sites in the SIO air sampling network', in *Trends: A Compendium of Data on Global Change* (Oak Ridge, TN: US Department of Energy) (http://cdiac.esd.ornl.gov/trands/emis/em_cont.htm).

Kepler, Johannes (1966) (edited and translated by Colin Hardie) *The Six-Cornered Snowflake* (Oxford: Clarendon).

Kitcher, Philip (2002) 'Creating perfect people', in Justine Burley and John Harris (eds) *A Companion to Genethics* (Oxford: Blackwell), pp. 229–42.

Kraut, Roger (1979) 'Two concepts of happiness', *The Philosophical Review*, **88**(2), April, pp. 167–97.

Kumar, Rahul (2003) 'Who can be wronged?', *Philosophy and Public Affairs*, **31**(2), pp. 99–118.

Kymlicka, Will (1989) *Liberalism, Community and Culture* (Oxford: Oxford University Press).

Kymlicka, Will (1990a) *Contemporary Political Philosophy* (Oxford: Oxford University Press).

Kymlicka, Will (1990b) 'Two Theories of Justice', *Inquiry*, **33**, pp. 99–119.

Kymlicka, Will (1995) *Multicultural Citizenship* (Oxford: Oxford University Press).

Laslett, Peter (1992) 'Is there a generational contract?' in P. Laslett and J.S. Fishkin (eds), *Justice Between Age Groups and Generations* (New Haven: Yale University Press), pp. 24–47.

Laut, Peter (2003) 'Solar activity and terrestrial climate: an analysis of some purported correlations', *Journal of Atmospheric and Solar Terrestrial Physics* **65**, pp. 801–12.

Layard, Richard (1980) 'Human satisfactions and public policy', *Economic Journal*, **90**, pp. 737–50.

Layard, Richard (2005) *Happiness: Lessons from a New Science* (London: Allen Lane).

Leopold, Aldo (1949) *A Sand County Almanac with Other Essays on Conservation from Round River* (Oxford: Oxford University Press).

Levenbrook, Barbara B. (1984) 'Harming someone after his death', *Ethics*, **94**, pp. 407–19.

Levy, Neil (2002) 'The apology paradox and the non-identity problem', *The Philosophical Quarterly*, **52**, July, pp. 358–68.

Liepert, Beate G. (2002) 'Observed reductions of surface solar radiation at sites in the US and worldwide', *Geophysical Research Letters*, **29**, pp. 1421–33.

Lomborg, Bjørn (2001) *The Skeptical Environmentalist: Measuring the Real State of the World* (Cambridge: Cambridge University Press).

Lomborg, Bjørn (2004) 'First things first', *New Scientist*, **184**, October, p. 23.

Macklin, Ruth (1981) 'Can future generations correctly be said to have rights?' in Ernest Partridge (ed.) *Responsibilities to Future Generations* (Buffalo: Prometheus Books), pp. 151–5.

Markandya, Anil and Halsnaes, Kirsten et al. (2001) 'Costing methodologies', in Bert Metz, Ogundlade Davidson, Rob Swart and Jiahua Pan (eds) *Climate Change 2001: Mitigation* (Cambridge: Cambridge University Press), pp. 451–95.

Marmor, Andrei (2003) 'Intrinsic value of economic equality', in Lukas Meyer, Stanley L. Paulson and Thomas W. Pogge (eds) *Rights, Culture and the Law: Themes from the Legal and Political Philosophy of Joseph Raz* (Oxford: Oxford University Press), pp. 127–41.

Marshall, Peter (1993) 'Thinking for tomorrow', *Journal of Applied Philosophy*, **10**(1), pp. 105–13.

Maugham, W. Somerset (1971) *Of Human Bondage* (London: Pan Books).

McCarthy, James J., Canziani, Osvaldo F., Leary, Neil A., Dokken, David J. and White, Kasey S. (eds) (2001) *Climate Change 2001: Impacts, Adaptation, and Vulnerability* (Cambridge: Cambridge University Press).

McCormick, M. Patrick, Thomason, Larry W. and Trepte, Charles R. (1995) 'Atmospheric effects of the Mt Pinatubo eruption', *Nature*, **373**, 2 February, pp. 399–404.

McDonald, Matt (2005) 'Fair weather friend? Ethics and Australia's approach to global climate change', *Australian Journal of Politics and History*, **51**(2), June, pp. 216–34.

McMahan, Jefferson (1981) 'Problems with population policy', *Ethics*, **92**, October, pp. 96–127.

McMichael, A.J. et al. (1996a) 'Human population health', in Robert T. Watson, Rmarufu C. Zinyowera, Richard H. Moss and David J. Dokken (eds) *Climate Change 1995: Impacts, Adaptations, and Mitigation of Climate Change* (Cambridge: Cambridge University Press), pp. 561–84.

McMichael, A.J., Haines, A., Sloof, R. and Kovats, S. (eds) (1996b) *Climate Change and Human Health* (Geneva: World Health Organisation).

McMichael, Anthony and Githeko, Andrew et al. (2001) 'Human health', in James J. McCarthy et al. (eds) (2001) *Climate Change 2001: Impacts, Adaptation, and Vulnerability* (Cambridge: Cambridge University Press), pp. 451–85.

McMichael, A.J., Campbell-Lendum, D.H., Corvalan, C.F., Ebi, K.L., Githeko, A., Scheraga, J.D. and Woodward, A. (2003) (eds) *Climate Change and Human Health: Risks and Responses* (Geneva: World Health Organisation).

Metz, Bert, Davidson, Ogundlade, Swart, Rob and Pan, Jiahua (eds) (2001) *Climate Change 2001: Mitigation* (Cambridge: Cambridge University Press).

Meyer, Aubrey (2000) *Contraction & Convergence. The Global Solution to Climate Change* (Totnes: Green Books).

Meyer, Lukas (2004) 'Compensating wrongless historical emissions of greenhouse gases', *Ethical Perspectives*, **11**(1), pp. 20–35.

Michaels, Patrick (2004) *Meltdown: The Predictable Distortion of Global Warming by Scientists, Politicians and the Media* (Washington DC: Cato Institute).

Michaels, Patrick and Balling, Robert C. (2000) *The Satanic Gases: Clearing the Air About Global Warming* (Washington DC: Cato Institute).

Milankovitch, Milutin (1920) *Theorie Mathematique des Phenomenes Thermiques produits par la Radiation Solaire* (Paris: Gauthier-Villars).

Mill, J.S. (1974) *On Liberty* (London: Penguin).

Miller, H.I. and Conko, G. (2001) 'The perils of precaution', *Policy Review*, **107**, June/July (http://www.policyreview.org).

Mirrlees, James (1980) 'An exploration in the theory of optimum income taxation', *Review of Economic Studies*, **38**, pp. 175–208.

Mirza, M.M.Q., Warrick, R.D. and Erickson, N.J. (2003) 'The implications of climate change on floods of the Ganges, Brahmaputra and Meghna rivers in Bangladesh', *Climatic Change*, **57**, pp. 287–318.

Mitchell, J.F.B. and Karoly, D.J. et al. (2001) 'Detection of climate change and attribution of causes', in John T. Houghton et al. (eds) *Climate Change 2001: The Scientific Basis* (Cambridge: Cambridge University Press), pp. 695–738.

Morris, Christopher W. and Epstein, Arthur (eds) (2001) *Practical Rationality and Preference: Essays for David Gauthier* (Cambridge: Cambridge University Press).

Nagel, Thomas (1979) *Mortal Questions* (New York: Oxford University Press).

Narveson, Jan (1991) 'Gauthier on distributive justice and the natural baseline', in Peter Vallentine (ed.) *Contractarianism and Rational Choice: Essays on David Gauthier's Morals by Agreement* (Cambridge: Cambridge University Press), pp. 127–48.

Narveson, Jan (2002) 'Liberty and equality – a question of balance?', in Tibor Machan (ed.) *Liberty and Equality* (Washington DC: Hoover Institution Press, 2002), pp. 35–59.

Nozick, Robert (1974) *Anarchy, State and Utopia* (New York: Basic Books).

Nurse, Leonard A. and Sem, Graham et al. (2001) 'Small island states', in James J. McCarthy et al. (eds) *Climate Change 2001: Impacts, Adaptation, and Vulnerability* (Cambridge: Cambridge University Press), pp. 843–75.

Nussbaum, Martha (1999) 'Women and cultural universals', in M. Nussbaum, *Sex and Social Justice* (Oxford: Oxford University Press), pp. 29–54.

Nussbaum, Martha (2000a) 'Aristotle, politics and human capabilities: a response to Anthony, Arneson, Charlesworth, and Mulgan', *Ethics*, **111**, October, pp. 102–40.

Nussbaum, Martha (2000b) *Women and Human Development: The Capabilities Approach* (Cambridge: Cambridge University Press), 4–15; 70–96.

Nussbaum, Martha (2001) 'Adaptive preferences and women's options', *Economics and Philosophy*, **17**(1), pp. 67–88.

Okin, Susan (1989) 'Reason and feeling in thinking about justice', *Ethics*, **99**(2), pp. 229–49.

O'Neill, John (1993) 'Future generations: present harms', *Philosophy*, **68**, January, pp. 35–51.

O'Neill, John (1995a) 'Future generations: present harms', *Philosophy*, **68**, January, pp. 35ff.

O'Neill, John (1995b) *Ecology, Politics and Policy* (London: Routledge).

O'Neill, John (2001) 'Meta-ethics', in Dale Jamieson (ed.) *A Companion to Environmental Philosophy* (Oxford: Blackwell), pp. 163–76.

O'Neill, Onora (1996) *Towards Justice and Virtue* (Cambridge: Cambridge University Press).

O'Neill, Onora (2000) *Bounds of Justice* (Cambridge: Cambridge University Press).

Oliver, John E. and Fairbridge, Rhodes W. (eds) (1987) *The Encyclopaedia of Climatology* (New York: Van Nostrand Reinhold).

Oreskes, Naomi (2004) 'The scientific consensus on climate change', *Science*, **306**, p. 1686.

Overy, Richard (1997) *Russia's War* (London: Penguin).

Paden, Roger (1996) 'Reciprocity and international justice', *Public Affairs Quarterly*, **10**(3), July, pp. 249–66.

Page, Edward (1998) *Intergenerational Justice and Climate Change* (Coventry: University of Warwick).

Page, Edward (1999) 'Intergenerational justice and climate change', *Political Studies*, **47**(1), pp. 53–66.

Page, Edward (2000) 'Justice between generations and the problem of posthumous harm', *Keele Research Paper*, **26** (Keele: Keele University).

Page, Talbot (1983) 'Intergenerational justice as opportunity', in Douglas Maclean and Peter Brown (eds) *Energy and the Future* (New Jersey: Rowman and Littlefield), pp. 38–58.

Parfit, Derek (1976) 'Rights, interests and possible people', in Samuel Gorowitz et al. (eds) *Moral Problems of Medicine* (New Jersey: Prentice-Hall), pp. 369–75.

Parfit, Derek (1984) *Reasons and Persons* (Oxford: Oxford University Press).

Parfit, Derek (1986) 'Comments', *Ethics*, **96**, pp. 832–72.

Parfit, Derek (1995) 'Lindley lecture: equality or priority?' (Kansas: University of Kansas), pp. 1–43.

Parfit, Derek (1998) 'Equality and priority', in Andrew Mason (ed.) *Ideals of Equality* (Oxford: Blackwell), pp. 1–20.

Parfit, Derek (2000) 'Equality or priority?', in Matthew Clayton and Andrew Williams (eds) *The Ideal of Equality* (London: Palgrave), pp. 81–125.

Partridge, Ernest (1981) 'Posthumous interests and posthumous respect', *Ethics*, **91**, January, pp. 243–64.

Partridge, Ernest (1990) 'On the rights of future generations', in Donald Scherer (ed.) *Upstream/Downstream: Issues in Environmental Ethics* (Philadelphia: Temple University Press), pp. 40–66.

Partridge, Ernest (2001) 'Future generations', in Dale Jamieson (ed.) *A Companion to Environmental Philosophy* (Oxford: Blackwell), pp. 377–89.

Passmore, John (1974) *Man's Responsibility for Nature* (London: Duckworth).

Paterson, Matthew (1996) 'International justice and global warming', in Barry Holden (ed.) *The Ethical Dimensions of Global Change* (London: Macmillan), pp. 181–201.

Patz, J.A., Gotheko, A.K., McCarthy, J.P., Hussein, S., Confalonieri, U. and de Wet, N. (2003) 'Climate change and infectious diseases', in A.J. McMichael et al. (eds) *Climate Change and Human Health*, pp. 103ff.

Pearce, D.W., Cline, W.R., Achanta, A.N., Frankhauser, S., Pachuri, R.K., Tol, R.S.J. and Vellinga, P. (1996) 'The social costs of climate change: greenhouse damage and the benefits of control', in James P. Bruce et al. (eds) *Climate Change 1995: Economic and Social Dimensions of Climate Change* (Cambridge: Cambridge University Press), pp. 179–224.

Pearce, Fred (1997) 'Greenhouse wars', *New Scientist*, 19 July, p. 43.

Pearce, Fred (2003) 'Heat will soar as haze fades', *New Scientist*, 7 June, p. 7.

Pearce, Fred (2005a) 'A most precious commodity', *New Scientist*, 8 January, p. 6.

Pearce, Fred (2005b) 'Tear up Kyoto or make it tougher', *New Scientist*, 28 May, pp. 13–14.

Penner, J.E. et al. (2001) 'Aerosols, their direct and indirect effects', in John T. Houghton et al. (eds) (2001) *Climate Change 2001: The Scientific Basis* (Cambridge: Cambridge University Press), pp. 289–348.

Pitcher, George (1984) 'The misfortunes of the dead', *American Philosophical Quarterly*, **21**, pp. 183–9.

Prather, M. and Ehhalt, D. et al. (2001) 'Atmospheric chemistry and greenhouse gases', in John T. Houghton et al. (eds) (2001) *Climate Change 2001: The Scientific Basis* (Cambridge: Cambridge University Press), pp. 239–87.

Preston, Ted (2004) 'Environmental values, pluralism and stability', *Ethics, Place and Environment*, **7**(1–2), March/June, pp. 73–83.

Putnam, Robert (1993) *Making Democracy Work: Civic Traditions in Modern Italy* (New Jersey: Princeton University Press).

Raffensperger, C., Tickner, J., Schettler, Ted and Jordan, A. (1999) '. . . and can mean saying 'yes' to innovation', *Nature*, **401**, 16 September, pp. 207–8.

Ramsey, Frank (1928) 'A mathematical theory of saving', *Economic Journal*, **38**, pp. 543–59.

Rawls, John (1971) *A Theory of Justice* (Harvard: Harvard University Press).

Rawls, John (1982) 'Social unity and primary goods', in Amartya Sen and Bernard Williams *Utilitarianism and Beyond* (Cambridge: Cambridge University Press), pp. 159–85.

Rawls, John (1993) *Political Liberalism*, (New York: Columbia University Press).

Rawls, John (2001) *Justice as Fairness: A Restatement* (Cambridge, MA: Harvard University Press).

Raz, Joseph (1984) 'Right-based moralities', in Jeremy Waldron (ed.), *Theories of Rights* (Oxford: Oxford University Press), pp. 182–200.

Raz, Joseph (1986) *The Morality of Freedom* (Oxford: Clarendon Press).

Raz, Joseph (1994) *Ethics in the Public Domain* (Oxford: Clarendon).

Regan, Tom (2004) *The Case for Animal Rights. 2nd Edition* (Berkeley: University of California Press).

Reilly, J., Prinn, R., Harnisch, J., Fitzmaurice, J., Jacoby, H., Kicklighter, D., Meilillo, J., Stone, P., Sokolov, A. and Wang, C. (1999) 'Multi-gas assessment of the Kyoto Protocol', *Nature*, **401**, 7 October, pp. 549–55.

Revelle R. and Suess, H.E. (1955) 'Carbon dioxide exchange between atmosphere and ocean and the question of an increase in CO_2 during the past decades', *Tellus*, **9**, pp. 18–27.

Rolston III, Holmes (1988) *Environmental Ethics: Duties To and Values In the Natural World* (Philadelphia: Temple University Press).

Rolston III, Holmes (1989) *Philosophy Gone Wild: Environmental Ethics* (New York: Prometheus Books).

Rosenburg, Alexander (1995) 'Equality, sufficiency, and opportunity in the just society', in E.F. Paul, F.D. Miller and J. Paul (eds), *The Just Society* (Cambridge: Cambridge University Press, pp. 54–71.

Routley, Richard and Routley, Val (1995) 'Against the inevitability of human chauvinism', in Robert Elliot (ed.) *Environmental Ethics* (Oxford: Oxford University Press), pp. 104–28.

Royal Society (1999) *Climate Change and Human Health* (London: Royal Society).

Ruddiman, William F. (2003) 'The anthropogenic greenhouse era began thousands of years ago', *Climatic Change*, **61**(3), pp. 261–93

Ruddiman, William F. (2005) 'How did humans first alter global climate', *Scientific American*, March, pp. 34–41.

Sattur, Omar (1991) 'Counting the cost of catastrophe', *New Scientist*, 29 June, p. 21.

Sauvé, Kevin (1995) 'Gauthier, property rights, and future generations', *Canadian Journal of Philosophy*, **25**(2), pp. 163–76.

Scanlon, Thomas M. (1981) 'Contractualism and utilitarianism', in Amartya Sen and Bernard Williams (eds) *Utilitarianism and Beyond* (Cambridge: Cambridge University Press), pp. 103–28

Scanlon, Thomas M (1999) *What We Owe to Each Other* (Cambridge: Harvard University Press).

Schär, C., Vidale, P.L., Lüthi, D., Frei, C., Häberli, C., Liniger, M.A. and Appenzeller, C. (2004) 'The role of increasing temperature variability in European summer heatwaves', *Nature*, **427**, 22 January, pp. 332–6.

Schimel, D. et al. (1996) 'Radiative forcing of climate change', in J.T. Houghton et al. (eds) *Climate Change 1995: The Science of Climate Change* (Cambridge: Cambridge University Press), pp. 65–131.

Schwartz, Thomas (1978) 'Obligations to posterity', in Richard I. Sikora and Brian M. Barry *Obligations to Future Generations* (Philadelphia: Temple University Press), pp. 3–13.

Sen, Amartya (1982) 'Equality of what?' in Amartya Sen *Choice, Welfare and Measurement* (Oxford: Oxford University Press), pp. 353–69.

Sen, Amartya (1984) *Resources, Values and Development* (Oxford: Basil Blackwell).

Sen, Amartya (1985) 'Well-being, agency and freedom: the Dewey Lectures, 1984', *Journal of Philosophy*, **82**, pp. 169–221.

Sen, Amartya (1992) *Inequality Reexamined* (Oxford: Oxford University Press).

Sen, Amartya (1999) *Development as Freedom* (Oxford: Oxford University Press).

Sen, Amartya (2004) 'Elements of a theory of human rights', *Philosophy and Public Affairs*, **32**(4), pp. 315–56.

Shue, Henry (1992) 'The unavoidability of justice', in Andrew Hurrell and Benedict Kingsbury (eds) *The International Politics of the Environment* (Oxford: Oxford University Press), pp. 373–97

Shue, Henry (1993) 'Subsistence Emissions and Luxury Emissions', *Law & Policy*, **15**(1), January, pp. 39–59.

Shue, Henry (1995) 'Avoidable necessity: global warming, international fairness, and alternative energy', in I. Shapiro and J.W. DeCew (eds) *NOMOS XXXVII: Theory and Practice* (New York: New York University Press), pp. 239–64.

Shue, Henry (1999) 'Global environment and international inequality', *International Affairs*, **75**(3), pp. 531–45;

Shue, Henry (2001) 'Climate', in Dale Jamieson (ed.) *A Companion to Environmental Philosophy* (Oxford: Blackwell), pp. 449–59.

Sidgwick, Henry (1981) *Methods of Ethics* (London: Macmillan).

Silver, Lee. M. (1999) *Remaking Eden: Cloning, Genetic Engineering and the Future of Humankind?* (London: Phoenix Giant)

Singer, Fred (2000) *Hot Talk Cold Science. Global Warming's Unfinished Debate* (Oakland: Independent Institute).

Singer, Peter (1972) 'Famine, affluence and morality', *Philosophy and Public Affairs*, **1**(2), Spring, pp. 229–43.

Singer, Peter (1975) *Animal Liberation* (New York: Basic Books).

Singer, Peter (1993) *Practical Ethics* (Cambridge: Cambridge University Press).

Singer, Peter (2002) *One World* (London: Yale University Press).

Slovic, Paul (2000) 'Trust, emotion, sex, politics, and science: surveying the risk assessment battlefield', in Paul Slovic (ed.) *The Perception of Risk* (London: Earthscan), pp. 391–412.

Smart, J.J.C. and Williams, B. (1973) *Utilitarianism: For and Against* (Cambridge: Cambridge University Press).

Smith, Joel B., Schellnhuber, Hans-Joachim and Mirza, M. Monirul Qader (2001) 'Vulnerability to climate change and reasons for concern: a synthesis', in James J. McCarthy et al. (eds) (2001) *Climate Change 2001: Impacts, Adaptation, and Vulnerability* (Cambridge: Cambridge University Press), pp. 913–67.

Smith, Steven R. (2001) 'The social construction of talent: a defence of justice as reciprocity', *The Journal of Political Philosophy*, **9**(1), March, pp. 19–37.

Smith, Steven R. (2003) *Defending Justice as Reciprocity: An Essay on Social Policy and Political Philosophy* (Lampeter: Edwin Mellen).

Smolkin, Doran (1994) 'The non-identity problem and the appeal to future people's rights', *Southern Journal of Philosophy*, **32**, pp. 315–29.

Snow, Robert W., Guerra, Carlos A., Noor, Abdisalan M., Myint, Hia Y. and Hay, Simon, I. (2005) 'The global distribution of clinical episodes of *Plasmodium falciparum* malaria', *Nature*, **434**, 10 March, pp. 214–17.

Stagg, J.M. (1971) *Forecast for Overlord: June 6, 1944* (London: Ian Allan).

Stainforth, D.A. et al. (2005) 'Uncertainty in predictions of the climate response to rising levels of greenhouse gases', *Nature*, **433**, 27 January, pp. 403–6.

Stanhill, Gerald and Cohen, Shabati (2001) 'Global dimming: a review of the evidence for a widespread and significant reduction in global radiation with discussion of its probable causes and possible agricultural consequences', *Agricultural and Forest Meteorology*, **107**, pp. 255–78.

Steiner, Hillel (1983) 'The rights of future generations', in D. McLean and P.G. Brown (eds) *Energy and the Future* (Totowa, NJ: Rowman and Littlefield), pp. 151–65.

Steiner, Hillel (1991) 'Markets and law: the case of environmental conservation', in M. Moran and M. Wright (eds) *The Market and the State: Studies in Interdependence* (London: Macmillan), pp. 43–58.

Steiner, Hillel (1994) *An Essay on Rights* (London: Blackwell).

Stott, Michael and Gupta, Sujata et al. (2001) 'Human settlements, energy, and industry', in James J. McCarthy et al. (eds) *Climate Change 2001: Impacts, Adaptation, and Vulnerability* (Cambridge: Cambridge University Press), pp. 381–416.

Stripple, Johannes (2002) 'Climate change as a security issue', in Edward A. Page and Michael R. Redclift (eds) *Human Security and the Environment* (Cheltenham: Edward Elgar), pp. 105–27.

Sumner, Wayne (1996) *Welfare, Happiness and Ethics* (Oxford: Oxford University Press).

Svenskmark, H. (1998) 'Influence of cosmis rays on Earth's climate', *Physical Review Letters*, **81**, pp. 5027–30.

Taylor, Charles (1994) 'The politics of recognition', in Amy Guttman (ed.) *Multiculturalism: Examining the Politics of Recognition* (Princeton: New Jersey), pp. 25–73.

Taylor, Paul (1986) *Respect for Nature* (Princeton: Princeton University Press).

Temkin, Larry S. (1993) *Inequality* (Oxford: Oxford University Press).

Temkin, Larry S. (1995) 'Justice and equality: some issues about scope', *Social Philosophy and Policy*, **12**(2), pp. 72–104.

Temkin, Larry S. (2000) 'Equality, priority, and the levelling down objection', in Matthew Clayton and Andrew Williams (eds) *The Ideal of Equality* (London: Palgrave), pp. 126–61.

Temkin, Larry S. (2003a) 'Egalitarianism defended', *Ethics*, **113**, July, pp. 764–82.

Temkin, Larry S. (2003b) 'Equality, priority or what?', *Economics and Philosophy*, **19**, pp. 61–87.

Temkin, Larry S. (2003c) 'Personal versus impersonal principles: reconsidering the slogan, *Theoria*, **69**(1–2), pp. 21–31.

Thjell, P. and Lassen, K. (2000) 'Solar forcing of the Northern Hemisphere land air temperature: new data', *Journal of Solar-Terrestrial Physics*, **13**, pp. 1207–13.

Thompson, Janna (2000) 'The apology paradox', *The Philosophical Quarterly*, **50**, October, pp. 470–75.

Tol, Richard S.J. (2002) 'Estimates of the damage costs of climate change', *Environmental and Resource Economics*, **21**, pp. 47–73.

Tol, Richard S. J. (2003) 'Is the uncertainty about climate change too large for expected cost–benefit analysis?', *Climatic Change*, **56**, pp. 265–89.

Trenberth, K.E., Houghton, J.T. and Meira Filho, L.G. (1996) 'The climate system: an overview', in J.T. Houghton et al. (eds) *Climate Change 1995: The Science of Climate Change* (Cambridge: Cambridge University Press), pp. 51–64.

Tungodden, Bertil (2003) 'The value of equality', *Economics and Philosophy*, **19**, 2003, pp. 1–44.

Twain, Mark (1996) *Following the Equator and Anti-imperialist Essays* (New York: Oxford University Press).

Tyndall, John (1861) 'On the absorption and radiation of heat by gases and vapours', *Philosophical Magazine*, **22**, pp. 169–94.

United Nations (1995) *United Nations Framework Convention on Climate Change* (London: HMSO Books).

United Nations Economic Commission for Europe (UNECE) (2004) 'Trends in Europe and North America', *The Statistical Yearbook of the Economic Commission for Europe 2003* (Geneva: UNECE).

Vallentine, Peter (ed.) (1991) *Contractarianism and Rational Choice: Essays on David Gauthier's Morals by Agreement* (Cambridge: Cambridge University Press).

Van den Belt, Henrik (2003) 'Debating the precautionary principle: "guilty until proven innocent" or "innocent until proven guilty"?', *Plant Physiology*, **132**, July, pp. 1122–6.

Van Dyke, Vernon (1982) 'Collective entities and moral rights: problems in Liberal-Democratic thought', *Journal of Politics*, **44**(1), February, pp. 21–40.

Van Dyke, Vernon (1985) *Human Rights, Ethnicity, and Discrimination* (Westport, CT: Greenwood).

Waldron, Jeremy (1987) 'Can communal goods be human rights?', *Archives Europeenes de Sociologie*, **27**, pp. 294–320.

Waldron, Jeremy (1988) *The Right to Private Property* (Oxford: Clarendon).

Watson, Robert. T., Zinyowera, Marufu C., Moss, Richard H. and Dokken, David J. (eds) (1996) *Climate Change 1995: Impacts, Adaptations and Mitigation of Climate Change: Scientific–Technical Analyses* (Cambridge: Cambridge University Press).

Weart, Spencer R. (2003) *The Discovery of Global Warming* (London: Harvard University Press).

White, Stuart (1997) 'Liberal equality, exploitation, and the case for an unconditional basic income', *Political Studies*, **45**, pp. 312–26.

White, Stuart (2003a) 'Fair reciprocity and basic income', in Andrew Reeve and Andrew Williams (eds), *Real Libertarianism Assessed: Political Theory after Van Parijs* (London: Palgrave), pp. 136–60

White, Stuart (2003b) *The Civic Minimum: On the Rights and Obligations of Economic Citizenship* (Oxford: Oxford University Press).

Wigley, Tom (1998) 'The Kyoto Protocol, CO_2, CH_4 and climate implications', *Geophysical Research Letters*, **25**(13), July, pp. 2285–8.

Wigley, Tom (2005) 'The climate change commitment', *Science*, **307**, 18 March, pp. 1766–9.

Winters, H.A., Galloway Jnr, G.E., Reynolds, W.J. and Rhyne, D.W. (2002) *Battling the Elements: Weather and Terrain in the Conduct of War* (Baltimore: Johns Hopkins University Press).

Woodward, James (1986) 'The non-identity problem', *Ethics*, **96**, July, pp. 804–31.

Woodward, James (1987) 'Reply to parfit', *Ethics*, **97**, pp. 800–816.

World Commission on Environment and Development (WCED) (1987) *Our Common Future* (Oxford: Oxford University Press).

World Resources Institute (2003), *World Resources 2003–2004: Decisions for the Earth: Balance, Voice and Power* (Washington DC: World Resource Institute) (available online at: http://governance.wri.org/).

Index